MISFIT MODERNISM

The Pennsylvania

State University Press

University Park,

Pennsylvania

MISFIT MOD- ERNISM

QUEER FORMS OF DOUBLE EXILE
IN THE TWENTIETH-CENTURY NOVEL

OCTAVIO R. GONZÁLEZ

Library of Congress Cataloging-in-Publication
    Data

Names: González, Octavio R., author.
Title: Misfit modernism : queer forms of double
    exile in the twentieth-century novel / Octavio
    R. González.
Other titles: Refiguring modernism.
Description: University Park, Pennsylvania : The
    Pennsylvania State University Press, [2020]
    | Series: Refiguring modernism | Includes
    bibliographical references and index.
Summary: "Revisits the theme of alienation
    in modernist literature, finding an alterna-
    tive aesthetic centered on the experience of
    double exile. Explores examples drawn from
    the cultural groupings of the New Negro
    movement, Parisian expatriates in the 1920s,
    and the queer expatriate scene in Los Angeles
    before Stonewall"—Provided by publisher.
Identifiers: LCCN 2020016973 | ISBN
    9780271087139 (hardback)
Subjects: LCSH: Alienation (Social psychol-
    ogy) in literature. | English fiction—20th
    century—History and criticism. | American
    fiction—20th century—History and criticism.
    | Modernism (Literature) | Queer theory.
Classification: LCC PR830.A42 G66 2020 |
    DDC 823/.9109353—dc23
LC record available at https://lccn.loc.gov
    /2020016973

Part of the Coda to this book is copyright © 2017
Johns Hopkins University Press. It first appeared
in *ASAP/Journal* 2, no. 2 (2017): 274–75.

Published by
The Pennsylvania State University Press,
University Park, PA 16802-1003

The Pennsylvania State University Press is a
member of the Association of University Presses.

It is the policy of The Pennsylvania State
University Press to use acid-free paper.
Publications on uncoated stock satisfy the mini-
mum requirements of American National
Standard for Information Sciences—Permanence
of Paper for Printed Library Material, ANSI
Z39.48–1992.

Bloch était mal élevé, névropathe, snob
et appartenant à une famille peu estimée
supportait comme au fond des mers les incal-
culables pressions que faisaient peser sur
lui non seulement les chrétiens de la surface,
mais les couches superposées des castes
juives supérieures à la sienne, chacune
accablant de son mépris celle qui lui était
immédiatement inférieure. Percer jusqu'à l'air
libre en s'élevant de famille juive en famille
juive eût demandé à Bloch plusieurs milliers
d'années.

Bloch was ill-bred, neurotic and snobbish, and
since he belonged to a family of little repute,
had to withstand, as on the floor of the ocean,
the incalculable pressures imposed on him not
only by the Christians at the surface but by all
the intervening layers of Jewish castes superior to his own, each of them crushing with
its contempt the one that was immediately
beneath it. To pierce his way through to the
open air by raising himself from Jewish family
to Jewish family would have taken Bloch many
thousands of years.

—**Marcel Proust,**
In Search of Lost Time

TO

In honor & in memory of my mother
Eva Figueroa ("La Piedra").

This book is also dedicated
to my partner
Brian Fuss

and is in honor & in memory
of my stepfather
Santiago Figueroa

&

my father
Julian Simon Ramírez.

CONTENTS

PREFACE
Queer Forms of Double Exile in the Twentieth-Century Novel

Looking back on this project, I'm tempted to say the genesis occurred some-where in the final pages of Wallace Thurman's first novel, *The Blacker the Berry* (1929). "No one is a total misfit," reads Thurman's free-indirect narration, focal-izing the novel's protagonist.[1] Emma Lou Morgan, the besotted protagonist of *The Blacker the Berry*, tells herself that there is still hope for her, that no one need be a "total misfit." My hermeneutic suspicion—my spider-sense—pricked up at this seemingly offhand sentence. What is a "total misfit"? I asked myself. More importantly, what did the notion of being a "total misfit" mean for a char-acter like Emma Lou Morgan, in the fictional Harlem of the Roaring Twenties? And what did the phrase mean for Thurman himself, whose authorial intention employed it as a sign of complete social estrangement? There is something to this modernist vocabulary of being a "misfit"—and of being a "*total* misfit," the absolute version of the same predicament. Emma Lou Morgan's predicament is that she is "too black," in the discourse of the novel; she is ostracized by her own family for having darker skin. Her family is a proud member of the so-called blue-veined circle, a real historical phenomenon among late nineteenth- and early twentieth-century middle-class African Americans.[2] Emma Lou Morgan is thus born into a family—and a larger, segregated, white world, of course—that already discriminates against her because of her skin color. That this discrim-ination is originally based in the family unit itself is the point of Thurman's novel: the point being that the experience of alienation from the family itself, while suffering the slings and arrows of social discrimination in addition to that, makes for a hard life. Makes for a subjective experience of being a "total misfit."

A "total misfit," then, to build on the vocabulary of Thurman's first novel and the study of "misfit modernism" as a whole, is a feeling or subject-position of double exile, of internal displacement—displacement within the family unit itself, based on prejudices that are social, such as skin color (or gender, or sexu-ality; more on this later). This originary sense of internal exile—internal because one's own kin rejects the bonds of kinship, "rending [the] deepest fibers" between mother and daughter, father and son, and so forth—is then overlain by a larger circle of social marginalization.[3] Racism, sexism, class prejudice, and other aspects of large-scale structural oppressions constitute the second layer of exile from the good life—the life of majority cultural citizenship. To be doubly exiled, within this framework, is to carry two heavy backpacks; Peggy McIntosh's famous notion of the "weightless backpack of privilege" is examined, in novels I group under the rubric of misfit modernism, by exploring its opposite situation. But I examine not simply the weight of one oppressive social dimension—not only one backpack, heavy as one is. Not one heavy backpack, but two. And, of course, given the origins of this tale of the "total misfit," figures like Emma Lou Morgan are saddled with the first backpack when they are children. If not born with this extra baggage, as everyone is who deviates from one social norm or another, then this second burden is nonetheless acquired, imposed, early on in life.

The role of the family in the tale of the "total misfit," and in tales I call misfit modernism, is therefore fundamental to the double exile experienced in these stories. Now, I know what you're thinking: this story is hardly new at all! What on earth makes it "modern," much less "modernist"? The answer is deceptively simple. Novels like *The Blacker the Berry* and novelists such as Wallace Thurman were, precisely, exploring the conditions of doubly exiled figures in a particularly modern moment, in a particularly modernist way. Thurman's modernism is an aesthetic I call affective realism; his novel seeks to document the "adjustment proceedings" of Emma Lou Morgan's experience of double exile in a naturalistic idiom. (His use of free indirect style is a hallmark of this idiom; more on this later.) The moment is even more legible. *The Blacker the Berry* is set in the maelstrom of the "Negro Renaissance," the 1920s and early 1930s, as is Thurman's second novel, *Infants of the Spring* (1932). This epoch is widely considered the first African American cultural awakening; what came to be called the Harlem Renaissance went by many names, including the "Harlem vogue," or the cultural aspect of the much older "New Negro" movement. Emma Lou Morgan, for instance, knows about Alain Locke's special issue of *Survey Graphic*, which was later published as the *New Negro* (1925) anthology; this collection is widely considered one of the founding literary monuments of the Renaissance.[4] Thurman's *Infants of the Spring* doubles down on the social verisimilitude of his fiction: it is a roman à clef that features characters based on Thurman himself as well as Richard Bruce Nugent, Zora Neale Hurston, Alain Locke, and Langston Hughes. There is even a major scene in *The Blacker the Berry* in which versions of these real-life figures first appear: "Truman Walter" is a character that Emma Lou Morgan meets in a flat based on the infamous "Niggerati Manor," Hurston's self-deprecating term for the building in which many of these young luminaries lived.

The question of the modernism in *Misfit Modernism* is more vexed, and, as the subtitle of this study suggests, involves the question of literary form.

The modernism of Thurman, along with many of his contemporaries, involves multifaceted aspects. The easiest one is provenance: Thurman was perhaps the best educated of the "younger Negro artists" who lived in the "Manor" and threw fire—in the form of their incendiary arts journal, *Fire!!*—on the elite social figures, cultural institutions, and discursive norms that directed the Renaissance as a concerted project for collective black uplift. The modernism of these writers inheres in their being influenced by—some, like Larsen, used the term "distorted" by—canonical Anglo-European modernist forebears, dating back to the mid-nineteenth-century realism of Flaubert, the proto-modernism of Baudelaire, the naturalism of Zola, and the decadence of Joris-Karl Huysmans in France. The legacy of queer Anglo modernism—from the aestheticism of Pater to the decadence of Wilde—similarly makes an impact on this collective band of misfit modernists.

As this very partial list indicates, their modernism was often interpolated through specifically queer legacies in literature. Even authors like Nella Larsen and Jean Rhys were in part influenced by the predominance of queerness in modernist thought and literature, to the point that a critic, Heather Love, asks, "Is queer modernism simply another name for modernism?"[5] Well, not quite. But the importance of the queer canon to the formation of misfit modernism cannot be overstated.

The modernism of this band of misfits is also legible in the narrative forms they employed—precisely those originated and negotiated by earlier figures, many of them queer themselves. Thurman's free indirect style is complemented by a naturalistic approach to exploring the social determinants of Emma Lou Morgan's personal predicaments. (My gloss on the free indirect style: narration that freely adopts the frame of reference, emotional tone, and idiomatic expression of a character. While framed as the narrator's discourse by nominally maintaining the narrator's outside position, it blurs the distinction between narrator and focal character: *She couldn't believe her luck!* A Vulcan mind meld between character and narrator.) But free indirect narration is but one tool in the misfit modernist toolbox. Others include Larsen's extensive reliance on psycho-narration in *Quicksand* (1928), her first novel. Rhys, in the novel I analyze here—the first she published, *Quartet* (1929)—also delves into psychological depths by employing modernist modes of focalization, like hypothetical focalization, which serve to destabilize the real world of the novel, to vaporize it into an impressionist landscape. Hers owes much to the French modernists; Ford Madox Ford, Rhys's first literary mentor, famously made her read modern French novels to help her develop her minimalist, poetic style. Ford himself was an avatar of impressionism, an early modernist label whose most famous exponent was Joseph Conrad. Christopher Isherwood, the eminently queer writer in this band of misfits, employs a whole lexicon of modernist literary form, including the one-day-in-the-life novel made famous by "high" modernists such as Joyce and Woolf. As an early proponent of the "new objectivity" in literature—exemplified in the famous first line of *Goodbye to Berlin* (1939), "I am a camera"—Isherwood was himself a scion of the nexus of English modernists. He was famously hailed by Somerset Maugham as holding "the future of the English novel in his hands."[6] The future of the English novel, in this early twentieth-century context, meant the post-Edwardian, post-Joyce, and post-Woolf moment: a newer modernism, for a newer time. (All modernists were hyperaware of time, and of needing to be, as Rimbaud famously said, "*absolument moderne.*") Further, Pound's injunction to "Make it new!" remains influential even as the original modernist vanguard left the literary stage and made way for new generations. One of these was the brat pack of "younger Negro artists," Thurman chief among them. But Rhys, Isherwood, and Larsen were all, in different or related ways, members of these generations.

Style on the page was one thing; one also had to be *absolument moderne* in the salon and dress appropriately. The modernist term *misfit parlors* suggests the centrality of fashion to the modernist discourse of the misfit. (As John Sullivan writes, misfit parlors were "clothing stores that dealt in bespoke clothing which had been left at the tailor's shop for one reason or another because the customer had rejected it or couldn't pay."[7]) Pound famously affected his cloak; Djuna Barnes was a brilliant, model-beautiful journalist and artist in high demand in modernist salons; and Rhys herself was a chorus girl and mannequin, her feminine beauty as much a mode of modernist self-fashioning as the minimalist style of her fictional storytelling. For this reason—among others much more salient!—there is a confluence of author and novel, writer and writing, in this ragtag bunch that I group under the freak flag of misfit modernism. Self-fashioning as a modernist was an essential component of literary success. This form of self-fashioning—epitomized by the Wildean epigram "If one cannot *be* a work of art, one must *wear* a work of art"—is as much a real-life dimension of the works and their progenitors as the works themselves. The queer or queer-adjacent self-affectations of Pound and Wilde, no less than those of Thurman, Rhys, and Larsen—not to mention Isherwood—are features of their modernist projects. And these self-affectations were also keyed to their real, historical locations as social actors. The gender of modernity, to quote the title of Rita Felski's seminal study, was but one aspect of how reality intersected with literature, then as now.

ACKNOWLEDGMENTS

I would like to thank the friends, colleagues, and mentors who have helped shape this book in its varied stages of development. In particular, I especially wish to thank Jonathan Eburne, the series editor, for believing in this project, and Eleanor Goodman for her gentle, astute, and careful guidance in shepherding this manuscript to completion. I would also like to thank Rebecca Walkowitz, Marianne DeKoven, David Kurnick, Heather Love, John Kucich, and Elin Diamond for their unstinting support and for intellectual contributions to the formation of this book, from its earliest stages to its fruition. Heather Love's *Feeling Backward* was especially helpful in understanding the undertow of modernism as a formation that shapes our contemporary accounts of queer struggles against domination and assimilation. I also wish to thank Amber Jamilla Musser, whose mentorship in the last three years has been invaluable in helping me reframe the interventions of this book within broader conversations about race, sexuality, and gender. Along with Amber, I look to Rigoberto González, Evie Shockley, Carlos Decena, Allan Isaac, Tim Dean, Scott Herring, Kadji Amin, and David Kurnick as role models and inspirations for my intellectual, creative, and professional journey. Thank you for leading by example, for showing me what's possible.

I owe a debt of gratitude to my dear friends and colleagues Nimanthi Rajasingham and Philip Longo, who read many iterations of several chapters throughout the years and whose friendship and support are invaluable to me. I also want to thank friends and fellow travelers in modernism and twentieth-century studies, including Michael Leong, Nami Shin, Philip Tsang, Angus Brown, Lisa Mendelman, Roanne Kantor, Joshua Gang, Tyler Bradway, Roy Pérez, Elliott Powell, Stacie McCormick, Jean-Paul Riquelme, Samuel Alexander, Jennifer Mitchell, Melanie Micir, David Alworth, Jennifer Schnepf, Angela Allan, and Todd Nordgren. Their generous feedback, collaboration, and support helped me refine my ideas throughout this process.

The graduate program at Rutgers was my home for many years, and I owe a debt of gratitude to friends and colleagues there, including Richard Dienst, Ann Jurecic, Carolyn Williams, Andrew Goldstone, Joshua Fesi, Candice Amich, Debapriya Sarkar (for making me laugh the moment I met you), Michelle

Stephens (for reading more than you had to), Mark Doty, Harriet Davidson, Cheryl Wall, Chris Iannini, Sarah Balkin, Meredith McGill, Andrew Parker, Stéphane Robolin, Becca Klaver, Caolan Madden, Manuel Betancourt, Angelo Nikolopolus, Cheryl Robinson, and Courtney Borack. Before Rutgers, I spent two formative years at Penn State, where I was nurtured and became a modernist. I want to acknowledge my mentors, friends, and colleagues there, especially Janet Lyon (not least, for the last supper with mojitos before I left State College), and also Pia Deas, Michael Bérubé, Robert Caserio (for sparking my love for narratology), Jeffrey Nealon, Jane Juffer, Mark Morrisson, Patrick Cheney, Aldon Nielsen, Amy Clukey, Ersula Ore, Verna Kale, Andrew Pilsch, Shawna Ross, Joshua Weiss, and Liz Kuhn. And before Penn State, I spent two years under the tutelage of wonderful faculty at Hunter College, including Linda Camarasana and Cristina León Alfar, who also showed me what's possible, coming back to school after an extended "intellectual detox" from Swarthmore. Between those two stages of my life, I fell in with the "Pink Poets" gay mafia in NYC: Rigo, Dean Kostos, Jason Schneiderman, Michael Broder, Scott Hightower, David Groff, Walter Holland, and others; and two pink non-poets but inspirations nonetheless, Jaime Manrique and the late Bill Sullivan.

I am also incredibly grateful to my friends and colleagues at Wellesley College whose warmth and collegiality helped this project mature. In particular, I wish to thank Bill Cain, Dan Chiasson (still chasin!), Margery Sabin, Lisa Rodensky, Irene Mata, Layli Maparyan, and Selwyn Cudjoe for their generous feedback and mentorship during the early stages of the manuscript and early years on the tenure track. Others at Wellesley have made me feel at home, including my other colleagues in English: Frank Bidart, Kate Brogan, Margaret Cezaire-Thompson, Paul Fisher, Alison Hickey, Yu Jin Ko, Yoon Sun Lee, Cappy Lynch, Susan Myer, Jim Noggle, Tim Peltason, Larry Rosenwald, Vernon Shetley, Marilyn Sides, Sarah Wall-Randell, and Cord Whitaker. In the greater Wellesley community, I want to thank Nikki Greene, who made me feel welcome from before day one, as well as Susan Ellison, Petra Rivera-Rideau, Natali Valdez, Heather Bryant, Ryan Quintana, Julie Walsh, Brenna Greer, Simon Grote, Michael Jeffries, and many others, too many to list, for making me feel at home in New England (even when we had 100 inches of snow). And above all, I'd like to thank my students, past and present, for their inspiration. Last but not least, my gratitude to the anonymous readers for helping to refine the contributions of this book to modernist studies and queer theory.

The research in this book would not have been possible without grants and fellowships from the Andrew W. Mellon Foundation, the Woodrow Wilson Foundation, the Wilson Career Enhancement Fellowship, Rutgers School of Arts and Sciences, the Office of the Dean at Rutgers Graduate School, and the Office of the Provost at Wellesley College. A research sabbatical in 2017–18 provided much-needed time and resources as I revised the manuscript and pursued the archives for traces of the last author included in this book, Nella Larsen, mystery woman of the Harlem Renaissance.

But I could not have written this book without the support of my longtime companion, Brian Fuss, and the love of my family.

Portions of this research were presented and supported at various conferences and symposia, including the Modernism Seminar at Harvard's Mahindra Center for the Humanities, the Modernist Studies Association, the Modern Language Association, the American Comparative Literature Association, and the inaugural Black Queer Studies Graduate Student Conference at Princeton. Exploring the archives at the Huntington Library, Yale's Beinecke Library, the University of Tulsa's McFarlin Library, the New York Public Library, and the Schomburg Center for Research in Black Culture would not have been possible without the assistance and support of dedicated curatorial staff at each of those institutions.

Earlier versions of chapters 4 and 5 appear in article form in *Ariel* and *Modern Fiction Studies*, respectively. Part of the coda appears in the special issue on "Queer Form" in *ASAP/Journal*.

Introduction

The Modernist Misfit: Antisocial and Intersectional

I prefaced this book with Wallace Thurman's *The Blacker the Berry* and the notion of "being a total misfit." And how that phrase struck a nerve, suggesting an entire world—an entire worldview—immanent to the author who invented it, immanent to the narrator who reported it, and immanent to the character who "thought" it. There must be some hidden meaning in such a phrase, or even a pedestrian explanation for it. For Thurman wouldn't have described the notion in those terms if the notion of being a "misfit"—and, in extremis, being a "total misfit"—didn't already, in that historical time and place, mean precisely that. Mean the experience of double displacement, of alienation from one's home community (and one's home, at times) as well as from societal structures of domination. In other words, to answer the question often posed to me as a doctoral student—Why "misfits"?—well, the answer is immanent to the texts. Somehow, in my unconscious critical processing of Thurman's novel—and Christopher Isherwood's, Nella Larsen's, and Jean Rhys's—the constellation of similar lives written about in related ways shone by the light of terms like "total misfit" (Thurman), "unconformity" (Larsen), "nonconformist" (Isherwood), "underdog," and "doormat in a world of boots" (Rhys).

This last example is telling of the pessimistic, even dystopian, landscape of misfit-modernist novels. And I grant that these novels employ synonyms for consistent versions of the same semantic figure. But this introduction demonstrates the epistemological significance of this semantic figure for general modernist discourse, especially its fictional representation. Rhetoric about misfits circulates as an idiomatic expression with a double meaning—either specific to marginalized identities, or universal shorthand for any social outsider or maladjusted individual—and, as I argue, in both senses at once. By contrast, the novels studied in *Misfit Modernism* share a consistency of focus on double exile and a spotlight on a doubly dislocated, minoritized antihero. Their mood is defined by a pessimism that Elizabeth Hardwick calls a "biological melancholy" in *A Single Man*.[1] The other authors in this study, too, imbue their narratives with an almost palpable mood of "biological melancholy" that permeates the misfit-modernist structure of feeling.

A Modernist Band of Misfits

All four authors collected in this study suffered for being misfits in their careers as well as in their lives. Most painfully, Thurman and Larsen exited the literary stage early and abruptly. Thurman died from alcohol-related issues in 1934, only two years after he published the remarkable roman à clef of the Renaissance *Infants of the Spring* (1932). (Thurman's alcoholism can be read as self-induced suicide, a form of slow death, in the sense used by Lauren Berlant.[2]) Larsen lived a relatively long life; however, her literary career was cut short after a plagiarism scandal in 1930 and a painful divorce in 1933. As discussed in chapter 2, by the fall of 1937 Larsen had disappeared from the "New Negro" scene—ironically, by announcing her return to it.[3] She continued writing, unsuccessfully, after 1930. Yet her links to the cultural ferment of the Renaissance were severed, not least by Larsen herself. Larsen deliberately distanced herself from the elite friends and circles of the Harlem literati, a scene in which she had been an important actor. For years after, she was thought to have "passed" into the white world, and her self-driven disappearance fostered historical amnesia, which erased memories of her many legacies—including serving as the first black librarian at what became the Schomburg Center. While Thurman's death was radically premature, Larsen's social death was slow, though perhaps even starker, in how it effaced her literary and cultural legacy.

Both misfits as well as consummate literary modernists, Larsen and Thurman represent the American context that rendered toxic any deviations from nascent minoritarian cultural norms. These norms, as we will see in their respective chapters, were enforced by both majority and minority cultural formations. Larsen's protagonist Helga Crane drowns in the *Quicksand* (1928) of her choices, after being unable to reconcile being biracial. Harlem's black bourgeois milieu will not tolerate her living white ancestry, her belonging to a white family, and that family wanted nothing to do with her. Thus Helga Crane's double exile from these communities marks her misfit position. It is only by renouncing her racial and cultural hybridity, her individuality, that Helga Crane is "saved" by a black Southern preacher. Her salvation is a form of social death, a form of suicide, that impugns the rigidity of a social environment structured by the color line. This same rigid environment structures the psyche and social aspirations of Thurman's Emma Lou Morgan. Like Helga Crane, but in an ironic inversion of the color-coded "tragic mulatta" script that Larsen subverts, *The Blacker the Berry* (1929) features another instantiation of the intersectional modernist misfit. This time, the critique of the black bourgeoisie and of the anti-black racism of society centers not on a biracial protagonist but on one deemed "too black" by her own "blue-veined" family. Thurman's ironic tale explodes the trope of the tragic mulatta, while Larsen's modernizes it.

Fittingly, given his self-appointed role as *agent provocateur*, Thurman engenders a novel that Carl Van Vechten deemed rather mean-spirited. *The Blacker the Berry* thus creates an almost totalitarian environment of exile for its internally marginalized, gendered, and queered female protagonist. That it is her bisexual lover who betrays and humiliates Emma Lou Morgan serves as a fitting coda to Thurman's comprehensive critique of Harlem's—and the United States'—anti-black modern sociality. Thurman's heterosexist critique runs counter to his own heroine's same-sex encounters in the novel, not to mention the author's own ones in the real world. (Thurman was open about his love affair with a Swedish man who appears in *Infants of the Spring*; there are also reports of his being arrested for public exposure in Manhattan.) Moreover, the novel closes with a scene that includes a close-up of Alva, Emma Lou's faithless paramour, his face made physically repulsive by alcoholic cirrhosis and nightly carousing with "effeminate" boys. His face is a potent final symbol of Alva's queer male misogyny, directed at Emma Lou. And, ironically, Alva's objectification of Emma Lou—whom he dismisses, in their own home, as merely his child's "mammy"—symbolizes Thurman's own internalized homophobia. Unlike in *Quicksand*, there is not even the suicidal solace of disappearing into an impoverished enclave of Southern black culture. Indeed, Emma Lou walks out of *The Blacker the Berry*, forever frozen, while leaving this decadent scene of queer Harlem: black and brown, men and boys, sexually and socially intimate, creating their own world while excluding Emma Lou Morgan from it. It *is* a rather mean-spirited novel, most of all toward facets of Thurman's own complex intersectional identity.

So much for the queer-of-color utopia that many contemporary critics suggest is immanent in such cultural and social formations existent in today's world. Thurman's novel, written in the 1920s and critiquing the elitism of the New Negro, seems to disallow—or disavow—this imagined twenty-first-century future. As Thurman might have put it, "'Tis new to thee." He held no truck with utopian imaginings, even while centering his narrative on a modernist heroine oppressed by the racisms, sexisms, and snobbisms that she, in turn, internalizes from childhood. Thurman sought to show the social and affective *reality* of racism in America and how it affected black women in particular: those who, given their darker complexion, were seen as unsuitable mates for middle-class strivers such as the denizens of Striver's Row in Harlem. This realism cuts everything in its path, leaving only a path to walking out into the world, away from queer sexuality premised on male homosociality, itself premised on the double oppression of a black sister. Thurman's novel, in other words, seems to anticipate Kimberlé Crenshaw's intersectional critique of the male-centered Black Power movement and white-centered Second Wave feminism. *The Blacker the Berry* foreshadows the rise of intersectionality as a discourse of black women's empowerment. As I argue in chapter 3, Emma Lou Morgan's "intersectionality," her double identity, is interpellated as the condition of being a "total misfit."

Misfits Before and After Intersectionality?

Of what use is it to us, this discourse and figure of "the misfit"? At least, I argue, it's a historical recuperation of a forgotten twentieth-century epistemology, one this study focuses on, that projects complex, minoritarian perceptions and affections of doubly exiled citizens, the "total misfits" like Emma Lou Morgan, or Larsen's Helga Crane, or underdogs like "the Rhys protagonist." Is the notion of the modernist misfit diagnostic today? Can it be? What does it allow us to see, and what questions seem answered by this analogical figure?

A provocative set of questions is proposed by Jennifer Nash's *Black Feminism Reimagined*, whose subtitle (*After Intersectionality*) speaks to a certain critical and conceptual exhaustion with the paradigm of intersectionality.[4] The "after," of course, also speaks to the promise of Crenshaw's model of social difference. As the symbolic inversion of *queer*, or rather its antidote, *intersectionality* has dominated discourses in women's studies, and queer studies after the rise of queer-of-color critique. Nash's most provocative insight is in disentangling the discourse of intersectionality from black feminism itself. She argues, convincingly, that debates over who legitimately "owns" the paradigm of intersectionality— arguments about whether Crenshaw "invented" it, or merely coined the term, for instance—force black feminist critics into a defensive posture. Their intellectual labor is spent defending their turf, so to speak. And, Nash argues, cultural defensiveness over who can legitimately use the term without appropriating it, or over whether some critic or argument is intersectional "enough," perpetuates a "siege mentality." Ironically, Nash claims, endless debates about intersectionality recapitulate a racist dynamic that limits the bounds of black women's intellectual thought. Intersectionality becomes the last redoubt, the last area not colonized by white feminism. And other facets of black feminist discourse are subsumed under the rhetoric of intersectionality. What if, Nash asks, black feminism abandoned the defense of intersectionality and its identification with that paradigm as synonymous with black womanhood itself? Nash thus makes a bold claim for disaggregating the discourse of intersectionality from its conceptual identification with black feminism and its social identification with black womanhood. Symbolic ownership of the term, she argues, is poor recompense for limiting other areas of black women's theoretical interests and aspirations. Let intersectionality fend for itself, Nash suggests; there is more to black feminism—and black women—than is written in intersectional philosophy.

Like Janet Halley in *Split Decisions*, Nash suggests a turn back to the future: the radical notion that, at times, it is better to adopt a single- or double-lens analytic rubric rather than follow the now formulaic expectation that everything be intersectional. Indeed, both Nash and Halley suggest the exhaustion of intersectionality's usefulness as a paradigm, given its watered-down "citational ubiquity":[5] if the term has become a political football, then the spirit of intersectionality is lost, and only the dead letter remains as a pale tribute to the black feminist theorists—and black women's experiences—who lived through it, and developed it, from the dawn of the New Negro in the late nineteenth century.

In the spirit of Nash's scholarship, *Misfit Modernism* proposes another rubric to add to a reconceptualizing of critical discourse on social difference beyond the stalemate over the intersectional, in feminist thought, or the antisocial, in queer studies. The modernist rubric of the misfit, and the aesthetic structure of feeling I call misfit modernism, offer a new way to conceive of the referents of intersectionality without the baggage—affective as well as intellectual, following Nash—that seems to weigh down its application in the early twenty-first century.

In a second intervention, this study pushes beyond another critical quagmire: the schism between the intellectual legacy of white queer theory—sexuality-without-gender or race or any other mark of difference—and the overcorrection that I see in queer of color critics who insist on the bankruptcy of the antisocial thesis of homosexuality. This book demonstrates that even nonwhite gay-identified writers—beyond Isherwood!—found the structure of feeling of double exile a resonant cultural space for literary invention. The queerness of Larsen,

Rhys, and Thurman thus complicates the current identification of negative affects with white modernist queer archives, and the insistence on critical and affective utopianism as the province of queers of color. With the exception a few notable queer of color critics, like Darieck Scott and Hoang Tan Nguyen, the hostile takeover of queer theoretical discussion obeys this binary logic, of the "bad old days" of "bad feelings" based on a white queer structure of feeling and the new utopia of brown and black redemptive theorization and critical reclamation of lost voices and archives. The culturally exiled modernist misfit traverses this line diagonally, invested in the same antisocial impulses that Lee Edelman consolidates as "fuck the future."[6] As I discuss in chapter 2, Larsen's *Quicksand* ends in a paroxysm of "all-consuming hate" for the holy triumvirate of white *and* black society: matrimony, children, and God himself. No less than *A Single Man*'s narrative fantasies of murdering US senators who persecute homosexuals during the lavender scare, novels by Larsen, Thurman, and Rhys attack minoritarian cultural utopianism—or the "propaganda" of "uplift," in modernist idiom—as unmodernist literary values. Are Rhys and Larsen "queer"? Perhaps, but it might be best to say that they are certainly misfits wedded to a vision of nonconformity, of articulating the impasses of multiple worlds that traverse the identities of their protagonists. Worlds they themselves traversed, in their own lives, as women, as brown, black, non-American, non-British, and/or queer authors had to traverse in order to be legitimated as modernists. Their frustrations with the discourse of modernism are avenged in their tales of exilic misfits. These figures, though, are not recapitulations of the modernist Promethean archetype as Camus's *Stranger* and Joyce's Stephen Dedalus are. The latter antiheroes become all but majoritarian while retaining their anticonformist edge, in a paradox that defines mainstream modernism. What these *misfit* modernists did was integrate the minoritarianism of their lives into the modernist form of narration, creating a genuinely new—for their time— articulation of *intersectional* antisociality as a legitimate position of critique of majority culture *as well as* of the collusions of their *respective* communities with that modernist cultural wasteland. It is the work of this book to unforget the *culturally encoded* figure of the modernist misfit, particularly in her crossroads or "intersectional" position of double exile.

Misfits Among Us?

Indeed, this modernist archive is a reminder that these baleful minoritarian visions are not solely the province of white queer modernists—or contemporary white queer *theorists*. And unlike the optimism of a Richard Bruce Nugent in "Smoke, Lilies and Jade" (1926), Thurman focuses on pessimism and queer sociality as cruel, as excluding women or any who don't fully belong in their milieu. The queer is *already* antisocial *and* intersectional, in Thurman's account. The queerness of Larsen's *Quicksand*, by contrast, centers on the grotesque dimension of "reproductive futurity," which defines Helga Crane's childbearing as foreclosing her future, not enabling it.[7] Larsen's novel is thus a radical reimagining of the maternal as political, as Amber Jamilla Musser argues about Audre Lorde's work.[8] But *Quicksand* represents a bleak antisocial vision of reproductive futurity as "no future." This is the insight of an early twentieth-century biracial novelist like Larsen, part of a band of antisocial intersectional authors I call misfit modernists. This archive challenges the whiteness of the antisocial queer theory archive, which has been dismissed largely for its Eurocentric canon, but it also challenges the political optimism of intersectional approaches to queer theory, which tend to dismiss the antisocial as inherently privileged and white rather than locating the intersectional within the antisocial, and vice versa, as I examine in this book. Fittingly, and ironically, Larsen's antisocial vision of reproductive futurity is consistent with Edelman's—all the more striking because the racialized maternal body is inherently political and harnessed to visions of New Negro futurity in the novel itself. Larsen's horizon is thus one harnessing the negative energies of the misfit as an intersectional exile, as baleful a sense of the political as we find in Edelman's archive.

Larsen's intersectional feminist critique *avant la lettre* focuses on sexual subjugation and paternalistic violence against Helga's deeply vulnerable maternal body, which comes close to death during labor. Musser draws out the liberatory potential of Lorde's hyphenated identities—as a black lesbian feminist, as a poet and essayist, and, especially, as a mother. By so doing, Musser argues that Lorde eroticizes the bonds of motherhood among black women, many of whom were Lorde's lovers. Musser examines the radical potential of resignifying motherhood within the space of black lesbian feminism—a space of intersectional identities—as not only biological but also social and erotic, a means of sensual energy and a resource for political renewal. Larsen's novel, by contrast, presents a prescient counterpoint: black maternity not reclaimed but imposed, as the price to be paid for sexual satisfaction. Lorde's famous essay "Uses of the Erotic" seems to stand against this very notion of eroticism, which stigmatizes black women in particular as symbols of sexuality's transgressive force within a deeply anti-sex and anti-black culture. The controlling image of the Jezebel haunts Larsen's novel and drags down her protagonist.[9] Her maternal instinct is the agent that keeps her moored to her own oppression. To abandon her children in order to live her own life again, as an autonomous individual, would mean the "rend[ing] of deepest fibers." Helga Crane can't do it. And so she drowns in the quicksand of maternity and racialized gender norms that subdue her, no less than does the love for her children.

This glimpse of the modernist misfit in the situation of the "tragic mulatta" would seem pitifully anachronistic. The contemporary impetus is to forget and to erase these baleful accounts of tragic black womanhood, tragic black mother-hood, and the ongoing legacy of slavery that haunts Larsen's novel. (She felt the gaze of her husband as the "lash of a whip," indicating this link as instinctive and no less oppressive.) All *Quicksand* needs is black second-wave feminism, in other words, and the solution is not to take modernist novels about so-called inter-sectionality that seriously—especially those, like Larsen's and like Thurman's, that center on the intersections of gender and race and sexuality.

Perhaps adding these novels to a growing body of work on Afro-pessimism would do them greater justice. But if we do that, we miss the investment in modernism as a cultural formation, and in modernist narrative form, that defines Larsen's and Thurman's authorship (no less than Rhys's and Isherwood's). Individually, Thurman and Larsen saw themselves as part of the cultural wave of the New Negro that would usher in the integration of black sociality and cultural uniqueness into the great US melting pot. To ghettoize them as chiefly speak-ing to black constituents misses the importance of the Harlem Renaissance as a political application of culture—aimed squarely at the white US public, which then, as now, denied African Americans social, economic, and legal citizenship. So, Larsen and Thurman may "fit" into the paradigm of Afro-pessimism better than that of literary modernism, but their focus on "misfits" should caution against the impulse to fit them into only one category—be it race or gender or sexuality—that simplifies their multiple investments and identities. Their refusal to conform became the touchstone of their early novels, which centered on figures of "unconformity" and "total misfits."

So, queer theory's "aggressive impulse for generalization," which Michael Warner argues characterizes the anti-identitarian queer politics in the 1990s, *also* characterizes the language of the misfit in modernisms like those of Larsen and Thurman.[10] Radically general yet deeply particular—in terms of race and gender and sexuality, as well as class and region—the modernist misfits we encounter in *Quicksand* and *The Blacker the Berry* challenge this strict sepa-ration between queer, on the one hand, and intersectional indexes of power, on the other. The so-called antisocial thesis of homosexuality, in other words, was being developed by intersectional novelists like Thurman and Larsen—not to mention Isherwood and Rhys—in modernist eras and contexts.[11] These contexts include the Harlem Renaissance, which extends to Boise, Idaho, and Los Angeles, for Thurman, and Copenhagen and Denmark, for Larsen. They also encompass the *longue durée* of Rhys and Isherwood: the hybrid Caribbean–Left Bank bohemianism of Rhys, and Isherwood's peripatetic imaginings, border crossings, and cross-identifications from Weimar Berlin to the Vedanta Society of Southern California.

Misfits Beyond *Queer*

In "Rethinking Sex," Heather Love writes, "While *queer* was supposed to name [a] coalition of the marginal, it has not always lived up to this potential. . . . Given the widespread commodification of the term, as well as its history of uptake in sexuality studies, it is not clear if *queer* can continue to do this work."[12]

I think *misfit* can do this work.

Thus this study aligns contemporary understandings of *queer* with modernist understandings of being a *misfit*. In this introduction, I argue that the early twentieth century employed the term "misfit" in at least two overlapping yet distinct senses. One sense describes certain individuals as outside the social mainstream. The second describes individuals who belong to a certain kind of social group as misfits. Both senses overlap in the concept of *queer* that we use today: *queer* in the minoritarian sense, as a category of social identification, signals a member of the LGBTQ coalition. But *queer* also means a certain attitude, a certain oppositional, even anarchistic, political orientation: what Warner calls "resistance to regimes of the normal," "queers, incessantly told to alter their 'behavior,' can be understood as protesting not just the normal behavior of the social but the *idea* of normal behavior."[13] Warner's anti-identitarian focus has been justifiably critiqued as a metonym for queer theory, linked to the pioneering work of Gayle Rubin, which began by dissociating sexuality from other dimensions of social difference—especially gender but also, implicitly, race and ethnicity.[14]

Much ink has been spilled in trying to retain *queer* as an enabling critical term. But perhaps its half-life is over. It's telling that communities of gender and sexual minorities identify with the LGBTQ+ initialism and not with the simpler, chicer term from the 1990s. "What's Queer About Queer Studies Now?" is the title of a special issue of *Social Text*; by that point—2005—*queer* had become so expansive, and so vaporized, that it meant everything and nothing to do with sexuality, with gender, with social oppressions of any kind, type, or flavor.[15] Now, queer studies studies everything *except* sex. (I exaggerate only slightly.) Queer studies has bigger realms to conquer. Meanwhile, on the ground, queer and trans students, leaders, activists, and advocates speak in pronouns and initialisms and neologisms. (*Ace*, anyone? *Incel*?) It's time to talk about sex, again, as Rubin once said. Except she said it at the beginning, the big bang of queer theory. What is there to talk about when we talk about *queer* today?

What about talking about *misfits* instead? As I demonstrate in this book, the term and its associations enjoyed a wide circulation in the first two-thirds of the twentieth century. Martin Luther King Jr., early in his career, sermonized about the importance of becoming a "transformed *nonconformist*" in order to resist Jim Crow, sanctioned by religious authority.[16] In that sermon, King analogized the story of the early Christians, who resisted Roman persecution, with the struggle to restore civil rights for African Americans. The story of the twentieth century, it is said, is the story of overcoming fascisms of every stripe, and the idea of being a misfit suits these early accounts of hegemony as the basic fact of social life. Social life in this era was defined by Jim Crow, by deep divisions and entrenched powers that were questioned only as a result of this prism, this view into social life through the lens of conformity or nonconformity. One-Dimensional Man, as Marcuse called it.

Is it the case that the variety of social movements, not to mention their successes, have been utterly misunderstood, over- and underestimated? Do we perhaps need better words to use to describe the reality *back then*, and perhaps use these words to describe our realities *right now*? Are we living, today, as One-Dimensional Men? But we no longer speak of one-dimensional *man*; we no longer speak of *one dimension*. To do so is to ignore the matrices of social difference as well as the achievements of the social movements in challenging and diversifying our notions of social cohesion, ramifying our ideas about social struggle. We don't need the idea of the misfit, of conforming or not conforming within a one-dimensional world order, because the world is split into *n* dimensions (or intersections, to use the paradigm).

However, if this study shows anything, it is the capaciousness and elasticity of this modern notion. Generally, in modernist discourse, a *misfit* (definition 1: *any outsider within general society*) is a culturally anonymous "anyone"— that is to say, a generic nonconformist, usually coded as *man* and not a woman, *white* and not black or brown or yellow or green, usually of sound mind and body. By contrast, a *misfit*, definition 2, is *a member of a minoritarian community defined as a distinct collectivity, or an individual possessing durable or permanent cultural, psychosocial, or sociobiological characteristics alien to the institutions, norms, and values of majority culture.* Georg Simmel's sociological archetype of the stranger (*The Stranger* [1908]) fits this description:

a single-identity person who is marginalized within a majority culture but remains essential to it. Simmel's chief example for the minoritarian misfit is the Jew in Europe, historically barred from certain social institutions (such as landownership) but allowed to carve out a place of social, economic, or cultural exchange for the benefit of the larger populace. The stranger is thus the type of cultural misfit who represents a minoritarian *group* that self-identifies as such; this archetype also includes individuals marginalized by their disabilities, sexualities, racial coordinates, and other structural differences *before* these differences coalesce into discrete cultural-political "identities" throughout the long twentieth century. Modernist novels featuring these characters arguably helped jump-start discourses of self-legitimation, collective liberation, and recognition from majority culture, disturbing the first notion of the social as a homogeneous, unmarked, organic whole. The best examples in the American context are the great African American literary tradition and ethnic American immigrant fiction. In the early to mid-twentieth century, a literary exemplar is Alain Locke's *The New Negro* (1925). But this study's archive centers on nonconformists *within* these rarefied groups, as in Thurman and Larsen's fictional challenges to the modernist New Negro's straight masculine paradigm. (A figure like Langston Hughes is enticing because he seems to exemplify this cultural-nationalist position yet personally seems queerer than he let on. This is a major reason Hughes isn't a subject of this book: he did not accept the further burden of double marginalization due to his sexuality.) So authors in this archive are even further afield, more alienated, constituting the modernist *misfit*'s definition 3: *culturally articulated figures defined by their alienation from majoritarian values, norms, and institutions, as well from their own cultural groupings, which recapitulate those same systems.* This type of misfit experiences a double alienation enforced by the collusion of majoritarian norms re-created within minoritarian collectivities in their march toward progress. *This double displacement is what makes these modernist misfits "queer," in our parlance today.*

Maybe, just maybe, being—or feeling like—a misfit is still a useful way to understand individual discomfort with the hegemonies of everyday life, and with the hegemonies of social power operative in minoritized social groupings (definition 3), whose norms and values (especially sexual norms and values) ape those of the majority even as their culture resists hegemony. (This is the critique of the LGBTQ community's focus on gaining a foothold in conservative institutions like holy matrimony and the US military.) The stories of double exile studied here demonstrate diverse modernist writers' principled maladjustment and the "adjustment proceedings" (in Thurman's terms) necessary for these minoritarian subjects to negotiate their internal marginalization from majoritarian-*lite* communal norms of belonging.

A Modest Proposal

The concept of *queer* served its purpose in pointing out the disparity between social identities and their exclusions—often visited upon racialized, gendered, and sexual minorities—that social movements engendered in order to breathe politically free air. Perhaps the rhythm of conformity, rather than that of normativity, is the true beat for these older stations of the misfit—and for the newer stations of marginality that continue to haunt the halls of minoritarian belonging.

A term like *queer*, unlike one linked to a specific identity, has been used as a solvent of identity purposefully. *But perhaps we need a different solvent.* My modest proposal is not *Let's substitute "misfit" for "queer" and call it a day.* Rather, it is *Let's look at these modernist self-conceptions of social marginality and double exclusion and think about why the notion of misfit-ness was so powerful, frequent, and overutilized—even as it remains, today, underanalyzed—before we coalesced around the rubric and rhetoric of identity.* The narratives studied here suggest a way to have our *three-way* with difference, the way our modernist forebears did: by coalescing around three definitions of social misfits, thereby gaining purchase on the realm of the majority through the backdoor rhetoric of universal exclusion and minoritarian particularity. Misfits like the modernists studied here indicate an analytic, if not a diagnostic, of social reality before the social movements took firm hold—but also before our late machine age remixed these Sixties revolutions and incorporated them into an even greater assemblage of capitalist engineering. The misfit is a conceptual, and *historical*, *ménage à trois* between intersectionality, identity, and humanity. An interface that perhaps helps us see through an older age's thought about difference beyond the cul-de-sac of the identity categories, or the intersection that leads to so much incoming traffic. Thinking intersectionally might be easier when routed through the universalism—and political efficacy—of identity, but only if it leads to a solvent of identity toward reassembling the social as a truly inclusive, homogeneous heterogeneity: meaning, a *solution* in the form of a liquid structure of feeling, not evaporating with the infinite regress of adding identity categories to the mix, but moving like quicksilver through fingers of every color, of every length, size, and even number.

As we will see, a kind of protomaterialism, as proposed by Rosemary Garland-Thompson, should be embraced, given the *misfit* idea that anybody can, and is, and will be outside the social mainstream, in some shape or another, at some time or another, "for one reason or another." And that means everybody is potentially a misfit, as everybody is potentially "intersectional," as anybody is that crosses the multiple lanes of social traffic. But the aim is not to minimize the greater hurts of greater historical oppressions (those who are "more misfit" than others). It is to elevate everyone to the same level, without forgetting those differences and without surreptitiously allowing for the false universal to remain the default, as "nonintersectional." To remember the misfit is to remember that the intersectional is universal, and vice versa, without forfeiting the particulars of hierarchical differences that, again, render some more intersectional—more "mis-fit"—than others.

This doubleness of meaning in the concept of nonconformity, maladjustment, and nonbelonging in the discourse of the misfit is the subject of the next section, which seeks to stabilize the tension inherent in universalizing versus minoritizing notions of the term.

Epistemology of the Misfit

"For one reason or another every one of you weren't happily adjusted back on Earth. Some of you saw the jobs you were trained for abolished by new inventions. Some of you got into trouble from not knowing what to do with the modern leisure. Maybe you were called bad boys and had a lot of black marks chalked up against you."[17] So says the captain of the space mission to his new recruits in Robert Heinlein's "Misfit" (1939), one of his early stories. Focused on one of those recruits, Andrew Jackson Libby, "Misfit" centers on Libby's extraordinary mathematical and logical abilities. Libby's "genius" sets him apart even within this band of misfits, men considered dangerous or disposable enough to enlist in astro-colonization (65).

I cite this example as a privileged figure for the misfit's social maladjustment, nonconformity, and nonbelonging (definition 1). This kind of misfit, as Capt. Doyle's speech implies, does not "fit into" society "for one reason or another." But Libby's "intuitive knowledge of all arithmetical relationships" sets him apart from the bounds of human faculties, not to mention the rest of his crew (64). So Heinlein's story turns on Libby's uncanny computational capacity. The narrative illustrates a symbolic equation of man and machine, first by personifying a space-age "ballistic calculator" as a protocomputer comprising "three Earth-tons of thinking metal," which Libby "subconsciously thought of . . . as a person—but his own kind of a person" (65–66). After personifying the "thinking metal" as Libby's "own kind of a person," the narrator describes Libby as a human "calculator." In the climax, when the machine fails to track an asteroid's orbit, Libby begins blurting out astronomical coordinates, miraculously saving the colonizing mission: *"Four hours later* Libby was still droning out firing data, his face gray, his eyes closed. *Once he had fainted but when they revived him he was still muttering figures.* From time to time, the captain and the navigator relieved each other, but there was no relief for him" (66, emphasis added). Libby proves a better machine, a better "computer," than his beloved machine made of "thinking metal." *He* doesn't fail to "apply the data"; he might faint, but his superhuman mind keeps processing, unerringly accurate (66). Libby's autonomic computations save the day, if not the galaxy. Heinlein's sci-fi allegory thus recuperates a misfit into a super-antihero. The plot of "Misfit" equates Libby's person with the marvels of the space age: marvels that his computational superpower recuperates, in turn. (Echoing the story's paradoxical isometric logic about the superiority of mechanical calculation beyond the limits of a mechanical calculator, Libby's explanation for detecting any and every technical miscalculation is that the data just "didn't fit" [64].)

This glimpse into Heinlein's space colonization story illustrates the modernist idea of being a "misfit." As I discuss below, misfit discourse encompasses varying yet related issues of the individual's relation to society, normalcy, and commonality. The idea of being a "misfit" includes forms of nonconformity, nonbelonging, or maladjustment. The term performs heavy yet invisible epistemological labor. Thus Heinlein's story about a misfit never utters that word, except in its title. Fittingly, the rhetoric of misfit-ness applies at various levels of social discourse. As I show in this introduction, discourse about "misfits" was a powerful one in the early to mid-twentieth century. And in the history of ideas, I argue that *misfit* discourse is a precursor to terms and concepts related to identity that we now take for granted: identity and all of its semantic entailments, including culture (as in collective identity); intersectionality (as in multiple, complex, or intersecting aspects of identity); positionality (as in how identity shapes one's standpoint in the social order); and broader terms for social subjugation and hegemony, such as oppression, exclusion, and alienation; majority and minority and their lexical variants (including minoritarian); and community, solidarity, and home culture (or family). All of these important ideological abstractions, and more, date from the late twentieth to the early twenty-first century. More importantly, they displace an older rhetorical fabric, one covering a general society without culture and other false utopias: the rhetoric not of *identity* and *community* but of *misfits* and *society*.

But, as we see in this study, the rubric and rhetoric of the *misfit* is directed to address cultural differences and their intersection, including in the specific way developed by the authors in this study: double marginalization, or stories about culturally different protagonists whose identity and community are in conflict, which renders the *modernist misfit* doubly alienated—from her or his own kind as well as from broader society. As we will see, the paradigm for addressing myriad levels of individuation and enculturation, of oppression and liberation, was constituted through these different semantic and rhetorical fields: *before the rhetoric of "identity," we talked about "misfits."*

And yet writing about a "misfit" like Andrew Jackson Libby is different from writing about a "total misfit" like Emma Lou Morgan in Thurman's *The Blacker the Berry* (1929), or Helga Crane in Larsen's *Quicksand* (1928). Libby is as majoritarian as it gets. As "Andrew Jackson's" namesake, he is an avatar of American white-settler patriarchal individualism. This "misfit" is thus worlds apart from Rhys's "underdogs" and "doormats in a world of boots," as in her novel *Quartet* (1929), or Isherwood's multicultural "non-conformists" resisting the postwar nuclear-industrial complex in *A Single Man* (1964).

But how can this seemingly antiquated term meet all of these varied fictional uses? "Misfit" describes a default super-antihero like Libby, but also a modernist culturally inflected antihero like Thurman's intersectional Emma Lou Morgan and Rhys's deracinated Marya Zelli. The story I am telling is about how the term *misfit* oscillates between the "Libbys" of the hegemonic order and the "underdogs" and "nonconformists" so labeled for their gender, race, sexuality, nationality, and other structural "isms" of identity. Before the various Sixties liberation movements—which Isherwood's novel anticipates but does not yet envision—and the rubric and rhetoric of identity politics, the term of art was this oddly misfitting term about "misfits." I say *oddly misfitting* because of its rare elasticity and generality: encompassing both "Andrew Jackson" and queer, black, female, or (post)colonial protagonists, often inhabiting multiple identities.

Misfit's Ladder; or, Levels of Modernist Alienation

Representations of the modernist misfit in the early to mid-twentieth-century novel, then, include these increasingly minoritarian, increasingly contemporary understandings of the subject and the hierarchies of social difference. At the most general level, modernist fiction centered on the figure of the misfit represents maladjusted protagonists generically coded as general nonconformists, like Heinlein's space colonists. These are indicatively male, abstract-universal misfits. What sets them apart is their criminality or antisociality, which can be remedied or redeemed. In Heinlein's story, the captain of this band of misfits tells them that, "*every one* of you *weren't happily adjusted back on Earth*," furnishing the rationale for their enlistment and for the story's title. Yet Heinlein's Libby instances a special kind of displacement. In "Misfit," Libby is a one-of-a-kind human supercomputer. He is presented at first as a run-of-the-mill misfit, like the others. But Libby is special: his "disability" is a super-ability, which elevates as it excludes him. Less fortunate examples from this archive of unique-individual misfits, excluded due to their physical, mental, or emotional disposition, or a particular disability or debility, are the mainstay of what I call mainstream modernist fictions, such as Virginia Woolf's shell-shocked Septimus Warren Smith (*Mrs. Dalloway* [1925]) or Albert Camus's probably-on-the-spectrum, existentially adrift Meursault (*L'Étranger* [1942]).[18] Even in this sketch of fictional modernist alienation, we see that a misfit is *not* a misfit is not a misfit . . .

Increasing the political dimension of nonconformism, maladjustment, and nonbelonging within this fictional universe are figures who represent a cultural valence of minoritarian subjectivity in the context of majoritarian domination. These are modernist characters closer to our own epistemology of social power and subjectivity. They are excluded due to permanent systemic cultural differences set against oppressive social hierarchies. Here we can glean the discourse of empire and colony and other structural divisions based on gender, race, and sexuality, perhaps most famously figured by James Joyce's Stephen Dedalus (*A Portrait of the Artist as a Young Man* [1916]), whose burning alienation from Ireland and its stultifying normative institutions, such as the Church and the language of the English oppressor, subjugate the modernist antihero in cultural exile. And finally, in the smallest concentric circle within this modernist circle of alienation, we can discern misfits who inhabit multiple positions that are in conflict within the misfits themselves and are thus mutually constitutive yet disidentifying. These outsiders represent misfits who personify nonconformism at various social levels and within various kinds of cultural wholes, with the result being a story of double marginalization. The marginalization manifests as being ideologically or behaviorally set apart from broader society; from universal norms of physical, intellectual, or dispositional comportment; from culturally inflected, structural hierarchies that define different social bodies; and from their own cultural (even familial) home, for nonconformity with the communities, ideals, values, norms, or institutions created by and for their own kind, as in the fiction grouped under the rubric of misfit modernism.

To return to the example of Joyce: the astute reader will ask, why *not* Stephen Dedalus? He is as deeply exiled as any other figure in these books, and Stephen's alienation is keyed to his nonconformity within, and maladjustment to, the conservative Ireland of Joyce's youth. Joyce, too, satisfies the autobiographical criteria set for analyzing misfit modernism: his self-exile is also paradigmatic of the cultural misfit's displacement. And though Joyce could indeed constitute a chapter in this study, his case is different enough to merit some discussion in this introduction. First, and foremost, is the ironic distance Joyce maintains toward his antihero. *Portrait* is conceived with authorial irony that destabilizes the seriousness of Stephen's misfit consciousness. As Wayne Booth writes, "As the young man goes into exile from Ireland, goes 'to encounter for the millionth time the reality of experience and to forge in the smithy' of his soul 'the uncreated conscience' of his race, are we to take this . . . as a fully serious portrait of the artist . . . ?" Booth asks whether Stephen's rejection of the priesthood counts as a "triumph, a tragedy, or merely a comedy of errors."[19] The narrative instability qualifies the alienation of Stephen Dedalus in his own novel, rendering it perhaps a sign of immaturity rather than a painful reflection on double exile.

The second main reason to question whether Joyce is properly emblematic of the misfit-modernist archive is his second major antihero: Leopold Bloom. As with Stephen, Bloom is culturally alienated—a misfit if only for being a Jew in Ireland—and emasculated. But Joyce's vision for *Ulysses* is ultimately a comic one. As Stephen's interior monologue states in Telemachus, "*And no more turn aside and brood.*"[20] Joyce's modernist aesthetic, in other words, encompasses a vision of the misfit in Dedalus and Bloom, but it is by no means comprehended by this theme alone. Indeed, Joyce's loving and detailed re-creation of Dublin and Irish culture while in self-imposed exile is symbolic of his enduring attachments to a cultural nationalism that he held to all the closer for being alienated from it. (Joyce was a real Irish patriot, unlike his Citizen.) And third, concomitantly, the "biological pessimism" that Hardwick identifies in Isherwood's *Single Man*— and that extends to the other novels in this study—is ironized in Joyce's *Portrait* and sidelined for a comic, universal vision of humanity in *Ulysses*. And so the Joycean structure of feeling transcends the parameters of this narrower, and more painful, vision. His imperial-level canonicity—coregent of English letters, with Shakespeare and Milton—registers the arc of Joyce's authorial trajectory: a minoritarian on steroids, Joyce thoroughly transformed the terms of English fiction, no less than Henry James before him. That grand ambition and reception dissolves the focus on double marginalization of *Misfit Modernism*.

"A Writer of 'Misfits'" (1)

Employing the critical lens I call *immanent reading*, which draws out the significance of the *misfit* term and constellated concepts from the novels themselves, in this section, I provide a materialist sketch of the long and rich history of twentieth-century applications of the term and its evolving meanings. In the following section, I discuss how literary critics have analyzed the theme of the misfit. An important distinction from these historical treatments and the argument that this book makes, however, rests on the particulars of definition. As described below, Rosemary Garland-Thompson defines *misfits* and *misfitting* as the disjointed juxtaposition between body and environment, predicated on a materialist disability-studies theoretical framework. Her understanding of *misfit* is thus closest to my own, the misfit as a *cultural* as much as *social* position of nonconformity and maladjustment.

Evidence for the resonance between the early twentieth-century notion of the *misfit* and our contemporary paradigm for marginalized sociocultural *identity* is furnished by perhaps the most visible queer modernist, John (Radclyffe) Hall. In a letter to her lover, Hall writes:

> Why is it that the people I write of are so very often lonely people? Are they? I think that perhaps you may be right. I greatly feel the loneliness of the soul—nearly every soul is more or less lonely. Then again: *I have been called the writer of "misfits." And it may be that being myself a "misfit," for as you know, beloved, I am a born invert, it may be that I am a writer of "misfits" in one form or another*—I think I understand them—their joys & their sorrows, indeed I know I do, and all the misfits of this world are lonely, being conscious that they differ from the rank and file.[21]

Jack Halberstam, in an essay on Hall's *The Well of Loneliness*, cites this letter to argue for the female "invert's" use of fashion to express female masculinity.[22] Halberstam thus notes the importance of self-fashioning for modernist inverts like John Hall and her most famous creation, Stephen Gordon, *The Well*'s famously lonely protagonist. But Halberstam's argument does not complete the cognitive connection: the notion of being a misfit is presented but also elided, as self-evident in its meaning, as synonym for invert and other forms of outsider-dom. Halberstam never questions why Hall centers on this term in particular. Why not "outsider" or "outcast"? What special meanings does "misfit" convey that these other terms do not?

Emma Liggins also discusses Hall's letter.[23] Liggins does not gloss over the term, linking it (as Hall does) to the sexological category of the "invert." But the "misfit" in Liggins's account functions as a synonym for Hall's subcultural lesbian identity—interchangeable with "odd," "abnormal," "outlaw," and so on. While Liggins echoes the connection Hall makes in this letter, even construing notions such as "misfit identities," these are yoked to synonymous phrasings like "outlaw identities" and "lesbian identities."[24] Such substitutions seem to dissolve the specificity and salience of the term "misfit," a specificity invoked by Hall herself. Liggins and Halberstam gloss over the ambiguity of the term. Here, being a "misfit" is synonymous with a cultural identity that is benighted by general society—that of the sexological invert. But being a misfit, as Hall views it, also connects her to "misfits of one form or another"—not simply other "inverts" like her. Hall's letter, importantly, does not provide examples of what these other "forms" could be. Most abstractly, a misfit is anyone who occupies— whether for a moment or for a lifetime—the position of social outsider "for one reason or another" (Heinlein), in the generic sense that lacks the cultural and political meaning Hall invokes.

Of course, this sense of the misfit—the social, even *antisocial*, outsider, as we see in early social science reports—is famously personified as the baleful villain called The Misfit in Flannery O'Connor's short story "A Good Man Is Hard to Find" (1953). The Misfit's murderous shadow perhaps obscures much of the symbolic potential this term might once have contained. For even if O'Connor's dark emanation serves as a figure for "the Other *par excellence*," as Dan Wood argues, this Southern Gothic image is more mirage than reality: a dark fairy tale, perhaps.[25] The term circulated for decades to name the position of marginalized *people* and *populations*, individuals *and* collectivities, construed as the "misfits of the world," as evinced by Hall's letter.

Etymology of *Misfit*

The importance of this term as an umbrella concept not simply for social deviance but for cultural minorities—such as Hall's female "inverts" and so-called Sapphic modernists[26]—is the heart of this study, which articulates how visions of *cultural* "misfits of one form or another" are narratively formulated in the modernist novel.

Etymologically, the first meaning of *misfit* (1823) is sartorial: "A garment or other article which does not fit . . . the person for whom it is intended." But its meaning quickly slides into defining the "wearer" herself as a misfit, in the general sense of maladjustment to one's environment: "A person unsuited or ill-suited to his or her environment, work . . . [*especially*] one set apart from or rejected by others for his or her conspicuously odd, unusual, or antisocial behavior or attitudes" (1860).[27] The meanings of *misfits* in Hall's letter explicitly draws on this last definition. In the adjectival definition of *misfit*—"Of, relating to, or designating *social misfits*"—the *Oxford English Dictionary* cites articles in the *Journal of Educational Sociology* in 1929 and 1936: "These misfit *personalities* constitute an increasingly serious *social problem*," stressing the volitional aspect of being a misfit: maladjustment due not to DNA or built environment, but just a bad attitude.[28] Thus early understandings of the misfit are about abstract individuals' volitional "maladjustment" or "unsocial behavior."[29] These accounts provide evidence of the resonance of this discourse in the early twentieth century, during which the idea of *being a misfit* frames discussions of social problems *caused by* maladjusted individuals of all stripes and persuasions: abstract persons with no cultural label.

Yet early discourse also paints a vaguely social-Darwinist portrait of misfits.[30] For instance, a 1937 article, "First Aid to the Misfit," addresses "the maladjusted child."[31] Looking closer, maladjustment is increasingly ascribed not to volitional individuals but to structural factors, such as physical disability. The author, Helen Cummings, writes, "We *now* look upon these manifestations of misbehavior *as merely symptoms*" in order to uncover root "*causes* and remove them."[32] A "primary cause," Cummings adds, "has been found to be *physical disabilities* which bring in their wake a trail of emotional conflicts and conduct disorders by which the child seeks to escape the handicap of his physical nature."[33] These disabilities occur across the social field. Cummings shows how the discourse about misfits "now" finds root causes in the realm of natural or environmental differences, rather than the other way around, which centers on the individual as an autonomous social actor. The fault for being a misfit, then, progressively lies in our stars.

As with Hall's notion of being a "born invert," defined as a natural trait maligned by institutional norms that render that essence problematic (such as marriage), children with congenital disabilities, such as deafness or blindness, become "social problems" requiring "first aid to the misfit." Yet Cummings stresses the importance for educators to "prevent the acquisition of similar defects by *the normal, healthy* child" by providing "proper lighting and ventilation, the inculcation of good health habits and instruction in safety education."[34] The "born" "abnormal" child and the "normal, healthy child" can both be misfits. In both cases, they need "first aid," or accommodation. In both cases, the root "cause" is not willful behavior but natural or social forces, or their interplay.

Thus rhetoric about misfits develops an increasingly complex discourse about systemic forces impinging on individuals *and* environments, forces progressively fixed as categorical physical, psychological, and sociological differences, such as disability or sexuality. Structural aspects of one's *identity*, in contemporary terms. This transition in worldview regarding the origin of social differences supports volume one of Michel Foucault's *History of Sexuality*, which documents a Western epistemological transition from regarding sexual acts as behavior to conceiving sexuality as the essence of the individual. In this paradigm shift, deviant sexual behaviors are anthropomorphized into "personages," or negative avatars of newly construed norms of gender and sexuality, such as "the homosexual" for heterosexuality. This scientific shift develops clinical terms like "sexual deviate," "gender variant," "sodomite," and, of course, "invert." Hall's letter adopts this discourse in the reverse—as Foucault describes it—to speak on her own behalf.

The discursive mesh of cultural meanings surrounding the term *misfit* in the modernist era, as a structural understanding of maladjustment to collective norms "of one kind or another," seems oddly self-evident, yet curiously undertheorized. The modernist discourse of the misfit is elided even in scholarly interventions, such as Halberstam's, that invoke this term in the context of minoritarian subjectivity, such as Hall's "born invert." Why the resistance to carrying through the early modernist idiom of misfits into our own time? The answer lies, I think, in the term's conceptual lability, which causes cognitive dissonance—a cognitive dissonance reminiscent of Eve Kosofsky Sedgwick's claim about the figure of "the closet," or sexual identity itself, as we see in the next section.

"The Great Assassins of History"

A post–Second World War lecture by Roger Tredgold employs the discourse of the *misfit* as shorthand for antisociality in the abstract individual, but also for varied forms of structural subordination. The title, "Changes in Social Responsibilities—and the Misfit," bemoans the transformation in British society in the postwar era, which the speaker blames for the rise of "misfits" in the general population. The lecturer, a physician, focuses on people "who suffer . . . from mental deficiency or senile decay." The increase in number of the mentally ill or senile caused greater demand for their "institutional care," while families seemed unwilling to shoulder the burden—an aspect of weakening social bonds, in his view.[35]

The good doctor blames a host of factors for the rise in so-called misfits, including the "break-up" in family systems, the loosening of authority in the education system, and the influence of media, such as the wireless and television.[36] All of these forces and institutions have neglected their duty to instill a sense of collective responsibility in the ordinary citizen, according to Tredgold. And in light of this collective failure, misfits from all walks of life "appear in various guises—to the psychiatrist they will be anti-social psychopaths; to the soldier, barrack-room lawyers, or sometimes mutineers; to the magistrate and police, criminals; to the industrialist, trouble-makers, sometimes 'communists,' though they would not be communists in Russia, or anywhere else that Communism was in power. . . . Finally, to their parents, they are an abiding disgrace." And, in peroration, he concludes that "in past ages, they were often found at the bottom of some of the world's trouble-spots; and they have on occasion been played on by circumstances, or by the unscrupulous, to swell the ranks of the Great Assassins of history."[37]

This swelling description recapitulates—and expands—the distinction Eve Kosofsky Sedgwick makes between minoritizing and universalizing understandings of the closet. Even in Hall's letter, *misfit* includes "inversion" but is not exhausted by it, as her vision expands beyond sexuality: "misfits of the world *in one form or another*." Similarly, in Cummings and Tredgold, misfits come in many forms: the physically or mentally disabled, caused by congenital or environmental factors, but there are also gestures toward general situations where individuals are at odds with their environment ("being played on by circumstances, or the unscrupulous"). (I think Hall exploits this understanding of misfits.) Hence, scientific discourse about the social problem of "misfits" in the early twentieth century uncannily recapitulates one of Sedgwick's key arguments in *Epistemology of the Closet*: that understandings of homosexuality draw upon mutually exclusive explanations. The universalizing view posits that everyone can be a little bit of both, as in Freud's notion of childhood's polymorphous perversity. The opposite view, the minoritizing understanding, sees homosexuality as the attribute of a minority of the population: this is the "ten percent" or "born this way" model. The minoritizing paradigm is thus an ethnic model of queer identity, construing homosexuals as constituting a distinct class of persons and, therefore, deserving protection from discrimination. Sedgwick argues that homosexuality is seen in both ways at various times and with no sense of cognitive dissonance in this bifurcated epistemology, which would be evident if it treated any other issue beyond homosexuality itself (according to her). Such was the deranging power of queerness to Western epistemological foundations—a key foundation of knowledge itself is the sexual, as Foucault maintained, but Sedgwick added that this knowledge centered on the distinction between hetero and homosexual as if the fate of the world depended on it.

In this study, I make a similar claim for the connotative itinerary of *the misfit* as a figure for social deviance: it invokes both a universalizing category of individual maladjustment and a minoritizing category of, well, what we call a *minoritarian identity*, such as Hall's "born invert." Hall's letter, like the sociological discourses on misfits as social problem, seems to oscillate between both connotations of *misfit*. One is a misfit as an ordinary individual who simply doesn't fit in within his or her environment. That is the generic, social-outsider definition, the one that predominates in most treatments of the term as a catchall category. But there is another, culturally attuned definition: the misfit as a *collective* subject, representing a certain "species" of individual—such as Foucault's history of when "the homosexual became a species," or, in a gesture that exploits both senses, in the case of Hall's letter, "the invert," a minoritizing category drawn from the general class of misfits "in one form or another."

The centrality of this term to general social-deviance theory, in other words, as well as to discourses of minoritarian self-definition has been shockingly missed by practically everyone. Even Halberstam's deployment of Hall's letter glides over this interesting deployment of the rhetoric of the misfit as a generic *type* (all the ways one can be excluded from "the rank and file of society") and as a given *token*—the *specific way* that Hall and her kind are excluded from "the rank and file of society." The causes of misfit-ness are thus legion. Misfits are even caused by developments as broad as societal decay in itself. Hall's letter emphasizes that misfits come in many forms. A misfit is set apart, but the causes of such isolation can be congenital or accidental, durable or transitory.

Except some forms are permanent. The general meaning is blind to structural distinctions and views misfits as volitional subjects, such as criminals, who can be rehabilitated once they pay their debt to society. Such management of spoiled identity allows the misfit to become part of the fold once more. A misfit like Hall is not able to "pay" this "debt," because the debt is by definition a core state of being. And by insisting that inverts are misfits, Hall ironically neutralizes the stigma of sex-gender deviance by tying it to the universal meaning of misfit as general nonconformity, unencumbered by strata of difference that cannot be erased. Hall's love letter implicitly shows the two sides of the misfit's Janus-faced meaning, and it is not too much to say—reading *immanently*, as explained in my methodology—that Hall's letter constitutes an important literary invocation of the misfit as a cultural, even political, social category. Hall joins the cultural notion of the term to the universal sense of misfit-ness as contingent as it is individual. Hall's rhetoric, in short, argues for the individual and social dignity of "born invert[s]" as included in the world as any other "manner or form of misfit." Anticipating the single (gay) man of Isherwood's novella, Hall invokes a subordinated collective sexual identity and joins it to the abstract, universal dialectic of the social and the individual. Inverts are not only misfits, in other words; they are people, too.

Again, in Hall's invocation, we see a reverse discourse that Foucault defines as a key strategy for sexual minorities speaking on their own behalf. So far, so understood. But the linchpin in Hall's strategic deployment of the rhetoric of sexology to justify her love—her sexual and gender "identity," in our terms—is the terminology she uses. Perhaps like the term *cosmopolitan*, whose ancient roots were revivified in the modernist moment, *misfit*, too, becomes a conduit for renewed interrogations of the social dialectic. Perhaps terms like *misfit* function as discursive bridges between a universalizing discourse of "the individual" outsider, undefined by material oppressions such as gendered or racialized embodiment, and a burgeoning deployment of collective, cultural uniqueness—be it inversion or be it the New Negro, as we shall see—that elevates the status of the individual as representative of a structurally marginalized group. Thurman's Emma Lou Morgan, who need not be a "total misfit," exemplifies this burgeoning deployment of the rhetoric of misfit-ness beyond the realm of the false universals, of individual versus environment, toward the concrete particulars of minoritized individuals within concentric circles of cultural differences and beyond, to a social realm revealed as stratified structurally, rather than idealized as a homogeneous whole.

The conception of the misfit is therefore a key discursive ingredient in this shift, proclaiming the misfit as precursor to the notion of identity as the foundation of minoritarian community. In other words, the double meaning of "misfit," as invoked in Hall's letter and in the novels in this study, rests on the idea that anyone can be a misfit, but that certain kinds of people are more "misfit" than others. These kinds of people—the misfits of the world, in one form or another—are the stratified segments of cultural groups, ethnic sodalities, sexual subcultures, religious minorities, and the like. Each can invoke being a collective misfit, drawing on the generality of the idea to define abstract individuals. By so doing, ironically, such invocations elevate the claims of minoritarian difference, appropriating the dignity of universal individuality, thereby exposing the default individual's *lack* of gender, race, ethnicity, and other entailments as a fiction. When deployed in this double sense simultaneously, *misfit* as a rubric implies the falseness of the unmarked individual by *claiming* this universality in the realm of the particular.

Thurman's "total misfit" employs this double meaning. Emma Lou Morgan is ostracized for being *female while being "too black"*; a dark-skinned male would be able to "pass." The notion of a "total misfit" thus envisions a universal image of outsiderdom—evident in the impersonal pronoun "no one"—but joins it to the particular entailments of Emma Lou Morgan's embodiment within an oppressive environment, with the resulting internalization of her *embodiment* as oppressive.

Here we have glimpsed the strange, modern career of the term *misfit*, which generally means *social outsider* and thus appears in social science discourses concerned about broad sectors of society. But the idea of being a misfit narrows down, even in social-problem commentary, to structural particulars, which became the cultural basis for identitarian or minoritarian groups—such as disability-rights coalitions—in the march toward liberation.

"A Writer of 'Misfits'" (2)

But let us briefly return to a key exponent of the *culturally attuned* definitions of the misfit. As Hall's letter indicates, such an understanding of the term centers on a minoritarian consciousness: Hall's parenthetical remark to her beloved, "for . . . I am a born invert," indicates the causation between being a misfit and being a "writer of 'misfits.'" She adds that she "understand[s] them—their joys & their sorrows . . . all the misfits of this world are lonely, being conscious that they differ from the rank and file." What Hall understands is that it takes one to know one: she is "a writer of 'misfits'" because she is a misfit in a specific form, while this understanding extends to knowing "all the misfits of this world" and writing about "'misfits' in one form or another." The autobiographical chain of being is incredibly tight, and it extends beyond the autobiographical contingencies of Hall's situation—she does not only write about "born inverts," after all, but about a full range of sexual and gender dissidents, including, in that indelible scene in *The Well*, the young man in the Paris cabaret who calls Stephen Gordon *"ma soeur."* Thus even in the realm of sexual and gender "misfits," there is variation—Hall's "beloved" was feminine, unlike John Hall (or Stephen Gordon) herself. But the larger point is the significance of the *misfits of the world* being defined by their social exclusion, as well as the "writer of 'misfits'" being defined by her "understanding" of this exclusion because she experienced it personally.

However, while Hall describes how misfits feel, she did not develop a distinctive misfit narrative idiom at the level of form. By contrast, the novelists in this study endeavored to transform the contours of fictional form to represent narrative life-worlds from a "misfit" point of view. It is partially for this reason that, despite the importance of Hall's point of view on misfits and "inverts" as a kind of misfit, her hypercanonical lesbian novel does not occupy a chapter in this book. But this was by design. *The Well*'s famously middlebrow accessibility—its formal conventionality—serves an important ideological purpose. By so doing, however, Hall sacrifices the potential to explore the idea of "being a misfit" via modernist narrative form. As Hannah Roche claims, Hall's conventional or "Victorian" realism "boldly appropriat[es] an accepted (and heteronormative) genre," that of the Bildungsroman, to make an ideological "statement about the rightful position of lesbian writing . . . in ways more direct and profound than the audaciously avant-garde."[38] Facing an obscenity trial in November 1928, *The Well*, Roche reminds us, "offended adversaries with both the radicalism of its sexual politics *and the apparent conservatism of its prose*," a style that Woolf dismissed.[39] This formal conservatism is at odds with the transformative prose of misfit modernists like Rhys and Isherwood. Larsen and Thurman, as realists—Thurman developing a form I call *affective* realism—appear closer to Hall's novel and its (more properly Edwardian) realism. But Hall's conservatism is not merely a stylistic fluke; it lies at the very heart of her novel's design. *The Well* is a "born invert's" Bildungsroman. Thurman's *The Blacker the Berry*, by contrast, develops its realism of affect within a narrative structure that eschews the closures of what Roche calls Hall's "Victorian" realism. Isherwood's and Rhys's novels, in turn, are more recognizable experiments in modernist form—such as *A Single Man*'s single-day structure and *Quartet*'s deployment of limited points of view to construct its unsettling narrative mood. Larsen's *Quicksand*, again like Thurman's novel, employs a more recognizable realist code of narration, while its experimentation involves the modernist exploration of depth psychology in the technique of psycho-narration. But Larsen's novel is modernist also insofar as its exploration of Helga Crane's complex psychology serves to subvert, and thereby deconstruct, the stereotypical sentimental flatness of the nineteenth-century "tragic mulatta" character. Ironically, *The Well* exploits a sentimentalizing idiom—we could call it the realism of the *tragic congenital invert*—in order to argue for the decency, normalcy, and sheer humanity of its queer protagonist.

Other Modernist Misfits

Flannery O'Connor's baleful yet iconic character The Misfit has drawn the most critical commentary on this term, albeit without reflecting on the discursive history of "misfit" as the modernist term of art for describing social differences at varying, and overlapping, micro- and macroscopic levels.[40] Similarly, my conception of the cultural, intersectional misfit in the modernist novel differs from legacy understandings of modernism as a literary formation of the anti-hero with a thousand faces. In criticism, one can look to Paul Levine's "J. D. Salinger: The Development of the Misfit Hero" (1958) to trace a consistent critical idiom about modernist misfits as *social* outsiders, and perhaps even as *cultural* outsiders[41]—but not, as is the focus of *Misfit Modernism*, as narrative figures who occupy multiply inflecting identities and are displaced within both majority culture and within their cultural home. Existing critical formulations of the misfit in modernism, in short, tend to generalize the notion of nonconformity within the social field, presenting paradoxically transcendent antiheroic figures such as Joyce's Leopold Bloom even while they are culturally marginalized—because of Bloom's sexual nonconformity, as an uxorious cuckold, no less than because of his being a Jew. The "Everyman" label conventionally attached to Bloom is indicative of this more generic understanding of the misfit in modernism.

By contrast, this study mines a *discrepant* literary formation that ushers in an intersectional notion of being a misfit—by authors who are autobiographically entailed in their creations. Bloom's example—no less than that of Salinger's "misfit antiheroes," in Levine's essay—belongs to a normative vein in literary modernism wherein the social outsider is the modernist hero par excellence. Stephen Dedalus, no less than Meursault, occupies a paradoxically central antiheroic position in the modernist novel. As noted above, I don't believe that either Bloom or Dedalus—despite their cultural displacements—are defined *solely* through their identitarian predicaments. Far from it. Leopold Bloom's odyssey is fundamentally classic, comic, and cosmic. Stephen's tragicomic "brooding" and desire to "forge in the smithy of [his] soul the uncreated conscience of [his] race]," by contrast, signals the self-aggrandizing gesture of Refusal of mainstream modernism. And this gesture is indicatively that of a masculine universal subject position that is antithetical to an intersectional, culturally determined figuration as created by the discrepant authors studied in *Misfit Modernism*. Perhaps Joyce knew this, and that's why he deflated Stephen's aspirations as never to become realized, to remain *uncreated*.

In another high-modernist counterexample, let me draw on the minor character of Miss Kilman in Woolf's *Mrs. Dalloway*. In that novel, the overweight, queer, and unpatriotic Doris Kilman symbolizes the abject modernist misfit. She haunts the gilded halls of the Dalloways' townhouse. Miss Kilman is marginalized within the moral economy of that novel. The title isn't *Miss Kilman*, after all; it is Mrs. Dalloway who decides to buy the flowers herself (in the famous opening line of that novel). Clarissa as a protagonist recapitulates the antihero in the becoming-majoritarian vein of mainstream modernism, centered on a once-queer society matron.

The Misfit in Literary Criticism

A recent critical invocation of modernist form and misfits—though not of the *misfit* itself as a modernist discourse—is Rob Hawkes's *Ford Madox Ford and the Misfit Moderns*.[42] But Hawkes's notion of "misfit moderns" bears only a superficial resemblance to the argument in this book. As Hawkes's subtitle suggests—*Edwardian Fiction and the First World War*—his study is situated in an earlier period, which saw the emergence of impressionists such as Ford and Conrad. Hawkes's notion of Ford as a "misfit modern" centers on Ford's style as premodernist and post-Edwardian. Hawkes's study centers on the "misfit" of

Ford's aesthetic, neither a form of the "materialist realism" of the Edwardian era, as described by Woolf in her essays on "Modern Fiction" and "Mr. Bennett and Mrs. Brown," nor a form of high modernism, as in the stream of consciousness of Dorothy Richardson, Joyce, and Woolf herself. In no sense does Hawkes convey the culturally displaced condition of double exile that *Misfit Modernism* invokes as its overarching theme.

Uncannily, an author in this study was originally Ford's protégée: Jean Rhys. If an epistemology of the misfit in modernist discourse shows us anything, it is how ironically fitting notions of the misfit and the modern seem to be. The question may not be *Why are critical accounts centered on the misfit and the modern?* but, rather, *What seems to disconnect them from accruing the intellectual force of a coherent formation—such as occurred, famously, with cosmopolitanism and modernism?* Why are scholars still failing to discover the epistemological centrality of the misfit to modernism itself? The answer might lie not only in the political unconscious between all of these accounts of modernist misfit forms and formations. The answer might appear, instead, in the local node of cultural and aesthetic and social history that links Rhys and Ford themselves. If the conceptual apparatus of this book holds, then these questions allow us to investigate the taken-for-granted-ness of any invocation of the misfit and the modern, which serves mostly to preclude sustained investigation of the codevelopment of these symbolic codes in the twentieth-century history of ideas.[43]

Hence, a key intervention this book makes is the dual epistemology of the term. A misfit like Ford, no matter how aesthetically variant, is *culturally* as far from being a misfit—in the *misfit modernist* sense—as it gets. Hawkes in fact struggles with the cultural conservatism of Ford's most famous novel, *The Good Soldier*, granting its formal innovativeness but eliding the reactionary cultural values—and privileged social positions—of Ford's character systems and Ford himself. However ably Ford subverts these conservative institutions—not least the institutions that profited from world war—his life and work seem more of a piece with canonical narratives and understandings of modernism itself. Again, we see how the misfit's very marginalization is made universal.

Rhys makes for an excellent foil: no impresario or scion of English letters, she. And in broader contrast, she and the other authors in this study center on the social experience of *feeling like a misfit*—in the early twentieth-century sense of the term ("A person unsuited . . . to his or her environment . . . *esp.* one set apart from or rejected by others for his or her conspicuously odd, unusual, or antisocial behavior or attitudes"). So the minoritizing meaning of *misfit* governs this study as representative of doubly dislocated cultural selves, rather than that of Ford or other mainstream modernists plausibly seen as "misfits."

In sum, literary criticism of misfits superficially draws from the discourse that Hall invokes in her letter. This is an underexamined idiom arising in early twentieth-century writing, both literary and scholarly, which, as we have seen, centers on the idea of the misfit as universal nonconformity or minoritarian nonbelonging. Nonbelonging due to what we now call issues of identity, such as Hall's "born invert," or multiple, intersecting, dimensions of cultural person-hood as elaborated by the novels in this study: racial and gendered otherness, as in Thurman and Larsen, or transnational origin, gender, class, and sexuality, in the novels of Isherwood and Rhys. All of these fictional artifacts explore a condition of double exile: a cultural outsider displaced from majority culture and also alienated from her own kind. The novels in this study compose a collection of case studies somewhat dissimilar from one another, which test the limits of representation, in both aesthetic and political senses of the word.

The "Misfit" as Theoretical Construct

Such elasticity in the term *misfit* and its dual epistemology is one reason for its undertheorization. To date, there is one contemporary theory of "misfit-ness," which hearkens back to early twentieth-century understandings. Rosemary Garland-Thompson suggests that we take the *misfit* concept seriously as a way out of the quandary of single-identity politics, on the one hand, and, on the other, as a way to resolve the ambiguity in the notion of disability as a social rather than a corporeal standpoint. In "Misfits," Garland-Thompson proposes the concept as a way to move past a critical impasse in disability theory, between the social model of disability—a view in which "oppression . . . emanates from prejudicial attitudes," socially reproduced in concrete forms such as "architectural barriers"—and a radical model of disability that draws on materialist feminist understandings of impairments—such as pain and "functional limitation." Her work joins that of other disability theorists who distinguish "between [impaired] bodily states or conditions . . . and the social process of disablement" that views disability as sociopolitical, not biomedical. Thus Garland-Thompson writes, "People with disabilities become misfits not just in terms of social attitudes—as in unfit for service or parenthood—but also in material ways. Their outcast status is literal when the shape and function of their bodies comes in conflict with the shape and stuff of the built world."[44]

Thompson likes *misfit* as a concept because it focuses on the materiality of environment and embodiment without, however, "rely[ing] on generic figures delineated by identity categories." She adds that "encounters between body and environment that make up misfitting are dynamic. Every body is in perpetual transformation not only in itself but also in its location within a constantly shifting environment." Garland-Thompson specifies that although *"misfit* is associated with disability and arises from disability theory, its critical application extends beyond disability as a cultural category and social identity toward a *universalizing of misfitting* as a contingent and fundamental fact of human embodiment." She adds that "focusing on the contingency of embodiment avoids the abstraction of persons into generic, autonomous subjects of liberal individualism," a "foundational myth . . . of Western culture."[45] Garland-Thompson's framework thus centers on the interaction between body and world that is universal and yet radically individual, depending on context. Her concept of misfit thus opens up a twenty-first-century space for thinking through multiple dimensions of embodied social existence.[46]

Of course, as I have demonstrated, *misfit* was used in the early twentieth century to think through disability and other dimensions of embodied existence—*before* the identity categories that usurped that discursive space, and the cultural and political capital, which Garland-Thompson sidesteps as "reigning notion[s] of oppression" at once atomized and universalized, too reliant on liberal-individual models of personhood. Such a contemporary reliance on identity, as I have argued, reinstates this universal within the particular—as Hall does in her love letter—in distinction to the archive of *Misfit Modernism*, which questions this complicity between minoritarian and hegemonic codes of personhood such as social respectability, individual autonomy, and moral conventionality.

Drawing on Garland-Thompson's critique of the generic "individual" and unitary notion of "identity," and based on archival histories of the term's use, this study analyzes novels elaborating the semantic figure of the "misfit." Each novel centers on a figure who stands culturally apart, *even within their own home-worlds*, not to mention from majority culture. A figure who doesn't fit in with their home environment not because they are essentially different, but because they are seen as embodying a difference that sets them apart even from their own group. Furthermore, the kind of *misfit* that this study centers on departs from the framework of disability (as well as sexuality), profiting from Garland-Thompson's generous conception of being a misfit as radically embodied but also radically universal. Just as everyone will someday be disabled, so does this study's formulation of the misfit extend universally while retaining its culturally specific parameters. *Never* is the modernist misfit a transcendental subject. The figure that emerges from the pages of the authors collected in this study—and, partly, that emerges in the careers and personae of the authors themselves—is never a universal subject of modernist alienation. Rather, the narratives surrounding this figure are always focused on the cultural dimension of alienation as an embodied, and particularly nonuplifting, if not outright antisocial, form of intersectionality. And while intersectionality is a concept that informs this study, its particularity as an optic of black feminist theory seems particularly misfitting for a study that ranges transatlantically, is situated earlier historically, and engages nexuses of identity beyond that origin. Thus while using the term *intersectionality*, especially in its antisocial form, as I read it in the modernist novel, the idea of the misfit remains more flexible for its immanent circulation within these novels themselves: Thurman's narrator describes the notion of being a "total misfit," and Larsen's that of "unconformity"; Isherwood's that of "nonconformists," and Rhys's of marginalized underdogs (or "doormats"). In all of these cases, the novels elaborate each misfit's cultural particulars as sites of double alienation. Ranging from the US context of the Harlem Renaissance through the Parisian expatriate scene and the West Coast multiculturalism of postwar Los Angeles, all of these narratives formally "theorize" the subjectivity of a cultural misfit.

Novels of Double Exile: Chapter Descriptions

Using critical methods such as immanent reading, this study draws out the contours—the structure of feeling—of modernist literary novels focusing on what one might consider as *antisocial intersectionality*. I discuss the critical methodology developed from this book's archive in the first chapter, illustrating the symbolic parallelism of this hermeneutic approach and the broader aesthetic ideals of modernism as a cultural formation.

The authors featured in this study are not meant to be exhaustive; they are instead the most visible emblems, the most resonant evidentiary examples of the semantic figure of the misfit and of a literary formation I call misfit modernism, within the archives of the transatlantic modernist novel. The theoretical framework provided by these case studies that span the twentieth century delivers a "proof of concept" for the resilient theme of the modernist misfit and its exploration of antisocial intersectional subjectivity—before these terms were coined—or living between two cultures and being unwanted by both. This last part is essential and distinguishes this study from others that focus on the narratives of modernity from the point of view of racial, ethnic, sexual, or gender oppression. To remember the misfit is to question anew how the progressive political march toward group liberation pressures intersectional individuals to conform to universal notions of agency, autonomy, and liberal individuality. And to remember the misfit is to also question how ethnic and other minority cultures also pressure intersectional individuals to conform to certain notions of uplift and communalism—as well as agency, autonomy, and liberal individuality—despite their counterhegemonic social contexts.

Chapter 1: Methodology

The first chapter explores the style of close reading I call *immanent*, by way of rereading Raymond Williams's influential account of the structure of feeling. I argue for the importance of nonaided close reading, or noninstitutional frameworks for understanding misfit modernist fiction. Immanent reading takes a stand in the so-called method wars for the nuance of close textual attention to the novel form, over and above trends of interpretation that draw on theoretical frameworks adopted from other fields of (scientific) knowledge, such as recent "turns" to midcentury sociology and cognitive psychology, not to mention quantitative or "distant" reading approaches. More importantly, as shown in the chapter on Jean Rhys, official discourses of close reading is a way of deflecting from a troubling misfit aesthetic or structure of feeling. Concomitantly, immanent reading is a way to stay close to troubling misfit structures of feeling. I view certain critical approaches as tactics for managing such narrative structures of feeling—deflecting by turning to psychoanalysis, for instance, in the succor offered by respectable concepts such as melancholia rather than the messy, immanent, aesthetic structure of feeling misfit modernists compose in their troubling fiction. For instance, the Rhys chapter argues that institutionally recognized powerful theories steamroll over the misfit's worldview, which is not legitimized by existing institutions or shared by others.

Chapter 2: Nella Larsen

The second chapter is the first case study, which focuses on Harlem Renaissance novelist Nella Larsen and *Quicksand* (1928). This debut novel centers on Helga Crane, a biracial and bicultural young woman whom the narrator describes as a "despised mulatto." Larsen's novel subverts the sentimental nineteenth-century literary trope of the "tragic mulatta" and modernizes it in the nonetheless tragic figure of Helga Crane. This chapter describes Larsen's formal technique of *psycho-narration*, used to convey deep insights into her protagonist, insights that the protagonist herself may not share. Larsen's novel thus intercedes in the tragic-mulatta stereotype by delving into her heroine's complex psychology—a feat hitherto unknown in modernist novels about black female protagonists. By creating a complex psychological portrait of Helga Crane, Larsen's novel serves to humanize and dramatize the cultural and racial boundaries a "despised mulatto" was forced to obey, despite these cleaving her very sense of self. As the narration puts it, "Why couldn't she have two lives, or couldn't she be satisfied in one place?" That the question is rhetorical emphasizes its force. There is no place, at the time, for someone who trespasses the color line with her very being, as Helga Crane does by having a white mother and black father. The homogeneity—and its Jim Crow enforcement—of each of her "two lives" means she must choose one or the other, which presents an impossible choice that is as existential as it is deeply intersectional. Helga Crane's submersion in the quicksand of her final choice—to marry a black preacher and lose herself in a Southern folk community—is akin to her destroying what makes her special to begin with: her doubleness of identity and vision, resonant as a form of double exile, but resonant nonetheless. The loss of her complexity is the tragedy of the novel, not the fact of Helga Crane's biraciality (as would be the case in naïve, sentimental treatments of the "tragic mulatta"). Unlike most critiques of *Quicksand*, this chapter centers on the narratological dimension that Larsen employs to explore the subjectivity and antisocial intersectionality of her protagonist.

Chapter 3: Wallace Thurman

The Larsen chapter also demonstrates how immanent reading can provide a pathway to understanding a complex psychological portrait of double exile, an approach I recapitulate, at a higher, more complex level, in the third chapter. Chapter 3 centers on the archive of Wallace Thurman, a key figure in the Harlem Renaissance, although less well known today than his contemporaries Zora Neale Hurston and Langston Hughes. Thurman was a provocative writer and editor known for his critique of class-bound New Negro ideals of uplift and respectability. Thurman sought to challenge the burden of representation on the New Negro artist (the "racial mountain," in the words of Langston Hughes), a burden chiefly represented by the influential writings of Alain Locke and W. E. B. Du Bois. *The Blacker the Berry* addresses the prevalence of intraracial prejudice within segments of the bourgeois black community. Thurman's novel represents the systemic ostracism and internalized stigma that shadow its protagonist, Emma Lou Morgan.

This chapter argues that Thurman's fiction operates according to an aesthetic ideal that I call *affective realism*: the dedication to documenting the painful realities of feeling unrelieved by uplifting narrative arcs in the context of representing intersectional subjectivity as a form of double exile. Thurman's novel calls this experience of intersectionality the "adjustment proceedings" of social prejudice and internal exile from one's community. Moreover, the narrative discourse employs a social-Darwinist paradigm in its naturalist idiom, representing what it calls "the haunting chimera of intra-racial prejudice" as a sociological phenomenon. In this mode of affective realism, while it focuses somewhat on social determinants—most important, Emma Lou's upbringing and family—it is the sharp delineation of the feelings of exclusion that distinguish this novel.

The Blacker the Berry thus represents a phenomenology of racism within Harlem. This internal critique and internal presentation centers on an affect the narration codes as "lonesomeness," a term repeatedly used to name Emma Lou's experience of double exile. The second key term in the novel is "total misfit," which reinforces the sense of isolation that the doubly exiled undergo. In social terms, Emma Lou as a "total misfit" registers her exclusion not simply from white culture but from Harlem's thriving artistic scene. Emma Lou's ostracism by figures known to Thurman—and even by a figure modeled on Thurman himself—ironically distances the author from the social movement that gave him voice to begin with.

Chapter 4: Jean Rhys

With the fourth chapter, we cross the pond by way of the Caribbean modernism of Jean Rhys. The transatlantic crossing made by Rhys, in other words—also reflected in Larsen's Dutch West Indian ancestry—mirrors the transatlantic leap made by misfit modernism as a whole. This diasporic crossing defines the porousness of national borders that defined the biographical itineraries of the authors in this study. Moreover, this national hybridity defines modernism as a whole, but as regards the subjects of this book, however, this crossing of national boundaries remains incomplete, unfinished. The example of Rhys serves to highlight the unavailability of national identification for these misfit authors. As a white "Creole" native of the West Indian island nation of Dominica, as British but not English, Rhys was caught between multiple national and colonial fault lines that divided transatlantic modernity.

Rhys's early fiction represents these and other cultural intersections: race, ethnicity, class, gender, sexuality, and what could be called the pre-postcolonial condition. But her first published novel, a roman à clef about her affair with Ford Madox Ford, *Quartet* (1929), centers on a figure Rhys famously focused on throughout her career: the social "underdog," in Ford's words. Using the modernist narrative device of hypothetical focalization, Rhys's novel spends much time on what *might* happen, what someone *would* be thinking, what *could* be the case. To explore the case of the underdog, in modernist narrative form, entails in part creating the social reality or mood of being an underdog through the use of nonindicative moods. What is an underdog if not someone whose view of reality is reliably *not* ratified by the rest? The idea of the underdog—or, to borrow Rhys's idiom, "a doormat in a world of boots"—is telling, as it invokes the importance of societal power in the discourse of the modernist misfit. Rhys is special partly through her exploration of various states of being, not only of being a misfit due to cultural intersectionality—above all gender, nationality, and class—but of being treated as an underdog, or seeing oneself as an underdog, besides. Rhys's stating the case of the underdog, in *Quartet*, happens not simply through the "top-dog" antagonism of Lois and Hugh Heidler but, more importantly, through the very narrative infrastructure of the novel. Its deployment of focalization within third-person narration is the key to understanding the theme of intersubjectivity, and of the third-rail political dimension of the intersubjectivity between "top dogs" and "underdogs" in "this three-cornered fight."

My immanent reading of *Quartet*, as with the Thurman chapter, indicates how misfit modernism is defined partially through immanent *writing*: recapitulating the thematic in formal terms. Such an aesthetic procedure is perhaps the thing all modernisms have in common. But misfit-modernist novels formalize the themes of maladjustment and nonbelonging even as the narrative focuses on a cultural outsider who is doubly displaced. Like Marya, Rhys's other protagonists have no home to speak of and find no succor from majority culture, despite all the "Good Samaritans" who come to her aid. Instead, these "doormats" live in "a world of boots," a pessimistic vision of social reality: the underdog's vision, warranted by her culturally marginal, intersecting identities.

In the emblematic case of Rhys, the early novels are instances of how minoritarian subjects are represented as misfits, in her case as vaguely racialized, hypersexualized women who are "underdogs," marginalized in their own stories as decadent fallen women or weak New Women. But such misfit status is not simply an artifact of Rhys's unrealized literary talents, nor a symptom of the general absence of a feminist sense of community in her era, nor a shameful effect of Rhys's belated identification with her Caribbean heritage. In the case of Rhys, when *Wide Sargasso Sea* appeared, her earlier novels reappeared. Many critics in the '70s, including V. S. Naipaul, speak of the narrative logic of minoritarian overcoming. But Naipaul also speaks of the precocious timeliness of Rhys's early novels ("Rhys thirty to forty years ago identified many of the themes that engage us today").[47] In some sense, then, they are considered ahead of their time—and also hopelessly behind the times, simultaneously. Within the minoritarian frame, Rhys's preoccupation with misfits who represent socially stigmatized "inferior beings" seems antiquated, as embracing their own oppression. Within a larger frame, however, one encompassing the losses of human history altogether, which in Rhys's case include the horrors of the two world wars and the realities of colonization and decolonization in the West Indies, these novels seem timely for their depiction of a "friendless and worthless but pitiful woman," as Rebecca West once claimed.[48]

West adds that Rhys "proved herself to be enamored of gloom to an incredible degree," claiming that Rhys's "preference for gloom is not artistic but personal." But this notion of the personal is limited, and in our present historical consciousness we can better appreciate Rhys's exemplary attachment to the modernist misfit's experiences of "inferior being," of being doubly dispatched from subcultural collectivity while remaining in the margins of majority culture. Such negative early modernist images remind us of the price to be paid for narratives of development: integration into a collective identity and norms of majority culture, such as aggrandized agency, liberal autonomy, and self-possessed individualism. The cultural price might be losing the attachments to loss, including self-loss, itself. Some minorities do not enjoy this privilege and remain mired in the cultural shadows of "inferior being" that Rhys depicts consistently.

Chapter 5: Christopher Isherwood

The fifth chapter is on Christopher Isherwood; specifically, it analyzes the ideological parallax between Isherwood's "nonconformist" sensibility in the modernist novella *A Single Man* (1964) and his identitarian post-Stonewall memoir of Berlin in the 1930s, *Christopher and His Kind* (1976). The germ of this project began in the Isherwood archive, which deals extensively with the politics of sexuality as a legitimate social identity. A gay-rights activist *avant la lettre*, Isherwood was a modernist critic of what we now term heteronormativity *as well as* a critic of what we now call homonormativity or homonationalism.[49] Isherwood was ambivalent about the idea of homosexual *identity* and remained steadfast in his espousal of a modernist doctrine of impersonal individuality, aesthetic autonomy from political causes, and what today we recognize as a principled queer critique of the social sphere. Isherwood's writing evinces the complex politics of a queer-rights activist before Stonewall, while also withdrawing from state-sponsored political movements, which refused to dignify queers as legitimate minorities.

Hence, Isherwood was a gay liberationist before gay liberation. But *A Single Man* problematizes the politics of positive gay representation by extending beyond queer as an identity to discover a discourse of coalitional identities in multicultural Cold War Los Angeles—something defined by an anticommunal cultural pessimism that inflects Isherwood's modernist resistance to the cultural logic of Stonewall, of asserting a visible, collective gay identity. Isherwood was never a "joiner": writing of his past self in the third person, Isherwood claims, "Not only was Christopher a homosexual, he was in his deepest heart, an individualist."[50]

The double exile in Isherwood's novel, and his broader archive, turns on the protagonist's ambivalence toward some facets of his queer identity and his sympathetic identification with other cultural groups as fellow "minorities" (or "minority-sisters," in the novel's parlance). Isherwood himself underwent chosen exiles, in a reverse migration away from his native Christian English identity and the war effort, on the one hand, and his increasing self-identification as a Hindu disciple and Americanized, "out" gay writer, on the other. The novel delves directly into questions of negotiating multiple identities in postwar Los Angeles, revealing the tensions among groups—such as "Negro" and "Swede," in the obsolete words of the narrator—and within such groups, as in the "minority-sister" phrase that represents queer belonging for Isherwood's protagonist. The novel portrays a model way of understanding "minority" identity through the lens of impersonal attachment and self-attenuation, which privileges empathy across identity forms that seem too often premised on antagonism—the "aggression of the minority," in the novel's terms.

Conclusion: Beyond the "Progress Narrative"

This introduction provides the theoretical and historical framework for the book. *Misfit Modernism* is a study of a particular trope, a figure of cultural nonconformity, of social nonbelonging and internal marginality, personified in the figure of the protagonist. This figure experiences what I term double exile—feelings of alienation and ostracism within the character's home community and within majority (white, male, bourgeois, heteronormative) culture. This figure of social exclusion and melancholy antisociality differs from the existential angst of the classic modernist antihero, as their cultural exile is grounded in minoritized identity: racial, gender, sexual, national, and class position might all play a role in their social exclusion. Their double exile is thus keyed to their intersectionality, and their often painful self-abasement and disidentification from homogeneous home or majority cultures, as represented in the historical contexts and literary forms of the transatlantic modernist novel. These contexts include the Harlem Renaissance, for the two (African) American authors in this study; the expatriate scene in Paris and London of the 1920s, for Jean Rhys; and the Berlin of the 1930s as well as the Los Angeles of the 1950s, for Christopher Isherwood, whose career traversed multiple modernist epochs and locales.

Not only are the authors in this study construed as "writers of 'misfits'" for writing about feeling like a "'misfit' in one form or another." But they are also writing their lives as "works of art," thus no less literary—or aestheticized. The notion captured in this book's title is meant to highlight the rupture of the boundary between historical identities and affiliations that are part of the history (or story) of being a "total misfit." The cross-identifications of Thurman, for instance—for whom Locke's injunction to draw inspiration from "Africa" was a nonstarter—were with modernism more than with a putative African vernacular culture. (He wasn't alone in this respect, of course; Countee Cullen's famous poem, "Heritage," pointedly asks, "What is Africa to me?") Their autobiographical writings signal the self-fashioning inherent in their self-invention: authors writing themselves self-consciously into being modern. Being modern then was what we call being modernist now, to distinguish aesthetic from historical dimensions of modernity. And being modern entailed a level of self-consciousness about personal effect and affectation that, as I noted, was created through social networking, self-fashioning, and other tools of interaction that supplemented the stylistic words on the page. One could not be modern—what we now call modernist—without being aware of how to be modern, as well as how not to be. That is what these authors' emphasis on being "modern" meant: like any fashionable style of dress, of comportment, of collective norms of social being. And in part, their modernism is what exiled them.

Moreover, as exemplary fictional accounts of double exile as a structure of feeling *"in solution,"* the novels explored in *Misfit Modernism* question a prevailing progress narrative of minoritarian collectivity. Christopher Nealon, in *Foundlings*, argues for a similar teleology for queer subjects in the twentieth century. His book locates early twentieth-century or modernist queer narratives—such as *The Well of Loneliness*—as originating a minoritarian tradition in the absence of a robust queer audience. Hence, Nealon entails a three-stage process for minoritarian (in this case, queer) narrative representation. He begins with the solitary queers of Hall's controversial novel and ends with queer writing that has its own preexisting audience. In the middle are figures such as Hart Crane, midcentury writers who originate within a shared sense of commonality but lack the articulated community of our contemporary identitarian moment of name-your-identity pride parades.

Love's *Feeling Backward* argues against this conventional mode of minoritarian cultural forgetting in the context of queer subjects and the "losses of queer history." Love faults the compulsory optimism of today's assimilating queers, for such optimism hides the "bad old days" of queer self-loathing. Nealon seems to deploy queer modernist texts such as Hall's in such a fashion, as a period relic of an unreconstructed solitary subjectivity formation, which indicates how far "we've come." More importantly, Love argues, such optimism forgets the *continuing* "bad days" of today. In other words, and in the terms of this study, modernist misfits are not simply artifacts of an earlier unreconstructed past. There might be "modernist" misfits in our supposedly postcolonial, postracial, postgay, and postfeminist present.

This introduction, and the study as a whole, questions the teleological narrative that glosses over the losses of minoritarian, and not only queer, history. "History," for me, includes fictional narratives and their reception, including our own contemporary attachments. As Love claims in the context of queer subjects, something about the "bad old days" is intensely affecting to this day. *The Well of Loneliness* is still the most widely read lesbian novel in English— although, Love reminds us, in a shockingly simple insight, it is also "the novel most hated by lesbians themselves."[51] Even as its narrative is less salient in our own time, Hall's novel presents a potential mirror for *misfit* subjects who, it is said, should not resemble the self-loathing, solitary, and alienated subjects of yesterday. Except, perhaps they do.

Misfit Modernism looks at narratives and authors whose lives and fictions contradict yet also corroborate this teleological framing of the process of becoming a minoritarian subject. I choose the term "minoritarian" and not identitarian because, as we have briefly seen with Rhys, such authors occupy various intersections of identity and fit uneasily within such matrices. Yet their fictions—and their lives, as well as the critical reception, which is colored by both realms of experience—seem to belie the minoritarian Bildungsroman of late modernity. This conceptual and historicist Bildungsroman operates as a three-part story of singularity, which then finds community, and finally this community finds its path to visibility and acculturation, if not assimilation, within a majoritarian framework. This framework exists at the level of cultural and aesthetic representation: canonization as legitimized minority experiences that then become all-but-majoritarian. Becoming is overcome.

In what sense is this now established narrative of minoritarian overcoming missing something vital—something that constitutes the central problematic of *Misfit Modernism* as a whole? In the sense that such a metaphor of minoritarian Bildung (1) apes majoritarian political values of affective optimism and personal autonomy and (2) reinforces evaluative aesthetic norms, such as formal sophistication and imaginative distancing of the personal from the aesthetic, with the "merely" personal rendered abject; indeed, (3) the minoritarian metanarrative of overcoming hinges on canceling out "earlier" stages—such as Rhys's rootless, lost urban protagonists. From the vantage point of minoritarian Bildung, such earlier stages—as in the refrain of Rhys's "earlier novels"—are retroactively seen as mere back-formation. By reconstituting the modernist novel about misfits and taking a second look at modernists whose lives and careers track along their nonconformist aesthetic preoccupations, we can better realize the persistence of a misfit structure of feeling defined by alienation from minoritarian community norms and from majority cultural ideals and their mirroring of one another. Modernist fiction about cultural misfits represents a salient critique of this double valence to minoritarian existence. Unless we understand the failures of assimilationist, even integrationist, cultural ideals of progress, we will forever ignore the misfits who refuse to bend to the will of the majority within the minority.

1.

Methodology

Immanent Reading

The evidence which literature may provide—and it is indeed evidence that is not available elsewhere—is accessible only if the literature is treated as literature. . . . [A]nd the literature which has to be taken into account ought to be selected on its merits as literature, and not on its external relevance to the more obvious movements of history. . . . When the literature is read as a highly aware and articulate record of individual experience within a culture . . . it will provide important evidence indeed.

—**Raymond Williams, 1950**

It is less important to like "good" poetry and dislike "bad," than to be able to use them both as a means of ordering our minds.

—**I. A. Richards, 1930**

This chapter explores the style of close reading I call *immanent*, by way of rereading Raymond Williams's influential account of the structure of feeling. I argue for the importance of nonaided close reading, or employing noninstitutional frameworks for understanding the modernist novel. Immanent reading, first and foremost, takes a stand in the so-called method wars, arguing for the importance of close textual attention to the novel form above trends of interpretation that draw on theoretical frameworks from other fields of (scientific) knowledge, such as recent turns to midcentury sociology and cognitive psychology, not to mention quantitative or "distant" reading approaches. More importantly, immanent reading is a way to stay close to troubling misfit structures of feeling. Thus I view institutional critical approaches as tactics for *managing* such narrative structures of feeling—deflecting by turning to psychoanalysis, for instance, and the succor offered by respectable concepts such as melancholia rather than the messy emotions named in the novels themselves, such as Wallace Thurman's "lonesomeness" in *The Blacker the Berry* (1929). It is this immanent approach that helped me understand and envision the minoritarian structure of feeling I call misfit modernism.

Revisiting the Structure of Feeling

Raymond Williams's influential concept of the *structure of feeling* is the point of departure for my critical approach. Williams formulates the idea of the structure of feeling—an idea that centers on subjective impressions of social experience—in *Marxism and Literature* (1977). These impressions are recorded in the realm of art and literature but are not limited to the aesthetic dimension. And they are subsystematic articulations of the immensity of social experience. Williams's examples of structures of feeling are drawn from socioeconomic classes or generations but are not "reducible to the ideologies of these groups or to their formal . . . class relations," he writes. He adds, "At times the emergence of a new structure of feeling is related to the rise of a class (England, 1700–60); at other times to contradiction, fracture, or mutation within a class (England, 1780–1830 or 1890–1930), when a formation appears to break away from its class norms, though it retains its substantial affiliation, and *the tension is at once lived and articulated in radically new semantic figures*."[1] With the last example, England 1890–1930, Williams signals the revolutions of modernism. Yet he also glosses over the transatlantic networks that define modernism and its movements. This transnational caveat to Williams's example serves to reframe a more substantive issue I have with the idea of the structure of feeling. Williams's essay begins far from where it ends up. It begins not with concrete examples tethered to concrete social forms—socioeconomic classes in England or tensions within a privileged class—but with the problem that his concept tries to resolve: how to process already-theorized experiences of the past, and how to understand the evolving experiences of what he terms individuals' "practical consciousness" and "practical experience" (130). The idea that "structures of feeling can be defined as social experiences *in solution*," as he writes, indicates that cultural-aesthetic forms develop "radically new semantic figures," as in his modernism example—these new semantic figures clearly referring to modernism's revolutionary experiments in form (133, 135). The structures of feeling Williams focuses on seem to slide from subjective (or "practical") experiences toward large-scale examples of entire generations or social classes that conclude his essay.

He begins, however, with the *subjective* in face of "relationships, institutions and formations in which we are still actively involved," what he calls "forming and formative processes" (128). In fact, Williams has this to say about "social consciousness," or his term for the fundamental basis of common reality given his Marxian framework: even when systems such as Marxism provide an account of "social consciousness," or the social order as a whole, "they are not a whole inventory even of social consciousness in its simplest sense." He cautions that forms of "social analysis"—such as "dominant *systems* of belief" or "influential *systems* of explanation"—"become social consciousness only when they are lived, actively, in real relationships." "Indeed," Williams adds, "*all consciousness is social*" (130, emphasis added).

Early on in his essay, Williams prefaces the notion of a structure of feeling as an inchoate or "embryonic" form of "practical consciousness" grounded in "practical experience," as distinct from "official consciousness" or "social analysis," or even "fixed social forms" such as economic classes (131). He defines, in turn, the structure of feeling as a "social experience which is still *in process, often indeed not yet recognized as social but taken to be private, idiosyncratic, and even isolating*, but which in analysis . . . has its emergent, connecting, and dominant characteristics" (132, second emphasis added). Originating from the "private, idiosyncratic, and even isolating . . . practical experiences" that inform an individual's "practical consciousness" arises the "evidence of *forms and conventions—semantic figures*—which, in art and literature, are often among the very first indications that such a new structure is forming" (133, emphasis added). There's a lot to be said, and that has been said, about the structure of feeling. But an element seldom discussed is the subjectivity of its original formulation, in new "forms and conventions" or "semantic figures" that belong to the cultural or aesthetic realm. Williams challenges the Marxian base-superstructure model, advocating for the agency of the letter in its most expansive sense: as a first response to an ongoing "cultural process," which formulates unarticulated aspects of social experience in tension with "official consciousness."

What is the "methodological consequence of such a definition," one might ask? Williams answers, "The specific qualitative changes are not *assumed* to be epiphenomena of changed institutions, formations, and beliefs, or merely secondary evidence of changed social and economic relations between and within classes"—the vulgar-Marxist reading of culture he preempts. "At the same time," Williams adds, "they are from the beginning taken as *social experience*, rather than as 'personal' experience or as the merely superficial or incidental 'small change' of society" (131). The conceptual journey in this influential essay thus sutures the social and the practical (or "lived") realm of experience. Art and literature are granted an important role in the ongoing "cultural process": not only as first responders but also as change agents who modify the structure of feeling already in place. They usher in "emergent or preemergent" changes to the social mood and social reality through the agency of their "semantic figures." How we get from individual consciousness to art and literature is the black box of aesthetic production.

So much for the revaluation of the "superstructure" as capable of changing the "base." More importantly, however, Williams argues for individual artistic emanations that may seem merely "private" or "idiosyncratic" but that later become legible as speaking for whole generations.

Preemergent Structures of Feeling

But what of the private visions that do not become legible, that do not speak for whole generations? Do they still exist? The argument in this book is that there are such creations, such structures of feeling, that may not define the contours of the very cultural formations they belong to, in part. They are the misfit "minority reports" of other first responders—alternative viewpoints as credible though not as legible as now established "official consciousness" would have it. And Anglo-American modernism is now as "official" a discursive apparatus, as Establishment, as any art movement ever was or, arguably, will be. What about the minority reports from misfit modernists? Of what consist their "semantic figures"?

The answer, in this book, is the semantic figure of the modernist misfit itself. And not simply the misfit as the modernist outsider we know and (have grown to) love, but the misfit as a "minority report" from so-called cultural minorities themselves. A figure defined by her doubly marginalized standpoint, intersectional within cultural milieus to which she belongs, but from which she is alienated, just as she is an outsider to mainstream social structures.

However, to argue this does not necessarily entail that the modernist idea of the misfit—as developed in these novels and the career arcs of the authors who penned them—endures as an emergent or preemergent structure of feeling in the twenty-first century. Indeed, hearkening back to Williams's tripartite notion of historical change—residual, dominant, or emergent—he makes clear that some cultural processes may or may not turn into full-scale "systems."[2] The abstract idea of the misfit in the twentieth century seems to evolve into a paradigm closer to our own notions of identity, and even of intersectionality, which were *fixed and formulated* well after. Hence, it is possible that the notion of the cultural misfit is *forever* an "emergent or preemergent" formation—lacking the mass-cultural approbation and historical specificities of individual social identities as they developed later in the century. In fact, part of the difficulty with seizing the misfit as a respectable, representable *idea* is precisely its backward-seeming-ness—and backward-feeling-ness, to echo Heather Love. It is for this reason that I turn to Williams's notion of the structure of feeling—seen, as I do here, less as a contained notion of a bounded collectivity and more as Williams initially conceives it, as a porous membrane, an individual scent in the air that only through historical change or cultural analysis can be said to coalesce into a bounded collective whole. This book does not primarily furnish a historicist account, but one based on a different set of concerns and conceptual paradigms drawn from the immanent aesthetic terrain of the modernist novel in discrepant minoritarian formations, such as those constructed (and lived) by the authors collected in this study.

So, the broadest version of the conceptual argument of *Misfit Modernism* is that the "semantic figure" of the modernist misfit *forms part of* a textually inscribed, culturally emergent, "embryonic" structure of feeling, which may never have achieved the dominance of more accepted and acceptable cultural paradigms within modernism. This project thus reexamines and dereifies Williams's original conception of structures of feeling in general. As noted, he takes great pains to justify that any idiosyncratic cultural vision can, and does, resonate as "evidence" of an "emergent or preemergent" structure of feeling. But as he begins his essay, Williams emphasizes the present-ness of these structures and bemoans their consolidation into "finished products." The feelings are a structure, but this structure is not crystalline—not "fixed, finite." The "procedure" of fixing "living presence" is a way of missing its vital, liquid state of matter: "all that is present and moving, all that escapes or seems to escape from the fixed and explicit and the known," which he critiques as too easily "grasped and defined as the personal: this, here, now, alive, active, 'subjective.'" He instead posits the idea of the structure of feeling to mitigate this critical "procedure," which divides the social/structural from the personal/emotional, and to revivify the notion of aesthetic–cultural process, to give it an autonomy that can only be called a modernist gesture by Williams himself. Even "the making of art is never itself in the past tense," he argues; it "is always a formative process, within a specific present" (128, 129). And this contemporaneity is what his notion seeks to capture in a theoretical concept as fugitive as the cultural process it seeks to describe.

Immanent Reading

The minoritarian basis for the concept of the misfit in *Misfit Modernism* rests on an innovative interpretive methodology—immanent reading—that mirrors the conceptual framework Williams adopts in this seminal essay. He privileges not simply the aesthetic dimension, contra the orthodox Marxist devaluation of culture—*"assuming"* art and literature as mere "epiphenomena" of social reality—but also of individual process. Private life becomes "social consciousness" even, or especially, when it seems most peculiar, most individual, most unconformist with the structures of feeling that currently prevail.

Indeed, it is funny that Williams devalues, in turn, Freudianism and psychoanalysis. For his understanding of the nether realm of "emergent or preemergent" cultural process is another word for the unconscious. But Williams's point is that *no* "official consciousness" gets to define or determine this nether realm that, nevertheless, he takes it upon himself to define. In the first long quote from Williams's essay, he uses the word "conscious" to describe what is happening in the bridging of practical experience to larger social forces: "the moment of conscious comparison," which, he vehemently argues, must not be subsumed by the "official consciousness" and become "formalized, classified, and in many cases built into institutions and formations." These "new semantic figures" are "discovered in material practice: often . . . in relatively isolated ways, which are only later seen to compose a significant (often in fact minority) generation" (132, 134). My point is that this "only later" may or may not happen. Williams's essay begins lamenting the "reduction" of the fruits of "practical experience" and "practical consciousness" into "official" accounts—including not just Marxism but also psychoanalysis—as "finished products" or mental commodities (128–29, 128). His essay thus oscillates between the past and present, the "current cultural process"—which finds formal expression in "emergent or preemergent" "semantic figures"—and the past, which he seeks to dislodge in favor of the present—and what he calls *presence*. (A notion akin to the modernist idea of the eternal present.)

Williams thus lays out a theory of radical immanence, in the order of literary and other aesthetic forms, that does not need to be explained or "formalized, classified, and in many cases built into institutions and formations." Later in the essay the structure of feeling congeals—is reified?—into a past that is consumable, classifiable, partly because it has already been lived; it becomes a generation or a class conflict. But before this, "emergent or preemergent" aesthetic forms of "evidence" of the new structure of feeling remain "*in solution.*" The chemical metaphors Williams uses are meaningful: the emergent or preemergent structure of feeling lies "*in solution,*" a "cultural hypothesis," "as distinct from other social semantic formations which have been *precipitated* and are more evidently and more immediately available" (132).

Here, my aims in revisiting the notion of the structure of feeling are twofold. Williams himself commits the same sin he decries. He relegates the emergent structures of feeling into "finished products" like the spirit of the age, of the socioeconomic class, of the generation, that capitulate his essay. He begins and ends with presence, but he allows the presence to congeal into social fact: a generation is a hard social fact, a commodity of feeling, not a structure of feeling, I would add. My second argument is that the formation—the *unseen* or hitherto *unarticulated* structure of feeling—that I am calling misfit modernism, created *and lived* by authors I am calling misfit modernists, is legible as "evidence" in the "semantic figure" of the modernist misfit.

As Williams writes, "not all art"—and to which I add, not all modernisms—"relates . . . to a contemporary structure of feeling. The effective formations of most actual art relate to already manifest social formations, dominant or residual, and it is primarily to emergent formations (though often in the form of modification or disturbance in older forms) that the structure of feeling, *as solution*, relates" (134). My conception of misfit modernism as a structure of feeling functions as a "modification or disturbance in older forms" of mainstream modernism, one held "in solution," but also, precisely, "as [a] solution" to the dominant narratives of modernism. These mainstream narratives of modernism elide minoritarian authors like those collected in this study. *A* solution, not simply *in solution*, the semantic figure of the misfit in the modernist novel serves as "the hypothesis of social formation" that is hitherto unseen in modernism; it is "distinguishable from other social and semantic formations" of this set of cultural-aesthetic movements "by its articulation of *presence,*" which Williams concludes is the evidence of practical experience transmuted into inchoate aesthetic form.[3]

All the authors in this study focus on the personified experiences of a lone figure—or a "lonesome" figure, to quote Thurman's novel's key term. They do this in an exemplary fashion, but of course, other authors could have been included. Similarly, Larsen's novel dwells on the "unconformity" of its protagonist, Helga Crane, and, more importantly, Helga's inability to "be happy in her unconformity."[4] Isherwood's "nonconformists" join Rhys's underdogs (or feeling like an "inferior being," a "doormat in a world of boots") to round out the quartet of voices I have chosen as exemplars of an emergent, or preemergent, modernist structure of feeling immanent in the semantic figure of the misfit. The misfit-modernist structure of feeling is one that ought not, following Williams, be subsumed under preexisting categories that are not drawn from the novels themselves.

Hence, *immanent reading* abides by Williams's tenet regarding the importance of unaided cultural thought. The cultural text contains within it all the meaning—the semantic figures—one needs to make sense of a social moment that appears evanescent. As a photograph captures that moment, literary novelists documented the figural life and presence of outsiderdom, of nonconformity, and of double exile in solution—not formulated as a clear, classifiable sociological landmark or piece of official consciousness but as a figure of practical consciousness. Williams cautions against established analytical rubrics other than his own, which was emergent or preemergent in this 1977 essay and which rests on Williams's propositions that immanence permeates cultural texts and that texts contain the semantic keys by which to decode them. Just such is my theory of immanent reading: to eschew the *taxonomies* of grand narratives of the unconscious (psychoanalysis) or historicism (Marxism), *though not their epistemological frameworks, per se*. This book emphasizes, with Williams, the conceptual and hermeneutical *priority* of aesthetic texts in the face of official classification schemes that too often serve to supersede them.

Close reading, as a mode of attention to immanent formal and thematic elements and thus understanding the text in isolation—as a significant resource for analysis—is a formalist hermeneutic associated with the New Criticism in the transatlantic context; French deconstruction and *explication de texte*, as Jonathan Culler reminds us; and Russian formalism, among other critical traditions.[5] Given these disparate strains of formalist critique, close reading as a concept is famously hard to define. As Jay Jin writes, "Close reading is far from being a homogeneous set of methodologies and practices."[6] Jin echoes Culler's suggestion that we should distinguish among different "modes" of close reading, rather than trying to stabilize it as a single practice. There are various modes of doing it—many ways of close reading, such as slow, reparative, deep, and close-but-not-deep—but there is a relatively stable idea of what close reading means, given its distant cousin, distant reading.[7]

This brings me to the *immanent* mode of close reading developed in this study, an intuitive hermeneutic for understanding modernist fiction. The second arc of *Misfit Modernism* is the argument that robust symbolic narrative genres, such as the novel, serve as structures of feeling in and of themselves. By so arguing, this book rests on contemporary understandings of critical interpretation beyond ideology critique, and beyond the "doxa" even of what qualifies as legitimate basis for critical interpretation.

Yet is my argument about the immanence of the modernist novel—at least, the novels spotlighting the culturally displaced misfit—merely recapitulating the aesthetic doctrine of the autotelic text? Is this simply repackaging the old wine of aesthetic autonomy in the shiny new bottles of immanent reading— and immanent writing? Yes—and no. The emergent analytical argument that grounds *immanent reading* is a mix of two vintages. One is the modernist doctrine of the self-contained work, though that doctrine usually applies to poetry, not the novel. And the novel, as a literary tradition, is above all a *social* form.

But the second vintage is my own concoction: an intuitive critical practice adopted in developing an understanding of misfit modernist novels, which leads to the hypothesis about a new way to read fictional form in general. *Immanent reading*, as cognate to the term *immanent critique*, refers to a method of close reading that involves a focus on the textual that will seem, at first blush, to employ magical thinking. And by this, I mean that *immanent reading entails drawing from a modernist novel*—for I've only "tested" this methodology on this distinctively literary formal tradition—*some keywords; a phrase (or set of phrases)—that hold the hermeneutic key to the novel's meaning as a whole.* Immanent reading thus might seem to be a "magical" methodology insofar as it places undue faith on the internal coherence (or immanence) of the modernist novel. The notion of the self-contained text is thus repeated with a difference: now there is a code that opens up a main pathway of understanding, one that uses the idiom and figures in the text as keys to that opened pathway. As a species of close reading, immanent reading rests on a presupposition about the autotelic nature of the modernist text, on the idea that the text presents us with immanent writing that is sufficient unto itself in answering its own symbolic questions. And in this sense, this hermeneutic framework is closest to the Freudian interpretation of dreams. For Freud's interpreter of dreams, the dream language was a fractal that contains within each part a version of the whole; everywhere in the dream is the meaning of the dream. Any fragment will yield the totality.

And so *Misfit Modernism*—and the notion of immanent reading—recapitulates, isomorphically, the aesthetic premises of the modernism that defines its object of study. A self-contained reading of a self-contained text. Immanent reading of immanent writing. Like Proust's madeleine dipped in tea, the phrase "total misfit" evoked, for me, an entire worldview of the early twentieth century in Thurman's novel. And also akin to Proust's mechanism of involuntary memory,

Misfit Modernism argues that the immanence of literary narratives can and does register entire worldviews, which lessens the need to turn to, say, midcentury sociologies of deviance to explicate what the novel formulates itself in diegetic and discursive terms as a "nonce" sociology. Attending to Thurman's narratorial voice in *The Blacker the Berry* is a key insight drawn from the intuitive approach of immanent reading, which fundamentally relies on literary evidence as a coeval branch in the tree of knowledge, with its own generative capability for capturing history, or even History. This logic follows Williams's isomorphic conception of structures of *feeling*—an approach that is impressionistic, given the undetermined nature of such structures to begin with. They are "*in solution*," a solution chemically being a "homogeneous mixture composed of two or more substances," which Williams distinguishes from "other social semantic formations which have been *precipitated* and are more evidently and immediately available."[8]

There is a critical explanation for why the novel is amenable to immanent reading—unlike philosophical treatises or memoir, for instance. As a fictional mode of narration, the novel has an ineluctable connection to social mimesis. As Marianne DeKoven reminds us, "The novel and history are *intimately connected* . . . in ways unique to the novel genre."[9] Modernism's formal innovations in the novel were limited, DeKoven writes, more so than the possibilities for formal rupture in other modes—namely, poetry and drama. In the long twentieth century, "radical formal innovation" in the modernist novel kept "pushing against the conventions of realism," DeKoven adds, but he also admits that some of these narrative conventions remained: "There were still plot, characters, action, Aristotelian beginning, middle, and end." Narrative innovations such as the famous stream of consciousness served in "undermining but not defeating those realist conventions," she concludes.[10]

Misfit Modernism argues that the novel's generic DNA is that of a social form of representation with realist underpinnings that even modernism could not totally uproot. And reading Williams immanently, the modernist novel can be *understood not only as "evidence" of a structure of feeling* but perhaps also as trying to create, discursively, what Williams himself thought the structure of feeling was: approaching the subverbal, the sub- or preconscious, and other kinds of postrationalist mental forms, through narration. Modernism's "higher" realism, after all, sought to capture the unformulated process of "practical consciousness" and "practical experience" that Williams ascribes to the structure of feeling. Reading immanently, the modernist novel can yield critical insights that are connected to the social, with all that entails, even when viewed through a formalist lens. Let us not fear the prison house of language evoked by this critical approach—given its surface similarities to the institutionalized and justly maligned New Criticism.[11]

As a subjective mode of close reading, immanent reading focuses on the representativeness of *certain* key words or tropes; moreover, they represent the key to the *novel*'s meaning, not that of "eighteenth-century England"—or twentieth-century England (or America) as a whole. Thus the claim that there is an *immanent* structure to modernist novels echoes a formalist premise consistent with Williams's own early formulation: "Not all great novels have a similar verbal pattern, but all have an essential structure which only close reading, or the more explicit process of literary analysis, will reveal." Williams adds, "Just as local attention to 'these words in this order' was necessary for a poem or for an extract of prose, so is it necessary for a larger work." And, as the epigraph notes, Williams argues for the importance of reading the totality of these words as "a highly aware and articulate record of individual experience within a culture" in which it originates.[12]

Is immanent reading merely New Criticism applied to the novel? Again, the answer is not exactly. The idea of a hermeneutic key is only that it opens the pathway to the greater understanding of the novel; it does not *entail*, as a restrictive doctrine, the exclusion of contextual considerations. Far from it. The idea is, contra New Criticism, a synthesis of the kind Ian Watt sought in his famed reading of the first paragraph of Henry James's *The Ambassadors*, between formalist approaches to the novel as a whole and the other considerations of author, place, and time that are best exemplified by historicist approaches. *Immanent reading is just such a synthesis, just such a "solution"*: it mixes and dissolves into a homogeneous mixture of heterogeneous elements drawn from psychoanalytic, Marxian, and materialist approaches to literature. Like Freud's interpretation of dreams, it assumes the symbolic legibility—or *synchronic figuration*—of the modernist novel as a total work of art. Eliot's "fragments I have shored against my ruins" is an indicative symbol. The critical enterprise, like the creative one, would do well to allow the social–psychic nexus that psychoanalysis and Marxism, to cite two major systems of analysis, understand as inescapably inscribed in the individual as well as the social body. Is it *literarily* inscribed in the narrative body? *Is* there a narrative unconscious, the ghost of meaning in the narrative machine—or what Genette calls narrative *mood*? Beyond Watt's claim about first paragraphs, immanent reading claims an idiosyncratic, private structure that such novels make manifest. Such a structure is not necessarily immanent in the first paragraph. Nor is such a structure necessarily recoverable in any predetermined dimension of literary and linguistic analysis: no claims to anything but, perhaps, diction in the form of keywords toward hermeneutic discovery and hermeneutic closure. My approach is, instead, like Williams's, impressionistic, confident in the nonrational logic that yields a reliable account of the dream—the novel—no matter how partial the understanding, how partial the recovered fragments, which still hold the key to all the rest. Nonrational does not mean irrational: it is a legitimate basis for literary creation, but also for humanistic critical inquiry.

2.

Narrating the Psychology of a "Despised Mulatto" in Larsen's *Quicksand*

Introducing the "Pleasure of Refusing"

The title of George Hutchinson's biography, *In Search of Nella Larsen* (2006), is apt. Mary Helen Washington famously dubbed Larsen the "mystery woman of the Harlem Renaissance" in a 1980 *Ms.* magazine article credited with igniting scholarly interest in Larsen. Along with other feminist reclamations of women writers—notably Alice Walker's search for Zora Neale Hurston, Larsen's contemporary—Washington's piece reawakened interest in an important novelist of the Renaissance.[1] But unlike Hurston, Larsen is an enigmatic figure whose documented literary career spans only a decade, from the 1920s to the 1930s. Hutchinson, in fact, problematizes the feminist project of reclamation as it concerns Larsen, arguing that Larsen is thereby integrated into a literary-cultural tradition within which she may not have fit, or wanted to fit, such as that of African American woman novelist, to quote the subtitle of Hazel Carby's study.[2] From the mid-1970s on, black feminist critics began revisiting literary history to reclaim women writers, partly in order to construct "alternative visions of black female authorship," in Hutchinson's words. He adds, however, that in the case of Larsen, "the position of biracial and passing characters"—the focus of Larsen's novels, *Quicksand* and *Passing*—"seemed beside the point."[3]

Moreover, Hutchinson cautions that in "the new feminist criticism, Larsen was legitimated by *being fit into* a sisterhood or black matrilineal pattern of descent extending from Phillis Wheatley to Alice Walker." In this "project of reclamation," Hutchinson continues, *"Larsen's exploration of the zone between the races, and its suppression both socially and psychologically* . . . came to seem merely a 'mask,' a ruse forced upon her by white people. Larsen's allegedly superficial emphasis on mulatto characters and passing had prevented her from more boldly investigating her real theme—black female sexuality, black sisterhood—and had compromised her worth as an author."[4]

I'll return to Hutchinson's incisive summation of Larsen's novels: the "exploration of the zone between the races, and its suppression both socially and psychologically." But, in this passage, Hutchinson questions Deborah McDowell's influential introduction to her edited collection of Larsen's novels.[5] In that essay, McDowell boldly claims that there is an unmistakable lesbian subtext of *Passing*. More broadly, she argues for both novels' focus on black female sexuality. But McDowell, in her influential yet controversial queer reading, also makes certain claims about the relative failure and tragic conventionality of Larsen's narrative endings. One novel, *Quicksand*, ends in marriage and maternity; *Passing* ends in another kind of "passing," or death. Specifically, the life of Helga Crane, the biracial protagonist of *Quicksand*, devolves until she is mortally weakened from giving labor for the fourth time, even as it concludes with Helga pregnant with her fifth child. *Passing* culminates in the death of coprotagonist Clare Kendry, seeming punishment for crossing the color line. So, McDowell argues, it would be left to future black women writers to envision liberated horizons for their fictional heroines.

Along with Hutchinson, I caution against this recovery project, insofar as it integrates Larsen into traditions that did not suit her personality or temperament and did not even exist during her brief literary lifetime. (Literary critic Rafael Walker concurs with Hutchinson in taking seriously Larsen's focus on biracial protagonists, arguing that "in distinguishing her heroines from the black women around them, Larsen draws a line within the color line, pressing us to take seriously her heroines' racial liminality."[6]) But, on the other hand, Hutchinson acknowledges that if Washington, Carby, McDowell, Davis, and others had not sparked interest in Larsen by locating her in the canon of distinguished black women writers, "who knows how long we would have had to wait for the resurrection of Larsen's work?"[7] Indeed, who knows if the "resurrection" would have occurred at all?

And so Larsen's authorial figure, and her slim corpus, are uncomfortably laid to rest alongside more representative "New Negro" women writers of the time. Yet there is scant evidence that Larsen cultivated friendships—literary or otherwise—with any of her fellow black women writers. Instead, Larsen was best friends with Dorothy Peterson, a diplomat's daughter who became the common link tying various figures in the Renaissance—from renowned sculptor Richmond Barthé to literary wunderkind Langston Hughes, who also served as Peterson's Harlem Suitcase Theater codirector, and from the distinguished multihyphenate James Weldon Johnson to the infamous multihyphenate Carl Van Vechten. Her deep friendships with Peterson and Van Vechten powered Larsen through her greatest triumphs, and her greatest losses, including the dissolution of her marriage; her withdrawal from both friendships signaled her self-imposed exile from the world of New Negro letters.

Indeed, Larsen was a misfit—or, in the words of her novel, an "unconformist"—even at the height of her fame as a novelist.[8] An interesting anecdote illustrates the paradox of Larsen's discomfited position within a cultural movement she excelled in. In honor of the publication of her well-received first novel, *Quicksand*, Larsen writes an ironic letter to Van Vechten, confiding to him that "on May Thirteenth, Sunday [1928], The Woman's Auxiliary [2 underlines] of the N.A.A.C.P. is going to give a tea for *me*!!! [7 underlines]. The good God knows why. I hope you will get an invitation because this will be a time when I will need all of my friends. You will be very pleased to know that *I was very gracious about accepting, though I wanted very much to have the pleasure of refusing*."[9] Larsen's ambivalence, and her dissimulated "pleasure of refusing" such a distinguished honor, is paradoxical indeed. Note her enthusiasm: she adds seven underlines for her personal objective pronoun, indicating her self-deprecating surprise at being so honored ("God knows why"). The invitation from the Women's Committee of the NAACP instantly upgraded Larsen's social status, from Mrs. Nella Imes, "Harlem matron," wife of Dr. Elmer Imes, to being celebrated in her own right as a literary phenomenon ("Nella Larsen" is the byline of her novels). And yet, as she herself makes clear, the pleasure of such recognition is mixed: there is another pleasure she admits to seeking—the "pleasure of refusing" that very honor. Although she "graciously" quells this impulse to refuse, Larsen can't help confiding in one of her closest friends, how much she wanted to refuse the invitation, even while demonstrating her enthusiasm in being so honored.

In this brief glimpse into Larsen's celebrated launch as a literary novelist, we view the double movement of her values: personal recognition finds its foil in the resistance to collective New Negro uplift she fears such recognition might entail. The notice from the *Amsterdam News* indicates the importance of this honor—not simply for Larsen, but "for the upward climb of the race": "James Weldon Johnson introduced Mrs. [Larsen] Imes by pointing out the significance of the literary movement to larger development, claiming that there should be a real place for the woman novelist of the group, as she had such a complete background of achievement to her credit in the upward climb of the race."[10] Among the distinguished guests were Grace Nail Johnson, Nina Gomer Du Bois, Alain Locke, and Van Vechten himself. Thus, while being inducted into the literary canon of the Renaissance movement, in which Johnson, secretary of the NAACP, indicated "that there should be a real place for the woman novelist," Larsen demurred from such belonging, such uplift.[11]

Indeed, Larsen's correspondence with Van Vechten and Peterson, in particular, is riddled with deprecatory comments—including self-deprecatory, in Larsen's struggle with double consciousness and its negative impact, internalized racism—about non-middle-class black people, to put it delicately. (Her letters drop the derogatory n-word liberally, in ugly fashion.)[12] For Larsen, "blackness" was as much a notion linked to lower-class status as to race. Her being from the working-class union of a white Danish immigrant mother and a black West Indian father meant that Larsen herself fell into this same lower socioeconomic status—unlike Peterson, Du Bois, Locke, and other college graduates that formed the New Negro elite. In this regard, her sardonic tone mirrors the elitism of Du Bois's "Talented Tenth." And, just as ironic, Larsen's working-class roots meant that she struggled to join, and to be accepted by, the black bourgeoisie. This vivid example touches on both themes in Larsen's literary biography: her resistance to black uplift and her quixotic "pleasure of refusing" the honors and privileges of elite African American culture, honors and privileges that she prized and cultivated as part of her novelistic persona.

Indeed, Hutchinson views Larsen as *"always an outsider."*[13] Here, "always an outsider" frames Larsen as a misfit due to the rareness, for its time, of her parents' multiply mixed sociocultural backgrounds.[14] Some Danish was spoken at home, and Larsen spent some childhood summers with her extended maternal family in Copenhagen. But added to this, after her mother's remarriage to another Danish immigrant, Peter Larsen, Nella became a misfit in her own home—the only "colored child" in a family of four, with a white half-sister.[15] As a teenager, Larsen took her secondary education at the teacher's college at Fisk University; she later audited college courses in Copenhagen after being expelled from Fisk. As an adult, Larsen navigated these intersections of the color line as well as of gender, class, nation, and cultural legacies. These prisms of minoritization socially followed Larsen everywhere, within both Jim Crow–enforced "white-only" and "colored" communities at home and abroad. She was not a "natural" member of the Talented Tenth, unlike her husband—the second black physics PhD in the United States. But neither was she ever accepted as a member of her white family, either. Larsen was thus overdetermined as a cultural as well as racial outsider, a misfit within homogenous cultures.

Her reaction to the NAACP tea in her honor emblematizes Larsen's double movement of attraction and repulsion. This self-conflicting movement can be summarized as the thrill of being recognized, cut with the acerbic "pleasure of refusing" such recognition, such belonging.

"I Arrive at Once": Larsen as a Misfit Modernist

Like the inverse image of Clare Kendry, in *Passing*, who loses her white husband when he discovers that she is black, Nella Larsen suffered matrimonial loss— her 1933 divorce from Elmer Imes was due to Imes's love affair with a white woman.[16] A few years after the divorce, Larsen cut off contact with her literary nexus of friends, confidantes, and associates of the Renaissance: her closest friends, Dorothy Peterson and Carl Van Vechten, and luminaries like James Weldon Johnson, Walter F. White, and Langston Hughes. Her letters and visits "dwindled, becoming shorter, fewer, and further apart until at last they ceased," in the words of Larsen herself, about Clare Kendry's "passing" into the white world.[17] George Hutchinson and Thadious Davis endeavor to fill in Larsen's "lost years"—from her last recorded visit to Peterson, on Sunday, June 20, 1943, to her being found dead in her Manhattan studio apartment on Monday, March 30, 1964.[18]

Like her major biographers—Larson, Davis, and Hutchinson—I, too, find plausible answers to the mystery of Larsen's life in her autobiographical fiction.[19] For instance, Davis claims that Larsen seems to have followed the path of the protagonist of *Quicksand* (1928), Helga Crane, who abandons her quest for modern self-definition in exchange for the security of marriage and childbearing in the Deep South. (For instance, Davis writes of Larsen's return to nursing after her divorce as a "kind of retreat that literally acts out the fears assigned to women characters in her fiction."[20]) Davis writes that "in the fall of 1937," Larsen "delivered 'reverse farewell messages' to her friends. 'On the night of the phone calls,' as some of them came to call it, she telephoned all of her friends with the same message: '*I arrive at once.*' She never arrived. After the dramatic message, she neither appeared nor was heard from again."[21] After a series of heartbreaks and partially fulfilled artistic ambitions, Larsen signaled her abrupt social disappearance, ironically, by announcing her imminent return from a trip to Brazil that her friends never believed she took. This odd coda seems fitting for so paradoxical a life. Davis adds, "Larsen evidently wanted to disappear; she intended that no one know her whereabouts, at least no one who would reveal them."[22]

But Larsen was not alone in her disappearance after the "Negro" was no longer "in vogue," to quote Hughes's memorable phrasing in the autobiographical *The Big Sea*. Along with Zora Neale Hurston's, Larsen's disappearance from the world of letters mirrors that of other Renaissance women writers—chief among them Jessie Redmon Fauset—many of whom were, until recently, all but forgotten, their work out of print or never published to begin with.[23]

Yet unlike many of her contemporaries—such as Hurston or Fauset, to whom she is usually linked for writing women-centered novels about the black middle class—Larsen remains a shadowy figure. The circumstances of her death, and her own rupture with the principals of the Renaissance in the 1930s, mean that the numerous manuscripts she produced in later years remain lost, perhaps forever. When Van Vechten began asking friends to donate their papers in order to preserve the rich archive of the Harlem Renaissance in letters, manuscripts, photographs, and ephemera, to be housed in Yale University's James Weldon Johnson memorial collection, Larsen refused to be collected, refused to be found (the pleasure of refusing?). By the time of her death, her unpublished manuscripts were not recovered.[24]

Beyond what little remains of Larsen's writing, Davis wonders why she produced so little to begin with. And why did Larsen give up trying to publish, after fourteen years of trying to land her fiction?[25] In answer, Davis cautions that Larsen "is not to be criticized for her failure to persevere" in her writing career, though she adds that Larsen seemingly "gave in without a visible struggle"; "despite her considerable courage," Davis surmises, Larsen's "internal resources were not sufficient to allow her to continue to write." "Her failure is our loss," Davis adds. "Larsen's story . . . is a sad one because it reveals the complex tragedy of a more subtle racism that twists and undermines the individual's sense of who and what is valuable."[26] And, Davis concludes, "during the thirty-four years between the publication of 'Sanctuary'" [in 1930] and her death, silence replaced Larsen's voice, but in that silence is the story of an African American woman writer unable to create in the face . . . of complex race and gender obstacles in society operating against her needs and of psychological dualism in her own personality fragmenting her responses to those needs."[27]

These words about Larsen's "failure" signal the end of Davis's literary biography. Yet it is here that the study of Larsen as a *misfit modernist* begins: in examining such supposed "failure" and its underlying causes, what Davis calls "the complex tragedy of a more subtle racism that twists and undermines the individual's sense of who and what is valuable." Davis's words fall as a final apologia, whereas I view her insight into Larsen's psychological character, her social situation, and her historical circumstances as indicative of sociocultural obstacles and internalized racism, a particularly toxic form of double consciousness (or "psychological dualism"). This internalized racism, Davis writes, served only to obstruct and "fragment" Larsen's responses to "complex race and gender obstacles ... operating against her needs." It is this fragmenting of Larsen's responses to those needs—or what Davis views as fragments—that the study of misfit modernists like Larsen can well teach us. Not as a role model of successful resistance to those "complex race and gender"—and class, and sexuality—"obstacles," but as an index of what we understand *as* successful resistance to them.

This study, then, interrogates the normative moralism inherent in diagnostic readings of modernist authors, like Larsen, who are perennial outsiders—or misfits—due in large part to their complex (or intersectional) identity. Larsen is emblematic of these complex obstacles, what black feminist legal theory came to call intersectionality. But my approach, unlike Davis's, in this example, does not seek to explain away such fragmentation but rather understand it as a legitimate, or at least self-legitimating, set of responses in a distinctive voice. This is Larsen's voice, the voice of an intersectional misfit in the modernist moment. Larsen registers this voice in the narrative form emblematic of organic social existence—the novel, the privileged mode of telling the story of modern life in the early twentieth century.

Larsen insisted on being known as a novelist, Davis reminds us—and this study suggests why. Since the development of the novel, this literary form engages the totality of the social as its purview. (Unlike, say, the lyric mode, which expresses the emotive subjectivity of the solitary speaker.) The modernist novel, in turn, positions itself against the bourgeois social order and the reproduction of docile individuals as citizens of *Bildung*. (This is what Jed Esty calls the modernist anti-Bildungsroman.)[28] A misfit modernist novel, by extension, takes this challenge to the organic social order, and its faithful reproduction in a fictional mirror, to another level: by adumbrating what Davis calls the "complex race and gender obstacles in society operating against her needs and of psychological dualism ... fragmenting her responses to those needs." All three dimensions—social, cultural, and psychological—are integrated into the novel about misfits like Helga Crane—and like Larsen herself. As Hutchinson writes (quoted above), Larsen explores "the zone between the races, and its suppression both socially and psychologically." Yet instead of being seen as "merely a 'mask,' a ruse forced upon her by white people," *Misfit Modernism* reads Larsen's exploration of these sociocultural impact "zones" as the dynamic terrain of modernity in narrative form.

I arrive at once. Where had Larsen arrived, when she abandoned her writing career for the nurse's uniform? And yet Davis believes that even "long after she began working again as a night nurse, she still insisted that she was a writer." Larsen, Davis argues, sought to hold on to a more distinguished social role than that of "a divorced woman working as a nurse," just as she had succeeded in transcending her (albeit glamorous) domestic role as one of the black elite, a "Harlem matron."[29] But why must we consign Larsen to this binary—either in or out, novelist or nurse, success or "failure"? The same dualism Davis finds in Larsen's psychology seems to govern how her biographers understand her career and her work. Indeed, long is the list of titles of Larsen manuscripts that are yet to be, and perhaps never will be, found.

This brief sketch of the biographical commentary uncovers an unfulfilled wish to recover Larsen from her self-imposed exile. Many critics, biographers, and scholars continue to pore over the scanty archives of her correspondence as well as the spotty records kept by Knopf, her publishing house, and Brandt and Brandt, the literary agency to which she submitted a coauthored novel, as well as records of her contact with foundations, schools, places of employment, and so on. Perhaps she herself wanted success, or nothing; glory, or oblivion. She wanted to "arrive," or, failing that—failing, in other words—to disappear forever. And it seems Larsen succeeded in this quixotic goal: succeeded in failing. And so we turn to her novels for some answers, to satisfy our wish to recover Nella Larsen as a modernist explorer of the misfit state of consciousness, a wish no less strong for its being, perhaps, impossible.

From "Tragic Mulatto" to "Despised Mulatto": *Quicksand*

No study of the modernist trope of the cultural misfit would be complete without articulating how this figure originates in an earlier instantiation: the so-called tragic mulatto, a figure that, in *Quicksand*, is invoked as a "despised mulatto."[30] Concomitantly, Larsen's own tragic life story epitomizes that of the modernist misfit, even as her fiction centers on characters who uneasily cross the color line, fitting neither in the black-bourgeois community nor in the narrow confines of their adoptive white families, ending in tragedy for both. As the book's introduction makes clear, this study distinguishes, yet finds thematic correspondences, between the dimension of the author and that of the fiction. Larsen—along with Thurman, Rhys, and Isherwood—are themselves "misfits" in the modernist subculture from which they spring. What makes them central to this study is that their fiction centers on precisely this formation, of double exile, as it draws from their respective autobiographies. Larsen's brief career as a Renaissance writer saw her as one of the most celebrated novelists among the "younger Negro artists," as Thurman famously hailed them in the anti–New Negro establishment little magazine *Fire!!* In short, authors like Larsen and other misfit modernists were marginal even within their marginal coteries, dropping off the radar from the literary scene entirely, as Larsen and Rhys did, in very different yet related contexts. Isherwood himself was not a "joiner," while Thurman, according to Dorothy West, drank himself to death, snatching defeat from the jaws of Hollywood victory, where he ended up in the early 1930s before his untimely death in 1934.

This opening chapter begins the study of the modernist misfit as a fictional figure, which distinguishes the literary formation I call misfit modernism. In so doing, this study, in conversation with Heather Love's study of queer histories of loss and negative feelings, expands that exposition of modern queer marginality and reimagines how we define "queer." Queer is a species of cultural outsiderdom that touches on, but does not center on, sexual dissidence. Larsen is a figure of *queer* modernism, in part, because she resisted the claims of any single identity: she never fit in because her identity was always complex, intersectional, heterogeneous, a source of permanent tension during the Jim Crow era in which she lived.[31] As Larsen's narrator writes about Helga Crane, a description that applies to Larsen herself, "She was, she knew, *in a queer indefinite way, a disturbing factor*" (42; emphasis added). This quote is drawn from the first chapter in the novel, which finds Helga Crane contemplating her escape from Naxos, a fictional amalgam of Fisk University and the Tuskegee Institute, which Helga likens to a "cruel educational machine" (50).

Helga Crane is the center of consciousness of *Quicksand*, as the impersonal narrator limns her perceptions and impressions in a complex tissue of free indirect style and psycho-narration. The novel's opening situates the protagonist in the "soft gloom" of her twilit room in Naxos (29). Why does Larsen's original novelistic creation see herself as a "disturbing factor" within the conformity that surrounds her? "The general atmosphere of Naxos, its air of self-rightness and intolerant dislike of difference" was not "the best of mediums for a solitary girl with no family connections. Helga's essentially likable and charming personality was smudged out" as a result (40). But Helga's biracial status—to which her lack of "family connections" alludes— is only the beginning of why she does not fit the "unmistakable Naxos mold" (42). She had been unable, or unwilling, to "conform" to the repressive social norms of Naxos, as her fiancé, James Vayle, had: "Helga . . . had never quite achieved the unmistakable Naxos mold, would never achieve it, in spite of much trying. *She could neither conform, nor be happy in her unconformity*" (42; emphasis added). A "disturbing factor" "in spite of much trying," Helga "had struggled in those first months and with what small success. A lack somewhere," she concludes: "she had considered it a lack of understanding on the part of the community, but in her present new revolt she realized that the fault had been partly hers. A lack of acquiescence. She hadn't really wanted to be made over" (42). And this attitude of "revolt," the narration reminds us, defies the class snobbery of the institution: "If you were just plain Helga Crane, of whom nobody had ever heard, it was presumptuous of you to be anything but inconspicuous and *conformable*" (43; emphasis added). Helga's lack of family is really a lack of a respectable black family; her mother's white family does not count: "Her own lack of family disconcerted them. No family. That was the crux of the whole matter. For Helga, it accounted for everything, her failure here in Naxos. . . . Negro society, she had learned, was as complicated and as rigid in its ramifications as the highest strata of white society. If you couldn't prove your ancestry and connections, you were tolerated, but you didn't 'belong'" (43). Moreover, as we see shortly, they cut her off entirely, effectively deracinating Helga Crane from any connections to family altogether. In the Naxos environment, Helga does not count because she was not a product of the black middle class, but that fact would have been ignored if she had proved to be "conformable." Helga Crane refused to accept her lower social status due to that accident of birth.

More specifically, what did Helga not want to "acquiesce" to? What exactly is the "Naxos mold"? Above all, uniformity in dress, speech, manners, and even thoughts. Again, Larsen sets the terms clearly in the first chapter. The conservative and intrusive moral and social pressures at Naxos are, ironically, outlined by "the banal, the patronizing, and even the insulting remarks of one of the renowned white preachers of the state," who had given the lunchtime sermon (37). Helga's interior monologue recalls the white Southerner's "insulting remarks":

> He had said that if all Negroes would only take a leaf out of the book of Naxos and conduct themselves in the manner of Naxos products, there would be no race problem, because Naxos Negroes knew what was expected of them. They had good sense and . . . good taste. They knew enough to stay in their places, and that, said the preacher, showed good taste.

> He hoped . . . that they wouldn't become avaricious and grasping,
> thinking only of adding to their earthly goods, for that would be a sin in
> the sight of Almighty God. And then he had spoken of contentment . . .
> pointing out to them that it was their duty to be satisfied in the estate
> to which they had been called, hewers of wood and drawers of water.
> (37)

The last phrase is significant. It's a scriptural quote from Joshua, indicating the Israelites's cursing of the Gibeonites to lives of menial drudgery and subservience.[32] The phrase reappears in W. E. B. Du Bois's "Of Our Spiritual Strivings," in which Du Bois famously condemns Booker T. Washington's accommodation of Jim Crow and emphasis on industrial education—Washington being the founder of Tuskegee.[33] Du Bois revolts against Washington's leadership and his ideology of self-reliance, which Du Bois—and Helga Crane, in this passage—views as *acquiescence* to the continued spiritual, political, and social repression of African Americans. She evinces a "lack of acquiescence" to Naxos and "the general idea behind the system" it represents (39): wholesale segregation, diminished social expectations, and, generally, political subservience and cultural whitewashing ("the white man's pattern" [39]). And the complexity of Helga Crane's situation is clear from this mental recapitulation of "the statements made by that holy white man of God to the black folk sitting so respectfully before him" (37). Helga's difference—her "disturbing factor"—helps her see through the speech, unlike the rest of the congregation, and hear it as voicing institutional Southern racism, the "respectful" acceptance of which Naxos views as part of its mission. And said mission is to function as "a show place in the black belt, exemplification of the white man's magnanimity" (39): "This great community, she thought, was no longer a school. It had grown into a machine. . . . Life had died out of it. It was, Helga decided, now only a big knife with cruelly sharp edges ruthlessly cutting all to a pattern, *the white man's pattern*. Teachers as well as students were subjected to the paring process, for it tolerated no innovations, no individualisms. Ideas it rejected, and looked at with open hostility. . . . Enthusiasm, spontaneity, if not actually suppressed, were at least openly regretted as unladylike or ungentlemanly qualities" (39; emphasis added).

Thus, from the beginning of the novel, during this extended retroversion, Helga admits that part of the reason for her outsider status, her "unconformity," was herself: she "hadn't really wanted to be made over," to become another "Naxos product" (37). Her perennial discontentment—her failure to accept these terms, which the preacher himself defines as "contentment," in his sermon—is, ironically, an indication of her race pride. Ironic because Helga does not herself see her "revolt" in these grand, political terms. And, perhaps, neither does the white preacher: note how he oddly links "good taste" to "good sense" ("They knew enough to stay in their places, and that, said the preacher, showed good taste" [37]). Indeed, notice, too, how the sermon ends with an admonition against "becoming avaricious and grasping, thinking only of adding to their earthly goods" (37). If "good sense" and "good taste" are linked, then to have *bad taste* is to breach the acceptable norms of Naxos and of the "magnanimous" white Southern establishment, personified by the preacher. The Naxos community "system" "tolerated no innovations, no individualisms. Ideas it rejected, and looked at with open hostility." And it is precisely in matters of taste that Helga Crane evinces her "individualism": "Most of her earnings had gone into clothes, into books, into the furnishings of the room which held her. All her life Helga Crane had loved and longed for nice things. Indeed," the narration adds, "it was this craving, this urge for beauty which had helped to bring her into disfavor in Naxos—'pride' and 'vanity' her detractors called it" (41).

Larsen herself was expelled from Fisk after her first year, apparently for being too ostentatious in her mode of dress. Hutchinson writes, "Larsen's feelings on leaving Fisk seem to have inspired her description of Helga Crane's feelings upon leaving a black boarding school"—the fictional Naxos—"at about the same age."[34] He includes some of the rules against displaying an "urge for beauty" in jewelry and dress at Fisk University around this time (1907–8): a "new rule had been passed," he discovers, which restricted "'the wearing of jewelry by young ladies to one ring, and requiring them to wear uniform on all social occasions, because a few have dressed in a manner contrary to the wishes of several of the faculty.'"[35] Hutchinson adds, "The faculty responded on June 10 [1908] by reaffirming the 'rules regarding extravagant and expensive dress and jewelry.'" "On June 13," he concludes, the faculty "'voted that the following students be not allowed to return to the university next year,'" a list of eleven names, eight of them women's, including that of "'Nellie Larsen.'"[36] The question of taste and sense that *Quicksand* raises in its first chapter, then, goes to the heart of rigid, class-based norms of "racial" comportment, whose policing brought about Larsen's expulsion from the first all-black community she ever experienced, "precipitating a major crisis in her adolescence."[37]

Narrating the Psychology of a "Despised Mulatto"

Most critics and scholars emphasize Larsen's departure from the "tragic mulatto" trope in her fiction. That hoary nineteenth-century figure was painted in broad pseudobiological strokes: a story of warring "blood," therefore constitutionally incapable of conforming to either black or white community. Instead, Larsen's biracial Helga Crane is a study of contrasts—but these are psychological, not (pseudo) biological. Her modernism inheres in her "intense" individuality and the depths below consciousness that the narrator mines. These depths are unknown to Helga Crane herself: this is precisely what makes her a modern, Freudian subject, divided not by "blood" but in her cultural allegiances, as the peripatetic narrative formally registers. Helga's sojourns to the black South, then to Chicago, then Harlem, then Copenhagen, then Harlem and finally the South again indicate her misfit status in every segregated community in which she yearns to live her life—or to begin a new life. The trouble with Helga Crane, in other words, is not her warring white and black "blood." It is the universal racial segregation that demands that she belong only to one community or the other—not both. And this, constitutionally, *is* impossible.

What is the role of biology in this story of the modernist misfit instantiated in the literary-cultural tradition of the "tragic mulatto"? And by "biology" I mean the embodied realm of sensation, affect, feeling, impulse, and instinct that *Quicksand* limns in its exploration of Helga Crane's interiority. Hutchinson formulates Larsen's novelistic project as the *"exploration of the zone between the races, and its suppression both socially and psychologically."* This general insight captures the complexity of Larsen's novels, in their ambidextrous handling of both social and psychological "suppression" of what Hutchinson calls the "zone between the races." This "zone" is another version of Du Bois's famous color line (Hutchinson's study is a biography of Larsen but also of the color line itself, according to the subtitle). But we can also understand that this "zone" between the races is embodied in the person of Helga Crane. As the daughter of a white immigrant mother and a black West Indian father, Helga Crane occupies this "zone" as a subject position. To describe Helga Crane as a "zone," however, deindividualizes her, which is precisely the opposite of Larsen's fictional project. I would revise Hutchinson's description of Larsen's novels as explorations of *the subjectivity* positioned "between the races" and this subject's "suppression both socially and psychologically." And it is the suppression of this subjectivity, personified in the protagonist, Helga Crane, that *Quicksand* indeed explores: Larsen employs modernist narrative technique for representing consciousness and *subconsciousness* to undertake this sustained exploration. The narrative is internally focalized through the perspective of Helga Crane and narrated by an external, impersonal narrative voice.

Quicksand employs various ways to detail the depth psychology of her protagonist, including that most impersonal mode of narration: *psycho-*

narration. Psycho-narration, according to narratologist Dorrit Cohn, who coined the term, presents a character's inner life at some distance from that character.[38] But this distance ironically grants greater, rather than lesser, access to the character's "transparent mind," the title of Cohn's seminal study of various modes for presenting fictional consciousness. Before outlining Larsen's deployment of psycho-narration in *Quicksand*, the vaporous notion of *focalization*, which encompasses narrative techniques like psycho-narration, itself needs to be clarified. According to Mieke Bal's *Narratology*, many "typologies" of focalization, or "narrative points of view," do not "make a distinction between . . . the vision through which" readers view the fictional world and "the identity of the voice that is verbalizing that vision."[39] Hence, for Bal—as for this study—there is a distinction between narrator and "focalizor," narration and focalization. Narration is not focalization: a character can serve as a filtering or focalizing agent, providing the angle of "vision" for story events and elements, while the narrator can serve to "verbaliz[e] that vision."

This distinction between narrator and focalizor holds in the case of *Quicksand* (as it does in Larsen's second novel, *Passing*). But this chapter centers on *Quicksand* rather than *Passing*, due to the former's focus on Helga Crane's mixed-race origins and modern subjectivity, premised on her social and cultural hybridity and "unconformity." *Passing*, on the other hand, is structured as a *pas de deux*: two protagonists and their complex and fraught intersubjective dynamics. As such, *Passing* is less about the subjectivity of a mixed-race protagonist as it is about the intersubjectivity of two such figures, focusing more on the twin forces of desire and disidentification that power Irene Redfield's and Clare Kendry's fraught dynamic.

Moreover, the distance between narration and focalization is important insofar as it allows us to understand psycho-narration, which has the curious effect of providing insight into a character's innermost recesses, *even those recesses that the character herself does not see or understand*. Unlike first-person *interior monologue*, which, following Cohn, provides direct, unmediated access to the verbal contents of a fictional character's "mind," psycho-narration allows access to nonverbal or subverbal mental contents. Cohn calls this aspect of psycho-narration the "cognitive privilege" of the narrator, where the third-person narrator enjoys "superior knowledge of the character's inner life" and the "superior ability to present it *and assess it*."[40] This last point bears emphasizing, as psycho-narration elicits insight into the character's inner life as well as, at times, evaluating that inner life in ethical, psychological, or other terms.

For example, in *Quicksand*, I was struck by the ascription of "instinct" to Helga Crane's inner life, as in the following instances. Beginning with the first chapter, the narrator of *Quicksand* emphasizes the instinctive basis for many of Helga Crane's feelings and reactions. Six instances describe the natural instinct that informs the protagonist's perceptions:

1. *Instinctively* Helga was aware that [the Naxos students'] smiling submissiveness covered many poignant heartaches. (11)
2. *Instinctively* Helga had known that [her fiancé] had placed the blame [for struggling to adjust to life in Naxos] upon her. (17)
3. That second marriage, to a man of her [mother's] race . . . so passionately, so *instinctively* resented by Helga even at the trivial age of six. (51)
4. They noticed her, admired her clothes, but that was all, for the self-sufficient uninterested manner adopted *instinctively* as a protective measure for her acute sensitiveness, in her child days, still clung to her. (74)
5. *Instinctively* she wanted to combat this searching into the one thing which, here [in Copenhagen], surrounded by all other things which for so long she had so positively wanted, made her a little afraid. (175)
6. *Instinctively* she had the knowledge that [Dr. Anderson] would be shocked. Grieved. Horribly hurt even. Well, let him! (261; emphasis added)

The "shock" that Helga anticipates Dr. Anderson feeling is her having sex with Rev. Pleasant Green the night before, toward the end of the novel. But all of these examples illustrate the cognitive privilege of the third-person narrator. As Cohn notes, this mode allows the psycho-narrator of *Quicksand* to assess Helga's perceptions in different ways, or on different terms. Hence, in examples 1, 2, and 6, the assessment confirms the factual basis of Helga's perception; these psycho-narrations of her inner life underscore the accuracy of Helga Crane's social perception: "instinctively Helga *was aware*," "*had known*," "*had the knowledge that*." But the other examples of psycho-narration rest on a different evidentiary basis: 3 and 5 indicate Helga's (instinctive) emotional response ("so instinctively resented by Helga"; "instinctively she wanted to combat this searching").

The remaining instance, in this series of "instinctive" reactions detailed by the psycho-narration, is perhaps the most interesting, for it makes a sweeping characterization of the protagonist (example 4). It thus asserts the greatest level of cognitive privilege enjoyed by the narrator and represents a rare instance where the narration takes on a more "authorial cast," in Cohn's words.[41] This authorial cast is, not coincidentally, focused less on Helga Crane's inner life than on the inner life of others, insofar as they perceive *her*: "They noticed her, admired her clothes, but that was all, for the self-sufficient uninterested manner adopted instinctively as a protective measure for her acute sensitiveness, in her child days, still clung to her" (74). This complex sentence begins by focalizing Helga's social interlocutors: "They noticed her, admired her clothes, but that was all." The rest of the sentence articulates what about Helga's comportment ensured that others kept their social distance: it was Helga Crane's "self-sufficient uninterested manner," which, the narrator continues, was "adopted instinctively as a protective measure for her acute sensitiveness, in her child days, [and] still clung to her." Again, this is a rare moment of cognitive privilege and social distance *between the narrator and Helga herself.* There is a highly impersonal—even imperious—point of view here, which involves a summary judgment of Helga Crane's total character, embodied in her "manner," and that manner is traced back to her childhood. It was "in her child days" that Helga "instinctively adopted" that manner of being, which repelled intimacy even in her adult life.

Psycho-narration here shows a penetrating insight that may or may not be available to Helga herself. Could Helga Crane realize that she had "adopted" her "self-sufficient manner" "*instinctively* as a protective measure," instinct being the opposite of reflective action? Moreover, Helga was a child when she adopted her self-protective hauteur, which renders her nearly unapproachable as a newcomer, as a stranger. And the group of characters in this new social milieu—here, a "very fashionable, very high services Negro Episcopal church" in Chicago—may not be aware of why they keep their social distance, either (73–74). It is the narrating agent that can provide this deep biographical sweep of Helga Crane's childhood, how she responded instinctively to her childhood surroundings, and how this "protective measure" continues to cocoon her from social interaction in present surroundings. Helga Crane does not seem to know all this, but the narrator does.

In this complex characterization, the narrator begins by presenting an external view of Helga's complex social reality, and then explains that this reality is caused by the quality of her social interactions, and these, in turn, are influenced by her *internal* workings, especially those that date back to childhood events and represent "instinctive" psychological adjustments to those events. What others perceive as Helga Crane's standoffishness is narratively explained as unconscious, unexamined psychological cover for her "acute sensitiveness." And this psychic chain of reactions is then tied back to Helga Crane's loss of her "birthright," as a six-year-old, when she was displaced in her own home by her mother's remarriage to a white man who wanted nothing to do with her: "That second marriage, to a man of her [mother's] own race . . . so passionately, so instinctively resented by Helga even at the trivial age of six."[42] But does such an external perspective count as focalization? As psycho-narration?

Perhaps it would help to cite the beginning of the passage, and what Helga had wanted to happen when she came to the "very fashionable" church even though she was "not religious" (73): "She hoped that some good Christian would speak to her, invite her to return, or inquire kindly if she was a stranger in the city. None did, and she became bitter, distrusting religion more than ever. *She was herself unconscious* of that faint hint of offishness [*sic*] which hung about her and repelled advances and arrogance that stirred in people a peculiar irritation. They noticed her, admired her clothes, but that was all, for the self-sufficient uninterested manner adopted instinctively as a protective measure for her acute sensitiveness, in her child days, still clung to her" (74; emphasis added). In the larger context of the passage, we see that Helga Crane's distinctive social "manner"—seeming "self-sufficient" and "uninterested"—exudes a "faint hint of offishness," about which, the narrator informs us, Helga "was herself unconscious." The fact that she herself is unaware of how she comes across defines the passage as psycho-narration. The narrator enjoys a sweeping understanding of how events in someone's childhood influence her social reception to this day, in addition to understanding how childhood events produce "instinctive" psychological adjustments in character (or "manner") that last into adulthood—even if *the subject* of these adjustments, and their social reception, is "unconscious" of them. Moreover, the sonic echo in both sentences further ties them together. The "offishness which hung about her" in one sentence rhymes with the "manner" which "clung to her" in the next.

The addition of the realm of instinct here, as elsewhere, serves to underline the *involuntary* nature of Helga Crane's somewhat antisocial manner—and the psychic matter for which said manner serves as "protective measure." And so does her being unconscious of both: how Helga Crane comes across, with an air of "offishness" that "repelled advances" and that exudes an "arrogance that stirred in people a peculiar irritation," and how this chilly social reception ties back to her instinctive (unconscious?) adoption of a (stand-) offish manner as a beleaguered child. Indeed, the choice of the term "adoption" is significant, as Helga Crane's rejection by her stepfather—and, by complicity, her mother— implies her needing to *be* adopted and her stepfather's failing to do so, at least emotionally. The child's response, the narrator implies, was to "adopt" herself: Helga's "self-sufficient" "manner," adopted to protect her "acute sensitiveness," is a symbolic, unconscious act of self-adoption. While still a child, Helga Crane became her own parent, and thus ceased being a child, in other words.

Psycho-Narration: Objective Insights into Subjectivity

In short, Helga Crane's lack of a familial home is synonymous with a lack of a cultural one. Neither her Danish relatives nor her adoptive middle-class black community in Harlem allow her the freedom to be herself—to occupy that zone between races. If the tragic mulatto trope is foundational to Larsen's modernist revision of it in *Quicksand*, this revision comes in the figure of the misfit. This handling of the sentimental tragic mulatta genre convention is well-trod territory in studies of the novel. Larsen's exploration of "the psychology of the thing," to quote Du Bois's review of *Passing*, is distinctively modern, according to the critical consensus.[43] But the means by which Larsen accomplishes this are less studied in the expanding scholarship. For it is her narrative control that yields *Quicksand*'s convincing psychological portrait of Helga Crane: in particular, Larsen's stylistic control over modernist techniques such as free indirect style and psycho-narration.

In a recent study of *Passing*, Gabrielle McIntire focuses on the narratological dimension of Larsen's second novel. McIntire argues, convincingly, that *Passing* "embed[s] confusions about the legibilities of race and desire within a *commensurately riddled narration* where none of its plot-lines or dominant preoccupations . . . submit to a definitive reading. Instead, all of these polyvalent concerns co-exist in a matrix of meaning which . . . suggests that an echolalic symmetry exists between broken sexual and racial epistemes and *the tasks of their telling*."[44] McIntire adds that "Larsen shows us that the vagaries of narration and interpretation are as prone to misrecognitions and mistakes as are race and desire; in other words, she reveals that race and desire are structured *as* forms of narration and are thus replete with potentially hazardous misreadings."[45] There is thus a narratological "symmetry" between what McIntire calls "broken sexual and racial epistemes"—whose fracturing in social reality allows for passing, or squeaking past the militarized zone between racial formations—and Larsen's mode of "telling," or narrating, the story. A more traditional approach—the realism or sentimental approaches of pre-twentieth-century mulatta fiction—would have rendered the novel a vehicle for reinforcing the zone, rather than trespassing it at the level of form as well as the level of content.

This intentional "symmetry" of narrative style and underlying theme is a hallmark of modernist literary fiction. And in *Passing*, as McIntire argues, Larsen's aesthetic purpose is to adumbrate the inscrutability of race as a shadow, rather than a substance. "Race" is only as real as shadows are—meaning, only as real as their substantive counterparts, and bearing no necessary relation to them, as a trick of light can make a shadow larger or different from its emanating object.

A similar argument about narratological symmetry can be made for *Quicksand*, except that the focus in Larsen's first novel is not on how the "shadow" of race, or the hegemonic construct of blackness as "race itself," can be manipulated, at times obscured—to borrow Du Bois's metaphorics in *The Souls of Black Folk*. Rather, Larsen's autobiographical story of Helga Crane focuses on interracial subjectivity and its own psychic shadows of meaning. In other words, the racial "shadows" in *Quicksand* are created by the heroine herself. They are shadows of the mind. And these shadows, by definition, are invisible to the emanating object. Or, perhaps, these shadows are all too visible. And adumbrating Helga Crane's subjective distortions of social reality, mediated by the gendered, racial, and sexual politics of her time and place, is the point of Larsen's psycho-narration.

As Cohn defines her neologism, which she encapsulates as "the narrator's discourse about a character's consciousness," "'psycho-narration' identifies both the subject-matter and the activity it denotes (on the analogy to psychology, [or] psychoanalysis)."[46] "At the same time," Cohn adds, this concept helps us focus on "the ironic or lyric, reductive or expansive, sub- or super-verbal functions that psycho-narration can perform, precisely because it is *not* primarily a method for presenting mental language."[47] Instead of presenting mental language—in the idiom and emotion of the character herself, as with free indirect narration—psycho-narration privileges the narrator's omniscience while plumbing the depths of the character's psyche. As a psychoanalyst seeks to uncover the unconscious and subconscious, the "sub-[verbal] or super-verbal," dimensions of mental life that escape consciousness, psycho-narration produces insights on these dimensions that are invisible to the psyche itself. It renders greater intimacy, paradoxically, than interior monologue—because the self is not privy to all it knows, but this subverbal or superverbal knowledge is "conveyed by a voice that can only belong to a clairvoyant, disincarnated narrator," the hallmark of fiction itself, according to Cohn.[48]

In sum, psycho-narration makes the distinction between narrator and focalizor decisive. Following Gérard Genette's typology, the narrator is "who speaks," as opposed to the focalizor, the character "who sees" (or "who perceives").[49] In *Quicksand*, the protagonist Helga Crane is the main focalizor—we perceive the story world through her eyes, and through her senses—even as the narrator is omniscient. (Helga is not the only character that the narrator focalizes, in other words. See, for example, Anne Grey's psycho-narration after marrying Dr. Anderson, Helga's former love interest [124].) With this constant access to Helga's "transparent mind," the narration is able to plumb the depths of her consciousness—and subconsciousness—in ways unavailable to the character herself. For example, chapter 15 opens with the following passage, during Helga's second year in Copenhagen, when she experiences "an indefinite discontent" directed at "her life," even at "herself" (110, 111): "Well into Helga's second year in Denmark came *an indefinite discontent*. Not clear, but *vague, like a storm gathering far on the horizon*. It was long before she would admit that she was less happy than she had been during her first year in Copenhagen, but she knew that it was so. And *this subconscious knowledge added to her growing restlessness* and little mental insecurity. *She desired ardently* to combat this wearing down of her satisfaction with *her life, with herself. But she didn't know how*" (110–11, emphasis added). The *indefiniteness* of the discontent is a hallmark of psycho-narration's capacity to articulate what to a character is subverbal, or preverbal—at the margin of consciousness ("this subconscious knowledge"). Psycho-narration knows what the character doesn't know—including, or especially, about herself. Such omniscient access to the protagonist here is of a piece with the novel's focus on modern psychology and biracial subjectivity.

But it is in the latter stages of the novel that the protagonist's *un*knowing becomes central to the narrative. From knowing what Helga Crane "instinctively" knew or was aware of, as seen above, the psycho-narration focuses on the temporality of this self-knowledge, and then on its gradual, eventual, evanescence. In the later chapters, the focus is as much on what Helga Crane does not know as on what she does. Beginning with the "indefinite discontent" of her second year in Denmark, which precedes Helga's return to Harlem and her quick downfall—her descent into the "quicksand" of multiple child-bearings and an unhappy marriage—the latter stages of psycho-narration focus on what continues to elude Helga Crane. Not simply contentment, or happiness, but knowledge itself. The distinction between perception and narration thus becomes sharper, as the focalizor becomes unmoored from self-knowledge, making mistakes that exacerbate this "indefinite discontent" into what amounts to throwing her life away.

The spatial metaphor in this passage—"like a storm gathering far on the horizon"—is also a temporal one. The metaphoric storm is coming. And Helga Crane is powerless to stop it—"She didn't know how" to "combat" its coming, which this foreshadowing renders as seemingly inevitable, a fact (and act) of nature. This fact of nature is Helga Crane "herself"—her not knowing how to solve the riddle of her identity and thus achieve contentment. It is no coincidence that after this chapter, upon her return to Harlem and her adulterous kiss with the now-married Dr. Anderson, the narrative focus is on Helga's "subconsciousness" and her "long-hidden, half-understood desire" (133). It is this lack of self-understanding that leads to her eventual downfall. And so the novel is hyperdescriptive of what the protagonist does not know, as her lack of self-knowledge, especially about her own desire (the "vague," "indefinite discontent"), grows into a "mental quagmire" (134).

The denouement of the novel, occurring after the climactic church scene—more on which below—stresses even more clearly this psychic link between self-knowledge and "half-understood desire." Chapter 20 begins with Helga having "given up thinking" (137). Rather than seeking to know, and to understand, herself and her "indefinite discontent," now Helga Crane seeks *not to know*, not to think. This moment ushers in the fall into narrative quicksand, during which bodily suffering means only mental escape can soothe her sorrow. Clearly, the path of the novel is carved by the psycho-narration, which scours the depths of self-knowledge, records the limits of that self-knowledge (as a horizon), uncovers that limit as partially sexual desire ("half-understood"), and, after Helga's consummation of her sexual desire with the unpleasant Rev. Pleasant Green, leads to a form of psychic coma and physical breakdown.

A quick textual analysis demonstrates how the psycho-narrator's use of key terms denoting Helga's consciousness (or "subconsciousness"), such as being *aware* of her feelings or others' motivations, begins to atrophy. Such decay in self-knowledge, and the desire to discover herself that the passage about "indefinite discontent" seeks to track, comes after Helga gains access to the ultimate knowledge, that of carnal desire. This desire is awakened, and then repulsed, by Dr. Anderson's kiss; his subsequent refusal to consummate his relationship with her leads to Helga's dramatic loss of self-possession, her winding up literally in the gutter, and her finding solace in a store that turns out to be a storefront church led by Rev. Green.

It is in the church scene that Helga becomes "unconscious of the words she uttered, or their meaning" (142). Even after the "orgy" of the evangelical prayer—during which she utters words she is unaware of uttering, let alone their meaning—Helga remains "still half-hypnotized," her "consciousness" still under the narcotic effect of the ironic conversion scene. And here we see the culmination of her struggle toward self-knowledge and understanding her desires: it is their sublimation in the religious fervor that seems to purify Helga Crane of this "indefinite discontent"—or, at least, for the time being:

A miraculous calm came upon her. Life seemed to expand and to become very easy. *Helga Crane felt within her a supreme aspiration toward the regaining of simple happiness, a happiness unburdened by the complexities of the lives she had known.* About her the tumult and the shouting continued, but in a lesser degree. Some of the more exuberant worshipers had fainted into inert masses, the voices of others were almost spent. Gradually the room grew quiet and almost solemn, and *to the kneeling*

girl time seemed to sink back into the mysterious grandeur and holi-
ness of far-off simpler centuries. (142; emphasis added)

From "indefinite discontent," Helga Crane achieves "simple happiness," one "unburdened by the complexities of the lives she had known." Thus it is not simply the other congregants who have "fainted into inert masses"—Helga, too, on the verge of fainting, responds to the overtures by the congregants to help her in her state of misery. Their ministering, typically for Larsen, however, has dark implications. She is called a "scarlet woman" and "Jezebel"—mistaken for a prostitute in her slinky red dress. Their help is predicated on saving Helga's soul. But at her lowest point in the story, after her rejection by Dr. Anderson and her drinking herself sick in order to forget, Helga needs fellowship and support, not moral judgment. Their aid comes at the price of Helga Crane's suspension of the self-defining quest for self-knowledge and solving the riddle of her "half-understood desire."

So, the scene—and the chapter—culminates in this passage, which reduces Helga Crane to a mere "kneeling girl," adopting a dispassionate viewpoint on her and her situation. Indeed, the narrator's choice of words is remarkable for the distance it implies. Even as psycho-narration takes up the slack almost immediately—"to the kneeling girl time seemed to sink back"—reducing Helga to a "kneeling girl" indicates the relative superiority of the narrator's vision, and the relative derogation of Helga's own consciousness. A mere "kneeling girl," now, Helga Crane is too easily seduced by the "miraculous calm" after the erotic, rhythmic, and cacophonous evangelical ritual, the concerted effort on the part of the whole congregation to save the "kneeling girl" from her own worst instincts. But those instincts—along with the insights and desires that arise in the course of the psycho-narration—are what make Helga Crane. It is thus no wonder that she is stripped even of her proper name at the end of this orgiastic religious conversion, the seeming exorcism of her passionate intelligence and quest for self-understanding. She becomes no one in particular—a figure on the floor—whose mental escape into "far-off simpler centuries" indicates her surrender of "the complexities of [her] lives" to the modern one.

And so the last section of the novel, after a brief interlude in a Manhattan hotel, takes place in a poor town in Alabama, where Helga becomes a pastor's wife and the "many lives she had known" become mere figments of memory. McDowell speaks for many in questioning the narrative logic of this ending; as with the ending of *Passing*, *Quicksand*'s finale raises questions about the likelihood of one Helga Crane becoming mired in the drudgery of rural poverty and perennial maternal labor. This problematizing of the ending of *Quicksand* serves to highlight the protagonist's dramatic descent—spatial metaphors being deliberate, in this novel—from an urbane, cosmopolitan mobility to the "far-off simpler centuries" of childbearing, childrearing, and domestic labor, as well as the "anesthetic satisfaction for her senses" that sex, sanctified by marriage, affords her (146).

But one way to understand the negative significance of Helga's ending up mired in the quicksand of constant maternal labor, a misfit within a poor, Southern black community—more limited than even Naxos was, in her own mind—is Larsen's deconstruction of the "tragic mulatto" narrative arc. That sentimental tradition also ends in the biracial figure returning to her (usually her) black roots, thereby ratifying a noxious American racist premise: the one-drop rule. In sentimental nineteenth-century fictions about the "tragic mulatto," such as Frances Harper's *Iola Leroy* (1892), the morally rigid mulatta turns down the lure of whiteness for the authenticity of blackness and the noble aspiration to uplift the race. (Even in Johnson's modernist *Autobiography of an Ex-Colored Man* [1912/1927], the narrator bemoans his cowardice in "choosing the lesser part," by passing as an ordinary white man, rather than becoming a great "race man.") Larsen does Johnson one better, with an ironic inversion of the "tragic mulatto's" implicit message of "separate but (trying to be) equal," the linchpin of the American racial imagination. *Quicksand* frames Helga Crane's return to the black South as the result of falling for the illusion of escaping into "far-off simpler centuries." This illusion is dispelled, once Helga Crane faces the reality of her impulsive choice to escape the complexity of her subjectivity in exchange for sanctified access to sexual expression as a pastor's wife. (And also to get her revenge on her former suitor, Dr. Anderson: "Instinctively she had the knowledge that [Dr. Anderson] would be shocked" at her marrying Rev. Green. "Grieved. Horribly hurt even. Well, let him!" [261].) Helga Crane's turning to her "black roots," typically for Larsen, is exposed as falling into bondage: subjugation to a patriarchal folk culture. Helga is punished *not* for crossing the color line (into whiteness) but for *not* crossing that line, for falling in line as the wife of a black preacher. Or rather, she punishes herself, agent of her own downfall, for believing in the succor of marriage as well as for viewing the Southern black community of "simple" religious folk merely as a means to escape from the "complexities of the lives she had known."

How convincing this last segment of the story seems is directly attributable to the success of the psycho-narration, which never leaves Helga's side, after the illusory respite after her conversion. What does occur in the novel's psycho-narration, however, is a decided shift. Focalization is signaled by nouns and verbs about vision and perception ("who sees"), and psycho-narration chronicles the deep sub- and unconscious modes of perception in the narrator's own words (and with the narrator's omniscient insight). Hence, key words and phrases that signal focalization include constructions like "being aware," "knowing," "noticing," and "subconsciously." A brief textual search for the word "aware," indicating unequivocally the presence of focalization in third-person narration, yields thirty-one separate instances in the novel. In each instance, the reference to "being aware" is linked to the character's perception; in most of these, the focalizor is the protagonist herself.

What is remarkable, however, is the degree to which the psycho-narration about Helga's awareness, in the final section of the novel, turns into a chronicle of what Helga Crane is *not* aware of. Indeed, during the first 134 pages of the novel, there are exactly two focalizing references to Helga's being *unaware*. One, meaningfully, occurs before she decides to depart Harlem for Copenhagen: "*Without awareness on her part*, Helga Crane began to draw away from those contacts which had so delighted her" (79; emphasis added). This psycho-narration foreshadows Helga's physical leave-taking. She detaches emotionally and socially first, even from those who had "so delighted her" and "lulled her" into feeling "peace and contentment," feeling "at last to belong somewhere," even to feeling "that she had, as she put it, 'found herself'" (75). This narratorial flourish at the end of the last quotation—"that she had, *as she put it, 'found herself'*"—indicates the legible narratorial distance and dramatic irony with which Larsen imbues even such seemingly unalloyed moments of joy and fellowship, of Helga's having, quote, unquote, "found herself." But, less than a year later, it is from this same fellowship—which "had so delighted her" one chapter earlier—that she withdraws, even without knowing it. But the narrator knows. (Helga Crane's second significant moment of "unawareness," before her shockingly deteriorating circumstances and outlook in the last section of the novel—from her return to Harlem from Copenhagen, to her marriage to Rev. Green and relocating to Alabama—occurs in Copenhagen and indicates a moment when she wants her interlocutor to think she is unaware, but she in fact knows all too well what is going on. The painter Axel Olsen, while painting her portrait, seems to proposition her—not asking for her hand in marriage, but rather proposing something much more fleeting: "Had he insinuated marriage, or something less—and easier?" [114]. Here, we can taste the tang of Helga's own idiom, which colors this moment of interior monologue in the free indirect style.)

Yet, beginning with the church scene in Harlem, after her return to the States, most of the references to Helga Crane's consciousness are about what she is *not* aware of, what she does *not* notice, what she *doesn't* know. Whereas the emphasis on what she "instinctively" knew predominates in the beginning and middle portions of the novel, the last third focuses on her loss of self-awareness and her diminished social awareness. From two instances of being unaware, of not knowing what was really going on, over the first hundred pages, we face six such signals in the space of twenty pages (79, 114, versus 138, 140, 147, 147, 149, 155).

In fact, the very reason that Helga enters the church is to find shelter from a lashing storm, which "lashed her and, scornful of her slight strength, tossed her into the swollen gutter" (138). An *immanent reading* of this novel would link this event with Helga's premonition in Copenhagen: "Well into Helga's second year in Denmark came *an indefinite discontent*. Not clear, but *vague, like a storm gathering far on the horizon*" (110, emphasis added). This storm, first appearing as a proverbial, even clichéd, metaphoric vehicle projecting Helga's "indefinite discontent," returns in the narrative as a climactic event—the return of the repressed. The storm "tosse[s] her into the swollen gutter," effectively manifesting as a larger-than-life natural force—larger and stronger than Helga's "slight strength." It is as if Helga's subconscious has externalized her psychological ill-being—the storm, after all, represents Helga's own "indefinite discontent"—rendering her as King Lear, blasted on the heath by the elements, which reflected his inner turmoil.

Helga Crane thinks she has found safe haven from the storm: a store—a different sort of temple, more congenial to her aesthetic self-fashioning than an evangelist church could ever be. "Helga Crane was not religious," we are told in no uncertain terms (66). So, dragging herself from the gutter, feeling "very tired and very weak," Helga "succeed[s] finally in making her way to the store whose blurred light she had marked for her destination" (138): "She had opened the door and had entered *before she was aware* that, inside, people were singing a song which *she was conscious of* having heard years ago—hundreds of years, it seemed. . . . *She was conscious too* of a hundred pair of eyes upon her as she stood there, drenched and disheveled, at the door of this improvised meeting house" (138–39; emphasis added).

Helga's entrance is thus marked by lack of awareness, by belated understanding: "before she was aware" of what she had stepped in to, she was already there. Even so, the passage focalizes this belated awareness, in terms of her "conscious" understanding, once she places the song and the people singing it in the proper context: an "improvised meeting house." Thus, despite her faulty vision—"marking" a "store" as "her destination," Helga accidentally stumbles into an evangelical church, one far removed from the stately, "very high" black Episcopal church she visited in Chicago (66). The contrast, however, rests not only on the fervor of the Harlem storefront meetinghouse but also on the urbane indifference of the Chicago congregation. In the earlier scene, Helga attends that church with the "hope . . . that some good Christian would speak to her, invite her to return, or inquire kindly if she was a stranger in the city" (66). None of this happens. And as a result, Helga "became bitter, distrusting religion more than ever" (66).

By contrast, the evangelical Harlem congregation is only too eager to extend their brand of kindly fellowship to a "pore los' sinner," a "scarlet 'oman," a "pore los' Jezebel" (140–41). The dramatic irony, in other words, is buttressed by structural irony, wherein the two church scenes are parallel yet diametrically opposed. In a structural narrative chiasmus, the succor and fellowship Helga Crane seeks in Chicago from the "very fashionable" Negro Episcopal church is finally granted, in Harlem, from the very unfashionable storefront church and its rhapsodizing, evangelizing congregation. But typical of Larsen, such fellowship and succor are no more than a baleful narcotic—a toxic "anesthetic" for Helga's "frayed nerves" (146, 139). Before becoming the "kneeling girl," Helga Crane had "sat down on the floor, a dripping heap, and laughed and laughed and laughed" (139). The narration adds, "It was into a shocked silence that she laughed" (139). The song stops "at the first hysterical peal" of Helga's laughter. The prodigal daughter returns, in a sense, coming full circle back to her lowest point in Chicago and thus losing her grip on reality and her sanity, given the "ridiculousness of herself in such surroundings" (139). It is this incongruity that the novel insists on, and it is Helga Crane's diminished perceptiveness, the "fraying" of her "nerves"—recorded by the psycho-narration—that this scene chronicles, foreshadowing the end.

Beginning with "before she was aware" she was entering a church, the psycho-narration focalizes Helga's (uncharacteristic) lack of perceptiveness:

> Helga too began to weep, at first silently, softly; then with great racking sobs. Her nerves were so torn, so aching, her body so wet, so cold! It was a relief to cry unrestrainedly, and she gave herself freely to soothing tears, *not noticing* that the groaning and sobbing of those about her had increased, *unaware* that the grotesque ebony figure at her side had begun gently to pat her arm to the rhythm of the singing and to croon softly, "Yes, chile, yes, chile." *Nor did she notice* the furtive glances that the man on her other side cast at her between his fervent shouts of "Amen!" and "Praise God for a sinner!" (140; emphasis added)[50]

In this passage, three explicit references to Helga Crane's diminished perceptions are flagged for the reader. Each instance seems to register a situation that is ominously different from that which Helga is aware of. Due to her bodily and mental distress, Helga Crane yields to the "relief" of tears while missing the import of social and sexual cues that surround her. Rather than uplifting her, these Good Samaritans make of her a "los' Jezebel," a "sinner" who must be saved, transforming Helga Crane into a caricature, a stereotype, a toxic, controlling image of black femininity. They disempower her by flattening her to this social shell. In order to save her, they must make her into a lost thing—or at least take her as being merely that: "lost," a word repeatedly used to describe Helga to the congregation. She is misrecognized as lost, but even if she were lost— and her "hysterical" laughter indicates a loss of decorum, if not more—Helga's true salvation is not in being saved. At least not by religious feeling. Her real salvation, given the arc of the character and the narrative, lies in continuing her epic quest to comprehend and apprehend her "half-understood desire," not to turn her back on it. It is in continuing her search for self-knowledge, not in relinquishing herself to the controlling image of being a "scarlet woman." But, as the narration reminds us, before the church scene, "Her self-knowledge had increased her anguish" (138). "Anesthetic satisfaction," in the form of sanctified sexual consummation, as well as the pound of flesh exacted by the congregation, are the only pleasures left to Helga Crane by the end of the scene; she is reduced to a "kneeling girl." Her mental acuity and emotional, physical, and spiritual poise, her self-possession, are the price of such small blessings.

The final section of the novel, then, emphasizes Helga Crane's unintentional, and then deliberate, loss of perceptiveness and mental acuity. First, as a result of mental strain, and then, as the result of the unimaginable pain she endures during childbirth, as well as the accumulated strains of having given up "the complex lives she had known" in order to secure her small piece of sensual satisfaction under the aegis of matrimony: "Helga Crane has deliberately stopped thinking" (144). Her internal deliberations before deciding to marry Rev. Green, and to abandon her former "lives," occur in the short chapter after her religious conversion: "It was a chance at stability, at permanent happiness, that she meant to take. She had let so many other things, other chances, escape her. And anyway there was God; He would perhaps make it come out all right. *Still confused and not so sure* that it wasn't the fact that she was 'saved' that had contributed to this after feeling of well-being, she clutched the hope, the desire to believe that now at last she had found some One, some Power, who was interested in her. Would help her" (144–45; emphasis added). The psycho-narration's focus on Helga's "confusion" and lack of certainty, in addition to the quotation marks implicitly undermining Helga's notion of having been "saved," indicate the distance and irony of the narrator vis-à-vis Helga herself. It's striking how the downward spiral that so many critics decry—for being narratively unconvincing, mostly—is predicated on the continued psycho-narration, but also how this technique reveals the confusion and faulty assumptions that plague the protagonist after her losing battle against stereotyped definition: as a "Jezebel" as much as a respectable member of the upstanding Harlem middle class, no less than as an exoticized black woman "curio" or "peacock" in Copenhagen, to be sold to the highest bidder as a wife.

In other words, the development of Helga Crane is a reverse one, appropriately enough for a novel titled *Quicksand*. Helga's sinking into the morass of endless labor—maternal and domestic—happens as a result of the challenges of living the complexity of her "lives" without anyone's helping her. The one figure who held the place of potential romantic fulfillment, Dr. Anderson, is, ironically, the figure Helga Crane thinks of when deciding to marry Rev. Green: "With the thought of yesterday came the thought of Robert Anderson and a feeling of elation, revenge. She had put herself beyond the need of help from him. She had made it impossible for herself ever again to appeal to him. Instinctively she had the knowledge that he would be shocked. Grieved. Horribly hurt even. Well, let him!" (145). This final reference to Helga's "instinctive" understanding of how her actions would impact another—the only man she belatedly realizes she ever loved (155)—signals Helga Crane's renewed clarity of mind, the accuracy of her "instinctive" awareness, lost in the church conversion scene and regained in that brief moment of "elation [and] revenge." The further irony is that the cost of this revenge is the destruction of Helga Crane's former life: as if to spite the man who refused to "help her," she accedes to another man whose help will be the ruin of her. It is only after her "disillusionment" with religion that Helga Crane finally regains the clarity of desiring "revenge" and wanting to escape the complexity of her undefined life:

> Within her emaciated body raged disillusion. Chaotic turmoil. *With the obscuring curtain of religion rent, she was able to look about her and see with shocked eyes this thing that she had done to herself.* She couldn't, she thought ironically, even blame God for it, now that she knew that He didn't exist. No. No more than she could pray to Him for the death of her husband, the Reverend Mr. Pleasant Green. The white man's God. And His great love for all people regardless of race! What idiotic nonsense she had allowed herself to believe. How could she, how could anyone, have been so deluded? (157; emphasis added)

And: "At first she had *felt only an astonished anger* at the quagmire in which she had engulfed herself. Made it impossible ever again to do the things that she wanted, have the things that she loved, mingle with the people she liked. She had, to put it as brutally as anyone could, been a fool" (159; emphasis added). The double bind of Helga Crane's life is exposed at the end of the novel, once she regains the perceptiveness into social and mental reality that she purposefully loses, in order to regain a sense of "elation and revenge" over the torment of her rejection at the hands of the only man she had ever loved. The narration thus focuses on Helga's return to clarity, albeit too late: her "astonished anger" at recognizing her self-deception, the folly of her choice to marry and return to the world from which she escaped—the "white man's God" that we encounter in the very first chapter of the novel. Except, now, her body is unable to escape—the major difference from earlier in her personal journey: "she had to admit that it wasn't new, this feeling of dissatisfaction, of asphyxiation. Something like it she had experienced before. In Naxos. In New York. In Copenhagen. This differed only in degree" (160). The only recourse left to Helga is the oblivion of sleep, of "not thinking," and—of "all-embracing hatred" (161).

From "A Queer Indefinite Factor" to "All-Embracing Hatred"

This "all-embracing hatred" is the queer antisocial note that defines the narrative consciousness of Helga Crane and the ending of *Quicksand*. This hatred is Helga Crane's baleful commentary on "the white man's God," religion, marriage, even her own children. Her ironic awakening from the "half-hypnotized consciousness" of the church scene finds her unable to extricate herself from the quagmire she has entered, half-willingly, half-blindly (143). From the veiled self-loathing that powers her decision to marry Rev. Green—in order to seek revenge on Dr. Anderson, as well as secure sexual "elation" within the sanctity of marriage—we see that loathing turned outward, finally, to become "all-embracing hatred" against social institutions that perpetuate a racist and sexist status quo. The radical antisociality of Helga Crane thus returns in full force, after the "obscuring curtain of religion [was] rent." And thus the conclusion of the novel comes full circle in more ways than one: not only back to Helga Crane's internal railing against the patriarchal "white man's God," not only back in the deep South, but, most importantly, *in the clarity and accuracy of her awareness as documented by the narration.*

Larsen's novel never leaves her psyche, documenting its lapses into self-serving blindness—"the obscuring curtain of religion," for instance, or the momentary glamour of being an exotic racial other in Copenhagen—with the psycho-narration functioning as foreshadowing, as in the following example: "In the days before her conversion, with its subsequent blurring of her sense of humor, Helga might have amused herself by tracing the relation of [Rev. Green's] constant ogling and flattering to *the proverbially large families of preachers; the often disastrous effect on their wives* of this constant stirring of the senses by extraneous women. *Now, however, she did not even think of it*" (148; emphasis added). Such a "disastrous effect" is precisely what Helga Crane incurs, while the psycho-narrator ironically foreshadows her capacity for self-blindness, her willingness to avoid thinking along the lines of her former self (the "blurring of her sense of humor").

Moreover, the final irony of the novel is how consistent Helga Crane's attitudes remain, once the reader realizes the self-deception that she effects. Her stance against marriage and childbearing, for example, returns once Helga Crane has maneuvered herself into becoming subjugated to the physical, maternal, and domestic quagmire of multiple childbirths and a "disastrous" marriage. Her former fiancé, James Vayle, had been shocked at her refusal to "contribute to [the] cause" of having children, which Vayle sees as incumbent on the black middle class: "We're the ones who must have the children if the race is to get anywhere" (132). By the end of the novel, Helga's resolution to never have children reverberates with bitter irony, once she is the mother of four, and the novel ends with her "beg[inning] to have her fifth child" (162).

The dialectic of knowledge and unknowledge, of awareness and unawareness, emphasizes the cognitive privilege of the narrator who can document both states in the protagonist's mind. Through psycho-narration, Larsen exposes the self-deceptions of her protagonist as well as how that protagonist finally sees through her self-deception—even if she holds onto it as "a kind of protective coloring, shielding her from the cruel light of an unbearable reality" (153). The choice of "unbearable" in this seemingly offhand moment is indeed "pregnant" with meaning: religion allows Helga Crane to escape the "unbearable reality" of bearing children she never wanted, for a man she fooled herself into wanting, only to satisfy her desire for "revenge" as well as her "half-understood desire" for sexual fulfillment. Precisely documenting how "*half-understood*" that desire is, however, is the triumph of Larsen's psycho-narration: the blind spots as well as the insights of Helga Crane's conscious, and unconscious, perception.

The first chapter of *Quicksand* prepares us for the "queer, indefinite factor" that Helga Crane represents: "A peculiar characteristic trait, *cold, slowly accumulated unreason* in which all values were distorted or else ceased to exist, had with surprising ferociousness shaken the bulwarks of *that self-restraint which was also, curiously, a part of her nature*" (39; emphasis added). Her penchants for "accumulated unreason" and "self-restraint" are at war with each other, making Helga Crane a study in psychological contrasts rather than a portrait of warring "blood." The passage concludes with her "characteristic" self-negating willfulness: Helga Crane "said aloud, quietly, dispassionately: 'Well, I'm through with that,' and, shutting off the hard, bright blaze of the overhead lights, went back to her chair and settled down with an odd gesture of sudden soft collapse, *like a person who had been for months fighting the devil and then unexpectedly had turned around and agreed to do his bidding*" (39; emphasis added). This pattern of resolution dissolving in the twilight of her mind—her "half-understood desire"—foreshadows the self-canceling attractions and repulsions of Helga Crane's trajectory. Her determination is instantly forgotten and turned into its opposite: that is the burden of her misfit status, where self-ownership means wading through an unknown world constructed in the ether of subconscious and unconscious impulses, "half-understood."

Conclusion: Plumbing the "Psychological Depths" of "Unconformity"

Larsen's novel thus positions its mixed-race protagonist as a perennial misfit. Helga Crane is endowed with a "queer indefinite factor" in every community to which she seeks to belong. Helga's queerness within—in the sense of that word as not fitting in, as it is employed in Larsen's novel—is a constant despite all of her peregrinations. But more importantly than Helga's "misfit" positioning, always finding herself an outsider to racial monocultures, Larsen's *Quicksand* articulates the contents of this misfit perspective. As we have seen, these contents are as much conscious as sub- or unconscious, and the novel details the downward trajectory of Helga Crane's ability to maneuver as a bicultural misfit. This downward trajectory, as I have argued, is detailed at the level of narrative form through the technique of psycho-narration, a stylistic feature of Larsen's and modernist fiction in general, that is understudied compared to the critical focus on free indirect discourse. Larsen's narrator opens the "transparent mind" of Helga Crane but does so by going beyond what even this insightful character can understand herself, about herself, in particular. The notion of Helga's "half-understood desire" thus indicates the importance of psycho-narration for articulating the contours of misfit consciousness *inasmuch as that consciousness is predicated on not knowing itself fully.*

Beyond this psychological portraiture, however, *Quicksand* articulates the ideological contours of Helga's misfit consciousness—and subconsciousness. These contours are radically anti-children, as we see in the section above. The ending of the novel is thus acutely ironic, insofar as Helga is trapped by her maternal "instinct" from escaping from the monoculture that asphyxiates her emotionally and, now, physically. For it is her love for the children, and memory of her own mother's abandonment, that prevents Helga from running away: "Of the children Helga tried not to think. She wanted to leave them—if that were possible. The recollection of her own childhood, lonely, unloved, rose too poignantly before her for her to consider calmly such a solution. . . . She couldn't desert them" (161). Back in Harlem, Helga Crane's modern, anti-child stance—as articulated to her former fiancé—is thus turned upside down, in a narrative arc that ends "when she began to have her fifth child." But the last section of the novel does not simply turn on this irony, however, no matter how tragic it is. For Helga Crane's eventual "rending" of the curtain of religion happens concomitantly; it is her faith in God—which she acquires in the conversion scene—that is finally shattered. Her downfall through lack of perception—after her rejection and emotional disturbance—is thus partially turned against, in her regaining of her usual consciousness. It is then that Helga Crane understands her unwillingness to abandon her children, as such an act would mean "a rending of deepest fibers" (161). This coincidence of the verb "rend" in both cases—"the obscuring curtain of religion rent" (157); "a rending of deepest fibers" (161) were she to abandon her children—indicates the unity of ideological conception that marks Helga Crane's final clarity. The further irony is that this clarity comes too late. This ideology of individualism has always been the core of Helga's peripatetic movement; her self-exile from Naxos is predicated on that school's "open hostility" on "individualisms" such as Helga's personal philosophy (39).

The ending of the novel, in other words, is consistent with the beginning; only the circumstances have changed, and dramatically so. But Helga Crane's postpartum convalescence leads to her ultimate rejection of her hasty religious conversion. And yet the last few chapters not only see the return of Helga Crane's anti-children philosophy. For example, the following passage documents her internal deliberations upon learning of the premature death of her fourth child: "after a short week of slight living," the infant had "just closed his eyes and died. No vitality. On hearing of it Helga too had closed her eyes. . . . She had closed her eyes to shut in any telltale gleam of the relief which she felt. One less" (158). This passage, in its blending of free indirect thought and psycho-narration, internally verbalizes Helga's own idiomatic intellection ("One less"), while the psycho-narrator delves into Helga's unarticulated consciousness: "a new idea had come to her" (158). But the point is more about the pointedness of her "relief" upon learning of her newborn's death. Such a shockingly unmaternal thought process is laid bare by Larsen's narration and indicates a consonance with the anterior "complex lives" Helga Crane had lived, when she articulated her refusal to ever bear children at all. The antisocial stance uncovered here is thus consistent throughout the narrative, and the anomaly is the church-scene conversion.

The ending of the novel, then, concludes with the original misfit consciousness of Helga Crane largely intact, even as her body is "used up" by the tolls of female sexual bondage within the institution of matrimony. As with the figure of Helga Crane being "like a person who had been for months fighting the devil and then unexpectedly had turned around and agreed to do his bidding" (39), the novel itself tracks this process from the inside out, within her consciousness, and then shows how she herself realizes this fact: that she had "unexpectedly" agreed to do the bidding of "the devil," even when her entire life was organized to avoid and resist his lures. These lures—sexual desire, marriage, children— are thus inverted by the queer consciousness of Helga Crane, the "white man's God" transformed into "the devil." What could be queerer than that?

Documenting the mental life of a modernist misfit—one labeled as a "despised mulatto"—is Larsen's triumph in *Quicksand*. Her protagonist's resistance to heteronormative institutions is shocking in a novelist whom many critics insist is merely an agent of a bourgeois consciousness. Davis's biography concludes with the following quotation from a 1925 letter from Larsen to Van Vechten:[51] "Larsen could not turn her need for expression and her experiences into fiction, for too closely had she allied her writing with the surfaces of 'amusing' social experience and *too little had she explored the psychological depths* charted and sketched in her subtexts."[52] I'd like to close this study of Larsen with an analysis of Davis's commentary, which is emblematic of the critical dismissal of misfit modernist texts. Texts like *Quicksand*, which destabilize the moral and cultural institutions of identity and community. Their destabilization is too toxic, it seems, not to be contained by the uplift of contemporary visions of authentic minority consciousness. Note Davis's assertion regarding what Larsen *could not* accomplish—rather than emphasizing the radically unstable assertions against religion, marriage, children, and even the family in her novel: this chapter, at the very least, analyzes how painstakingly *Quicksand* "explore[s] the psychological depths" in its *texts, not merely its "subtexts."*

If the evidence of Helga Crane's consciousness (and subconscious "depths") counts only as "subtext," rather than "text," then Davis's judgment of Larsen's fiction as merely focusing on the "surfaces of 'amusing' social experience" is correct. But the modernism of Larsen's fiction lies precisely in documenting how subjectivity negotiates the "surfaces of . . . social experience" and the "psychological depths" that are enmeshed in that experience. Davis continues by quoting Larsen herself: "'What things there are to write, if only one can write them,' [Larsen] mused in the mid-1920s. *Her list of 'things,' meant to be extensive* and tensile, *revealed a limited, oddly vapid sense of material:* 'Boiler menders, society ladies, children, acrobats, governesses, business men, countesses, flappers, Nile green bath rooms [*sic*], *beautifully filled, gray moods and shivering hesitations,* all *presented in an intensely restrained and civilized manner* and *underneath the ironic survival of a much more primitive mood. Delicious.'*"[53]

The interest for me, and for this study of misfit modernists like Larsen, is precisely in legitimating such authorial poetics of representation, which do not conform to established norms of social, cultural, or political value. Larsen's "vapid sense of material," in Davis's words, is in fact a wide-ranging enumeration of a social world that scales bohemia and demimonde, aristocrats and plebes ("flappers" and "acrobats" along with "countesses" and "boiler menders"). Above all, however, is the focus on *mood: "beautifully filled, gray moods and shivering hesitations . . . and underneath the ironic survival of a much more primitive mood."* Larsen's aesthetic vision is far from vapid but rather interested in the "delicious" contrasts of a "primitive mood" "presented in an intensely restrained and civilized manner." The oscillation between "surface" and "psychological depths," in Davis's words, is precisely the modus operandi of Larsen's modernist technique of psycho-narration, of narrating the interiority of a mixed-race protagonist that, at the time she was writing, was not considered a legitimate basis for fiction. As Rafael Walker reminds us, it seems that even in our own time, such narrative focus on a biracial, bicultural, "unconformist" consciousness is dismissed as inauthentic, the narrative of a "despised mulatto" dismissed as not "black enough," as (today) a form of false consciousness.[54] But that was precisely Larsen's point: the whiteness of black bourgeois society and the primitive mood of white avatars of aesthetic refinement like the modern painter Axel Olsen. The constant is the narrative "mood," or the texture of the narrative discourse as created by modernist techniques (or *modes*) like Larsen's adept psycho-narration.[55]

Yet, in *Quicksand*, the narrative constant is also the psychological exploration of a misfit (or "unconformist"), "despised mulatto" consciousness and the social hypocrisies she perceives in each cultural community she encounters, because none of them is really home: "As she stepped out into [Chicago's] moving multicolored crowd, there came to her a queer feeling of enthusiasm, as if she were tasting some agreeable, exotic food—sweetbreads, smothered with truffles and mushrooms, perhaps. And oddly enough, she felt, too, that she had come home. She, Helga Crane, who had no home" (62–63). Upon her arrival in New York, a week or so later, Helga instead began to "feel like a criminal" (74). For a misfit like Helga Crane, home is a utopia, a "queer feeling" rather than a place ("who had no home"), given her unconformity. Her ability to integrate into the Harlem black middle class makes her "feel like a criminal" because it is predicated on lying about her white parentage, because her biracial caste violates the norms of "pure" family, marriage, and religion that define most cultures as "homes," leaving misfits like Helga Crane out in the cold, or pretending to be someone they're not. The question of intent arises next: whether Helga chooses to not have a permanent "home," and whether her folly in marrying Rev. Green violates the "pleasure of refusing" conformity that is the predilection of the misfit—even if so doing means refusing the comforts as well as the norms of family, matrimony, and religion that constitute home. To redefine "home" itself—as a queer feeling?—is the direction that Larsen's novel points us to, as does her ersatz *ars poetica*, cited in Davis's conclusion: Larsen's catalog of domestic contents, transformed by an ironic aesthetic vision aiming at deeper psychological and social reality. This deeper psychology—unearthing "beautifully filled, gray moods and shivering hesitations"—is constructed primarily through Larsen's psycho-narration, told in her novel's "intensely restrained and civilized manner," its stylistic restraint and surface-level civility ensuring "the ironic survival of a much more primitive mood." Her distinctive, contradictory, misfit-modernist aesthetic ensures Larsen's survival, even if only two of her novels survive.

3.

Affective Realism

Feeling Like a "Total Misfit" in Thurman's
The Blacker the Berry

Misfits . . . are always first to flock to experimental movements.

—Theophilus Lewis, 1929

For Thurman, arguing against the older generation's insistence on
representational didacticism and idealism—for him, indistinguishable
from the bourgeoisie's obsessions with uplift and respectability—was
the consuming passion of his life.

—Amritjit Singh, 2003

Introduction: Refusing to "Appear in Public Butter Side Up"

Although a central figure in the Harlem Renaissance, Wallace Thurman is
obscured by his contemporaries Langston Hughes and Zora Neale Hurston.
Amritjit Singh and Daniel Scott, editors of the *Collected Writings*, admit that
Thurman tended to "walk . . . into dangerous racial and personal territory."[1]
Thurman admits that it was "difficult and risky" to critique the norms of the
New Negro cultural establishment as championed by leaders such as W. E. B. Du
Bois and Alain Locke. For example, in his short-lived little magazine, *Harlem*,
Thurman lambastes Du Bois for criticizing a novel by Rudolph Fisher, *The Walls*

of Jericho (1928). Thurman admits to becoming "angry and incoherent" upon reading Du Bois's review, calling such criticism "narrow and patronizing," even evincing patronizing "concern" for Du Bois himself.[2] Thurman concludes his diatribe by declaring that Du Bois "has served his race well; so well, in fact, that the artist in him has been stifled in order that the propagandist may thrive."[3]

In this searing critique, Thurman radically distinguishes his modernist aesthetic ideal of artistic freedom from the thrall of the Renaissance man's "propagandist" posture, here personified by Du Bois, which called for an aesthetic doctrine of collective uplift through representations of respectable black characters. For Du Bois, the literary presentation of such characters signifies "a step upward from Van Vechten and McKay," that is, from the "primitive types" depicted in Van Vechten's and McKay's *Nigger Heaven* (1926) and *Home to Harlem* (1928), respectively: the numbers runners, "sweetback" men, and women of easy virtue such as Thurman's own "Cordelia the Crude" (1926). These were Harlem Renaissance works Du Bois decried for their focus on the "worst" elements in urban black life.[4]

In this fraught critique of Du Bois, Thurman impugns the Harvard man's "propagandist" agenda as inimical to the artistic sensibility ("the artist in him has been stifled in order that the propagandist may thrive"). But he also devalues Du Bois and the Renaissance "race man" *tout court*, calling such a position mere posturing and hypocritical. In comparing the good doctor to a "denizen of Striver's Row," Thurman lambastes the materialism and assimilationism of the Talented Tenth, Du Bois's term for the African American college-educated elite. Hence, the central aim of Renaissance men such as Du Bois—leveraging positive black representations to uplift the race, especially in the eyes of the greater American public—is equated with selling out. Thurman caricatures the "denizen of Striver's Row" as "scuttling hard up the social ladder, with nothing more important to think about than making money and keeping a high yellow wife bleached out and marcelled." By so doing, Thurman calls out the most visible representative of the black cultural elite at this time for being in collusion with hegemonic white bourgeois values, and thus "pander[ing] to the stupidities of both black and white audiences."

More cuttingly, Thurman mobilizes a black cultural trope, that of a "high yellow wife," whose skin color is "bleached out" and hair is "marcelled," as evidence of the New Negro elite's Eurocentric sensibility. The race man as race traitor: Thurman was a caustic critic of the whole edifice of black elitism that subtended his own writings and was unafraid of biting the hand that fed him. Thurman was a significant figure of the Renaissance's *enfants terribles*, the generation of "Younger Negro Artists," which included Langston Hughes.

Thurman actively contributed to this generational schism, partially in order to become the philosophical leader of this generation, by writing jeremiads against the black cultural elite and the "propagandistic" aesthetic agenda of Du Bois and other thought leaders, such as Alain Locke, the "dean" of the New Negro Renaissance.[5]

Thurman's point regarding the hidden Eurocentrism of black cultural leadership is bolstered in another essay, "Negro Artists and the Negro."[6] In that essay, Thurman argues that the problem with the "bourgeois Negro" is that he "[fears] what his white compatriots think" and "feels that he cannot afford to be attacked realistically by Negro artists who do not seem to have the 'proper' sense of refinement or race pride. The American scene dictates that the American Negro must be what he ain't! And despite what the minority intellectual and artistic group may say it really does seem more profitable for him to be what he ain't, than for him to be what he is."[7] Thus Thurman made quite an effort to strike a radical pose against the progressive elitism of the New Negro establishment. For Thurman as well as for Hughes, writing about modern black life included gritty urban color and "unrefined" elements. The contemporary critiques made by Du Bois and others regarding younger literary authors such as Thurman centered on the notion of uplift and evincing sufficient "race pride," found wanting in Thurman, McKay, and Hughes, among others, because they focused so intensely on the "primitive" elements of Harlem life. Thurman sought to neutralize such critiques by calling for an aesthetic ideal of realism as an overriding artistic principle. Said principle sought to depict the "American Negro" "as he is" rather than as he "must be," which was what Thurman thought he was not ("must be what he ain't"). As Thurman writes in "Negro Artists and the Negro," the "Negro artist . . . will receive little aid from his own people unless he spends his time spouting sociological jeremiads or exhausts his talent in building rosy castles around Negro society."[8]

It is the principled refusal to erect those "rosy castles around Negro society" that sets apart writers like Thurman, who take it upon themselves to write oppositional "jeremiads" against the "sociological" function of artistic production espoused by the New Negro establishment. This establishment's values coincided with Eurocentric bourgeois norms of respectability, decorum, and, ironically, race pride. On the same page, Thurman adds, "Negroes in America feel certain that they must always appear in public *butter side up*, in order to keep from being trampled in the contemporary onward march. They feel as if they must always exhibit specimens from college rather than from the kindergarten, specimens from the parlor rather than from the pantry. They are in the process of being assimilated, and those elements within the race which are still too potent for easy assimilation must be hidden until they no longer exist."[9] This quote exemplifies Thurman's oppositional aesthetic ideology, based on relative autonomy from what he termed "sociological problems or propaganda," which threatened to render invisible (or "hidden") the "American Negro" as he was, in the "onward march" toward "assimilation" ("what he must be").

The imposition of this "propagandistic" burden on younger black artists constitutes Thurman's grievance against Du Bois's ideals of representation, summarized in Du Bois's notion that "all art is propaganda, and ever must be."[10] The New Negro elite's interest in racial uplift was oriented toward a mainstream white audience whose values measured positive or negative representation on the scale of respectability. As Thurman puts it, the Renaissance brief to uplift was a march from the pantry to the parlor, and from kindergarten to college. For Thurman, it was as important to depict the pantry, and the kindergarten, as it was to represent the "rosy castles" erected around New Negro society, whose privilege distanced them greatly from mainstream black urban life. Hence Thurman's call to depict the Negro "as he is," not "as he must be."

Chapter Overview

This chapter focuses on Thurman's first novel, *The Blacker the Berry* (1929), and argues for the relevance and importance of Thurman's anti-bourgeois, anti-uplift, *misfit-modernist* aesthetic. Thurman's noted contrariness, his negativity bordering on nihilism, is notable even in his self-characterization as "caviling."[11] His dissident vision sought aesthetic freedom and distance from the New Negro as a masculine, bourgeois, collective black identity. Thurman cultivated a negative minoritarian sensibility, defined in opposition to the aesthetic ideology of the New Negro.[12] Such cultural opposition is an early twentieth-century example of disidentification. Thurman's work is not in Locke's 1925 *New Negro* anthology, signaling his belatedness to the movement and his outsider status. His outsiderdom freshens Thurman's eye and sharpens the critical edge of his first two novels, *The Blacker the Berry* and *Infants of the Spring* (1932), as radically opposed to collective uplift and the reduction of art to propaganda, no matter how well intentioned.

His aesthetic of negativity draws on his outsider status with regard to Harlem's cultural and racial norms. As Dorothy West boldly put it, "He hated Negro society, and since dark skins were never the fashion among Negro upper classes, the feeling was occasionally mutual."[13] Noted for his "pessimism and defeatism," in Daniel Walker's words, for his acerbic negativity bordering on nihilism, Thurman had a fraught relation to the "Negro upper classes," as West recalls. She talks about the "mutual contempt" that black "high society" and Thurman had for one another. I draw on this archive of contemporaneous reception as an immanent structure of feeling that, I argue, is undertheorized as a formative influence on Thurman's subcanonization. The same forces of negative critical reception influence other misfit modernists in this study, indicating the rebounding effect of this negative minoritarian aesthetic, impacting the careers and afterlives of the authors as well as their underappreciated novels about modernist misfits.

Therefore, this chapter draws on the reception history of *The Blacker the Berry*, much of it negative, and the hermeneutic style I call *immanent reading*, which focuses on privileged terms in the text that serve as a key to its interpretation. Immanent reading eschews theoretical constructs extrinsic to that archive. My immanent reading of Thurman's novel draws on the consistency of negative affects that *The Blacker the Berry* produces. To do this, I draw from two immanent domains, one in the body of the fiction, and the other in that body's reception. This chapter thus centers on the resilient yet toxic agency of negative affects in *The Blacker the Berry* and in contemporaneous criticism of the novel. One immanent key word, beyond the "total misfit" I discuss in the introduction, is "lonesomeness," which speaks to the protagonist's dilemma of double exile. And the second affective keyword, "stupid" or "stupidity," is found in the body of an oft-cited contemporaneous review of the novel.

Hence, this chapter draws on an autobiographical vein of Thurman criticism and performs its own yoking of the autobiographical with the narratological, or, rather, my reading draws a picture of the correspondences and continuities in affect within the aesthetic order of the novel as well as outside it, in the time of its origin. The negative affectivity of the Harlem Renaissance—especially after Thurman included themes of prostitution and bisexuality in *Fire!!*, which provoked the rebuke of elders such as Locke and Charles S. Johnson—renders this period of cultural history charged not only from an aesthetic but from an affective point of view. This chapter thus focuses on a palpably negative novel, and a palpably negative author, and how critiques centering on either the one or the other, or both, responded in kind with negative affectivity. In the past, this consensus has made Thurman a minor figure and *The Blacker the Berry* an understudied novel. My chapter analyzes this entire aesthetic and cultural complex, centering on a novel whose protagonist has a "racial complex" and an author whom most critics tied to his protagonist as himself personifying the issue of racial inferiority that shadows—and, I argue, enriches—this difficult and affecting novel.

Thurman's focus on the negative in his literary and critical productions, as well as the critical conception of the relative "failure" of his finished works—in terms of Eurocentric aesthetic values, as we see below—is part of the reason he is a minor figure of the Renaissance. Yet Thurman led the Younger Negro Artists by editing influential journals such as *Fire!!* and *Harlem*. For this reason his literary legacy bears reexamination. More specifically, Thurman's anti-uplifting aesthetic challenged the established leaders of the New Negro movement. As Granville Ganter writes, the "moralistic case" against Thurman, based on his refusal to "celebrate" the community, was a strategy originating with Du Bois.[14]

More broadly, *Misfit Modernism* argues that the burden of uplift defining (and confining) minoritarian representation is a force against which modernist authors such as Thurman perennially struggled. Thus it is this "moralistic" valence in minoritarian representational norms that renders Thurman difficult to appreciate both in his own time and our own, with its own minoritarian norms of cultural uplift, positive representation, and burden of respectability. Indeed, our own contemporary progressive politics finds discomfort in Thurman's principled resistance to ideological litmus tests for minoritarian literature and art.

The Aesthetic Politics of Reception

Thurman's novel chronicles the series of rejections and social solitude that result from the protagonist's originary ostracism from the social and familial environment. Using the language of naturalism, *The Blacker the Berry* details Emma Lou's story as one based on the social determinations of exclusion and hardship. Emma Lou is thus doubly displaced from the outset: the first scene of the novel recounts her high school graduation, where she is the only black student in the school, and her feelings of solitude and ostracism within this white social world. Moreover, Emma Lou's family, which models itself as a branch of the old white Southern aristocracy, similarly ostracizes her, displacing her within her own home, rendering her a "total misfit" within her own family, in the words of the novel (256).

This double marginalization mirrors, yet transcends, Du Bois's definitive characterization of modern African American subjectivity as defined by the metaphors of "the Veil" and double consciousness in *The Souls of Black Folk* (1903). *The Blacker the Berry* represents Thurman's handling of this theme of modern black subjectivity. But Thurman's novel then asks, What happens to the tale of color prejudice when one is living solely or primarily inside the Veil (within one's own kind), instead of outside it? As he himself states about his first novel, Thurman took the modern tack of looking at the inner workings of black social life, rather than representing the more chronicled negotiations of black subjects in relation to white society. As Thurman writes in "Notes on a Stepchild," he "had concerned himself only with Negroes among their own kind, trying to interpret some of the internal phenomena of Negro life in America."[15] Note Thurman's impersonal use of the third person to write about himself, a trait shared with another misfit modernist, Christopher Isherwood, the subject of chapter 5. Thus Thurman's self-criticism hinges on "he," not "I"; on Negroes "among *their* own kind," not "our own kind." In these cases, Thurman detaches from personal interests and minoritarian community as well as from homogenizing "white folks" as a monolithic bloc. Thurman's cultural disidentification renders his writing situated and grounded yet resistant to claiming allegiance to the elite black community, given its bourgeois caste distinctions. He was much too individualistic as an artist to be subsumed under collective identity or interests: "He did not hate all white people, nor did he love all black ones. He found individuals in both races whom he admired. . . . He was not interested in races or countries or people's skin color. He was interested only in individuals."[16] Thurman's focus on individuals, however, does not preclude his interest in *minoritarian* individuals, and black individuals above all. He did not flee from the community but rather sought to "view the whole problem [of race in America] objectively, tracing things to their roots"—and, I would add, wallowing in the descent into the "problem" and its "roots."

A tale of internalized racism and intraracial prejudice, *The Blacker the Berry* describes the painful dynamics of modern urban "Negro Life." Bracketing the omnipresence of white social hegemony in order to present a close-up view of internal cultural experience, Thurman's novel represents black society as structured by the same brutalizing forces of racialization and oppression as the dominant white world outside the margins of the novel. As the second part of the novel's title makes clear (*A Novel of Negro Life*), Thurman represents what happens when a marginalized subject operates *within* her "own kind" but is also tragically situated outside of its normative social contours. This novel chronicles a doubly minor form of "Negro Life" experienced by intersectional subjects, such as Emma Lou Morgan, who are doubly marginalized. Her combined social attributes push her outside the charmed circle of belonging within her own cultural and familial formation as well as within the majority culture of white supremacy. Briefly, the plot of the novel centers on the fact that Emma Lou Morgan is "too black" for her light-skinned black family. The fact of her darker skin color combines with her gender (being born female rather than male) and her personal attributes (being ordinary rather than exceptional) to create a complex personality alienated from her own kind and from majority culture. Emma Lou Morgan is internally displaced due to black-bourgeois cultural norms and values (which Thurman dubs "Negro-white"), which mirror those of the dominant white world.

Of course, the title of the novel echoes the "old Negro saying," which is given in epigraph: "The blacker the berry / the sweeter the juice." Yet this title is ambivalent, in the sense of its rhetorical effect as a double gesture. *The Blacker the Berry . . . A Novel of Negro Life* functions as a phrase comprising a title and subtitle. Yet the use of an ellipsis, rather than a colon, constitutes one titular entity, thereby refusing by punctuation the distinction (and hierarchy) of title/subtitle that the phrase's syntax suggests. The syntactical ambivalence in Thurman's title mirrors the symbolic ambivalence represented by the narrative as a whole. For the title leaves out the gesture of redemption in the saying itself. *The Blacker the Berry . . . A Novel of Negro Life* echoes the syntax and the theme of the "old Negro saying," but the substitution of "the sweeter the juice" signals the novel's refusal to sugarcoat its tale. The subtitle signals Thurman's aspiration to realism, wanting to focus on the realities of early twentieth-century "Negro life," rather than the sweetening myth of proverb.

In an unpublished review essay, "This Negro Literary Renaissance" (1926), Thurman remarks on the sentimentality of 1920s "New Negro" fiction. Discussing the novel about passing, Thurman writes, echoing Wilde, that it is only in *novels* that black characters light enough to pass for white ever return to the fold, refusing the lure of whiteness. And commenting on Walter F. White's novel about passing, *Flight*, Thurman signifies on his own literary accomplishment in *The Blacker the Berry*. He states, coyly, in a parenthesis, that he would "leave to others [to render judgment on] the author of *The Blacker the Berry*." He adds that if "Mr. White had been a novelist *rather than a journalist . . .* [he] would have been able to make us privy to what the Negro who passes for white *actually feels and experiences*."[17] It is this idea about a special approach to literary fiction that I call Thurman's *affective realism*, which governs the aesthetic ideology informing *The Blacker the Berry*. His aesthetic of affective realism is legible in the phrase "actually feels and experiences." Thurman adds,

> While on the question of novels concerning Negroes who cross the [color] line, let us ask: when will some novelist emerge *courageous enough to give a truthful delineation*? To date, it has become a *literary convention* to have these fictional passers cross over into the white world, remain discontented, and in the final chapter hasten back from when they came.

There are several thousand Negroes who each year lose their racial identity, and of this number less than one per cent return to their native haunts. There is *in real life* none of that ubiquitous and magnetic primitive urge which *in fiction* draws them back to their own kind. This romantic reaction is purely an invention of the fictioneers.[18]

A staunch realist in the modernist vein, Thurman here deplores the "literary convention" of "romantic" "fictioneers." By so doing, Thurman marks his allegiance to an aesthetic ideal of realism—well before the likes of Richard Wright, I might add. Here, he does so in the use of social statistics to prove his point about the *unrealistic* treatment of passing in novels like White's.

Indeed, "This Negro Literary Renaissance" is a literary manifesto on par with Langston Hughes's influential "The Negro Artist and the Racial Mountain" (1926). Thurman's essay promotes his anti-uplift aesthetic, one tied to an almost toxic reality principle. His is a realist aesthetic centered on the subjective, the phenomenological, and the affective. In the "passing" example, Thurman spurns fictioneers' distorted accounts of passing, a phenomenon with different outcomes in real life. Instead, Thurman holds to the principle of realism, the acknowledgment that minoritarian subjects sometimes, indeed often, sold their birthright for a mess of pottage when they could. Such an anti-sentimental message is typical of Thurman's negative minoritarian aesthetic, indebted to the idiom of literary naturalism, which he uses to frame the "social problem" at the heart of this novel.

What is more, this minoritarian aesthetic has influenced the negative reception history of Thurman's inaugural novel. The reception of the novel mirrors that of its hapless protagonist. Like Emma Lou Morgan, *The Blacker the Berry* is largely disowned by its closest kith and kin: academicians who study the Harlem Renaissance have largely focused on the luminaries of this movement, such as Jean Toomer, Langston Hughes, Zora Neale Hurston, and Nella Larsen. Queer critics, on the other hand, when they turn to the Harlem Renaissance, tend to study these same figures, ironically, or the more recognizably "gay" figure of Richard Bruce Nugent. Thurman's work does not comfortably conform to a New Negro mode of literary representation. Neither does it conform to an unproblematically queer one: as Ganter explains, "Thurman was neither a picture of heterosexual virility nor was he exclusively gay. Combined with his lukewarm interest in promoting his black identity, Thurman has not found a comfortable place amid the progressive identity politics of post-1960s literary scholarship. In contrast to Richard Bruce Nugent, who has been welcomed by contemporary gay scholars, Thurman remains a wall-flower, neither self-consciously black enough, nor gay enough to serve as a Renaissance poster boy."[19]

I would add that Thurman is not recognizably *literary* enough, either. And this is despite Thurman's own exacting literary values and his leadership of the younger generation of New Negro artists—as evinced by his editorship of *Fire!!* and *Harlem: A Forum of Negro Life*. Thus, despite his avant-gardism, seen in the bohemian themes of *Fire!!* (bisexuality, polyamory, prostitution, and so on), Thurman's output was considered subpar relative to his own high literary standards. Nugent, for instance, complains about the first issue of *Harlem* in an eight-page handwritten letter to Dorothy Peterson. The letter begins, "Dear Dot: I suppose you have seen 'HARLEM. . . .' I was the most disappointed individual. . . . Wally could have done *so* much better with the format."[20]

Indeed, reception of *The Blacker the Berry* in the black press was mostly negative. Eunice Carter, in an oft-cited review in the National Urban League's *Opportunity*, assesses Thurman's novel in terms of bourgeois aesthetic values and finds it wanting. First, Carter acknowledges the novel's popular success ("a book that has run into several editions"). Yet Carter wonders whether Thurman's success speaks to the novel's "artistic achievement" or simply demonstrates that "Mr. Thurman has become a devotee of the most fashionable of American literary cults, that dedicated to the exploitation of the vices of the Negro of the lowest stratum of society and to the mental debauching of Negroes in general."[21] Thus criticizing the subject matter of Thurman's novel as kin to Van Vechten's and McKay's similar treatments of Harlem nightlife, Carter concludes, "McKay has done it better." Her review ends with words Thurman himself might have chosen in his own dismissals of the Harlem vogue: "One wishes for the chronicles of the Negro that same finished workmanship, that same polished perfection that characterizes the best in Anglo Saxon letters."[22] Ironically, Carter's insistence on a supposedly objective frame of reference for literary value ("finished workmanship") reveals her aesthetic Eurocentrism ("the best in Anglo Saxon letters"). Like Thurman himself, doubly ironically, she argues against publishing work by black authors that is insufficiently refined to stand on its own merits.

Indeed, Thurman was thus criticized for failing to abide by normative Eurocentric cultural-aesthetic values—including that of bourgeois respectability and literary sophistication—that he himself championed. For instance, in "Notes on a Stepchild," another posthumously published essay, Thurman declares his "spiritual kinship" with literary modernism. He name-drops canonical figures such as Joyce, Woolf, Mann, Stein, and Huysmans. Before writing *The Blacker the Berry*, Thurman reflects on how he began: by "taking as a motto Huysmans' '*I record what I see, what I feel, what I have experienced, writing it as I can, et voilà tout,'* he began his first novel, spending his non-writing hours trying to find a master among *the contemporary realists.*"[23] And, in "Nephews of Uncle Remus," Thurman critiques his artistic contemporaries: the "results of the Renaissance have been sad rather than satisfactory, in that critical standards have been ignored, and the measure of achievement has been racial rather than literary."[24] Carter's review thus mirrors Thurman's own critique of contemporary black writers.

What is more, Du Bois's review mirrors Carter's. His critique of *The Blacker the Berry* struggles to reconcile opposing impulses. Du Bois lauds Thurman's bravery in confronting an issue, intraracial color prejudice, that he agrees is "one of the most moving and tragic of our day."[25] Thurman's novel "frankly faces a problem" that exists and one that "most colored people especially have shrunk from, and almost hated to face."[26] Yet, like Carter's, Du Bois's review applies aesthetic standards to measure the novel's achievement. Again, it is ironic how both reviewers fault Thurman according to the standards he himself championed: here, the "measure of achievement has been" not "racial," but "literary."

But Du Bois's critique goes beyond aesthetics. He also judges the novel according to "racial" standards. Du Bois begins with a sympathetic account of the novel: "Here is the plight of a soul who suffers not alone from the color line, as we usually conceive it, but from the additional evil prejudice, which the dominant ideals of a white world create within the Negro world itself."[27] Du Bois's review then turns to a biographically oriented critique of Thurman: "The author [who tells a story such as Emma Lou's] must believe in black folk, and in the beauty of black as a color of human skin. I may be wrong, but *it does not seem to me that this is true of Wallace Thurman. He seems to me himself to deride blackness*; he speaks of Emma's color as a 'splotch' on the 'pale purity' of her white fellow students and as mocking that purity 'with her outlandish difference.'"[28] Thus Du Bois criticizes Thurman himself for the novel's discourse of intraracial prejudice. Citing an excerpt from the novel as proof that Thurman is not sufficiently race-proud, Du Bois blames the author, not the racist discourse that the novel depicts, ventriloquizes, and criticizes: "It seems to me that this *inner self-despising* of the very thing that he is defending, makes the author's defense less complete and less sincere, and keeps the story from developing as it should."[29] He views the novel as a symptom of its author's internalized racism rather than as Thurman's indictment of the Talented Tenth as a "pigmentocracy."[30] Du Bois thus scapegoats Thurman, representing the issues Emma Lou faces as merely Thurman's own. Such imperatives of uplift—or denying "self-despising," or eradicating it—are the essence of the logic and politics of collective identity. Thurman's novel is a satirical treatment of this logic, exposing the harsh irony attendant on a culture that demands bourgeois decorum from its well-heeled members, yet signally excludes those members who do not embody "Negro-white" respectability in their skin color, if not their mannerisms.

Indeed, Du Bois's commentary is doubly ironic. In the same review, he lauds Larsen—the subject of chapter 2—and her second novel, *Passing*, even as he challenges Thurman for not being race-positive. The irony inheres in both novels' "mulatto" milieu, that of an upper-class black bourgeoisie that *The Blacker the Berry* satirizes. Emma Lou Morgan's maternal grandmother founded a "blue-vein circle" in Boise, Idaho, a self-anointed "superior class" of light-colored black folks, so called because "all of its members were fair-skinned enough for their blood to be seen pulsing purple through the veins of their wrists."[31] As outlined in the narrative discourse of the novel, the blue-vein circle's credo was "'whiter and whiter every generation,' until the grandchildren of the blue veins could easily go over into the white race and become assimilated so that problems of race would plague them no more" (19). It is this milieu that *Passing* also documents, albeit from the safely entrenched position of an Irene Redfield, someone who can and does easily pass for white. Larsen's *Passing* is a critique of this echelon of the black bourgeoisie. But it does not focus on, nor does it question, the toxic doctrine of skin-color hierarchy as it affects the darker-colored members of this class, which is the raison d'être of Thurman's novel. Irene's "race-conscious Puritan" values are ironically critiqued, but not systematically rebuked, as they are in Thurman's novel. *The Blacker the Berry* renders these values hollow through the suffering of Emma Lou at the hands of the "Irene Redfields," who govern the urban and urbane black milieus of the early twentieth century.

Finally, Du Bois is unable to see the aesthetic and ideological distance the narrator maintains from those prejudiced words and worlds.[32] He misses moments when the narrator intervenes, situating Emma Lou's "self-despising," or her family's motto of "whiter and whiter every generation," as *toxic* values. Du Bois seems to miss the aesthetic distance between the novel's (racist) discourse and its (anti-racist) ideological commitments. Put another way, the novel is largely narrated in the free indirect style to render an impersonal yet subjective view of the social problems that haunt its protagonist. Part of what Du Bois finds lacking are moments that sufficiently verbalize against the blue-vein doctrine. But Thurman's literary aesthetic was heavily influenced by the modernist turn toward interiority and subjective points of view, along with abandoning a moralizing, omniscient narrator that functions as the center of conscience as well as consciousness.

For Thurman, the modernist novel was not a vehicle for propaganda, not even (or especially) for New Negro uplift. His reference to "contemporary realists" shows us that his approach to composing modern fiction was a form of realism, one keyed to "internal" black social reality, as quoted above. (Thurman's focus rests on the internal in social and psychological terms, as we will see.) In "Nephews of Uncle Remus," Thurman formulates his aesthetic vision thus:

> Every facet of life can be found among Negroes, who being human beings, have all the natural emotional and psychological reactions of other human beings. They live, die, hate, love, procreate. They dance and sing, play and fight. And if art is the universal expressed in terms of the particular, there is, if he has the talent, just as much chance for the Negro author to produce great literature by writing of his own people as if he were to write of Chinese or Laplanders. He will be labeled a *Negro* artist, with the emphasis on the Negro rather than on the artist, only as he fails to rise above the province of petty propaganda.[33]

By trying to "rise above" "petty propaganda" in *The Blacker the Berry*, Thurman was accused of promoting the racism that the novel criticizes. The dimension of external racism is situated, in his novel, within the upper-caste black social milieu, the blue-vein circle, which ostracizes Emma Lou even as she is one of their own. But the novel also focuses on internalization: Emma Lou's absorption of the same toxic values that poison her mind and spirit. This double movement of the novel renders its richness as both social document of intraracial color prejudice, which is the usual reading, and as an aesthetic representation of subjectivity faced with social marginalization by one's own kind, in the context of white supremacy.

I am interested in the individual element that Thurman is known for and in reading his individualism not as a retreat from social concerns, but as narrative exploration of the modernist "total misfit" and her "self-despising" subjectivity. After all, Thurman said he wanted to represent "all the natural emotional and psychological reactions" of his characters in their "particular" milieus. The relative absence of a force against the blue-vein circle, or against Emma Lou's sense of inferiority given her darker coloring, allows the novel to seem complicit in the racial propaganda it exposes. But let's remember, Thurman's style—refusing to show the "butter side up"—assumes a reader interested in the representation of "real" "psychology" as well as social reality. In the real world, there is no arbiter to intervene against the blue-vein circle, and so it does not appear in Thurman's novel.

Other critics have located the "self-despising" in Emma Lou herself, and in Thurman by proxy. In a typical vein of criticism, Thurman wears a "female face," in Thadious Davis's formulation, which allows him to adopt the veil of gender to investigate not just intraracial color prejudice but also queer sexual desire. Given Thurman's biography—which encompassed bisexuality and darker skin color—Emma Lou Morgan becomes Thurman's fictional face.[34] Her "self-despising" again becomes Thurman's own. In summary, protagonist, novel, and novelist are aligned and circumscribed as mired in racial self-hate, as retrograde instantiations of what Davis calls the "necessary black subject" of African American fiction.[35] The critical bent, therefore, collapses the aesthetic order and narrative distancing effected by the novel. Reading *The Blacker the Berry* as an uncompli-cated extension of Thurman also allows the novel to be dismissed, as Du Bois does, on racial, as opposed to literary, terms. And as Carter illustrates, Thurman's novel has also been dismissed on aesthetic grounds ("McKay has done it better"), which are, ironically, consistent with *Thurman's* own principles of critical discern-ment. On aesthetic *and* ideological grounds, *The Blacker the Berry* just can't win.

Affective Realism in *The Blacker the Berry*

Critics thus far have reinforced Du Bois's identification of Thurman with his novel, and both with Emma Lou Morgan's central problem: the "tragedy of her life was that she was too black," the narrator informs us (11). Uncannily, art imitates life, as the novel seems to anticipate the biographical readings it has inspired. Thurman's narrative employs the free indirect style to great effect, blurring the lines between Emma Lou Morgan's racial consciousness; that of her family, beholden to the doctrine of the "blue-vein circle"; and that of the impersonal narrator. Hence, when Du Bois uses the narrator's descriptions of Emma Lou's "outlandish difference" as evidence for *Thurman's* own espousal of such views, Du Bois slides around the web of narrative layers and their result-ing ironies. As Gaither underscores, the protagonist is not the narrator, nor are these fictional devices reducible to Thurman's authorial aesthetic.[36]

Departing from this premise, I would like here to enter the world of Thurman's novel. After the plot summary, I expand on my claim that *The Blacker the Berry* presents an intriguing narrative of self-abandonment that challenges both supporters and critics of Thurman's novel. My argument goes beyond Gaither's notion that Emma Lou Morgan is an ingenue who embodies the central irony of the novel as satire. Instead, my reading departs from another critic's notion that Emma Lou Morgan is a figure in a "perpetual state of victimhood."[37]

The Blacker the Berry tells the story of Emma Lou Morgan, whom the reader first encounters on the day of her high school graduation. The narrative follows

Emma Lou's peregrinations from her hometown of Boise, Idaho, first to Los Angeles to attend the University of Southern California, back to Boise, and then to Harlem. The setting is roughly contemporaneous with the date of the novel's publication: there are mentions of Van Vechten's *Nigger Heaven* as well as Locke's *New Negro* (219, 142). The novel is divided into five sections: Part I narrates Morgan's experiences in Boise and her years at USC. Part II recounts Emma Lou's entry into the Harlem of the New Negro, where she expects to find a black community more accepting of her darker skin than the blue-vein circle or the black collegiate circle. Part III shifts the narrator's focalization to a key secondary character, Alva, who becomes Emma Lou's paramour. Part IV recounts a 1920s Harlem cultural phenomenon, the rent party, which forms the basis for Thurman's successful Broadway play.[38] The last section, "Pyrrhic Victory," involves Emma Lou Morgan's final escape from internal and external marginalization.

Throughout, the narrator presents the protagonist's central problem—"the haunting chimera of intra-racial color prejudice" (72)—using the bleak, deterministic idiom of literary naturalism. The narrative frames "the tragedy of her life" as largely the result of environmental influences, as a response to the accidents of genetic inheritance (gender, skin color, etc.). Indeed, the narrative goes out of its way to impugn Emma Lou's family for their prejudice against darker skin. This familial matrix implants the "complex of inferiority" that shadows Emma Lou Morgan; the novel dramatizes the Countee Cullen verse "My color shrouds me in," which is the novel's second epigraph. Emma Lou's collegiate experiences reinforce this originary exclusion; her experiences in Harlem only recapitulate the same "tragedy." Everywhere she goes, from Boise to Los Angeles to the "New Negro Mecca," she faces the color line within black communities. As with Larsen's *Quicksand*, geographic displacements are only temporary escapes from these psychic and social exclusions, which must be faced rather than evaded.

However, there appears to be a profound contradiction in the Thurman corpus. As we have seen, Thurman's aesthetic was opposed to the "propagandist" persuasion of Du Bois. In "This Negro Literary Renaissance," Thurman links his aesthetic to that of other experimental artists of the movement, classing his work alongside Hughes's: "*Fire!!*, like Mr. Hughes' poetry, was experimental. It was not interested in sociological problems or propaganda. It was purely artistic in intent and conception. Hoping to introduce a truly Negroid note into American literature, its contributors had gone to the proletariat rather than the bourgeoisie for characters and material, had gone to people who still retained some individual race qualities and who were not totally white American in every respect save color of skin."[39] Thurman thus defines his work as experimental writing, himself a key member of the "Younger Negro Artists" and their aesthetic counterprogramming. Like others of his coterie, such as Hurston and Nugent, Thurman aimed to depict social reality rather than romanticize it for opportunistic reasons ("more profitable for him to be what he ain't").

Thurman opposes what he terms "romantic propaganda," criticizing novels like Walter White's *Fire in the Flint* (1924). He dismisses the latter for being both commercially successful and, what for him amounts to the same thing, of satisfying the lowest common denominator in the American reading public. This is work that Thurman thought "followed the conventional theme in the conventional manner, a stirring romantic propaganda tale [that] recounted all the ills Negroes suffer in the inimical South, and made all Negroes seem magnanimous, mistreated martyrs, all Southern whites evil transgressors of human rights. It was a direct descendant of *Uncle Tom's Cabin*, and had the same effect on the public."[40] The aesthetic opposition of "experimental" and "artistic" work to "sensational" and "propagandistic" fiction echoes Thurman's disdain for the "conventional manner."

Thurman's literary sensibility would rather champion what he considers the school of "damned" writers of the Renaissance, such as Hughes and McKay, and their "experimental" "primitivism"—their *realism of the proletariat*, damned by the New Negro intelligentsia, exemplified by Du Bois, which excoriated such accounts as pandering to white tastes. Thurman, in so doing, advances an aesthetic principle for black fictional representation opposed to the illusions of "fictioneers," one that instead would represent "the American Negro" "impersonally and unsentimentally."[41] Doing so, he knew, would forfeit the New Negro stamp of approval: a previous example was *Fire!!* magazine, which Thurman had tried to get banned to create a *succès de scandale*. (It didn't work.) Thurman anticipated negative reviews by "polite colored circles" that awaited *The Blacker the Berry*, which, he lamented was "castigated and reviled."[42] Thurman and his coterie saw an aesthetic hierarchy between the "respectable" (among whom he counts White, Larsen, and Jessie Fauset) and the "damned" among his contemporary novelists. Thurman adds that "only among the damned is there any show of promise, any kernel of talent."[43]

Yet it is at this juncture that a central contradiction arises between Thurman's professed aesthetic values of "experimental realism" and an artistic production that includes the aforementioned short story "Cordelia the Crude" and the play he wrote based on it, *Harlem*. Thurman's turn to the stereotyped "conventions" of melodrama in his Broadway play was for "box office reasons," according to Hughes.[44] While deploring the conventional sentimentality of White's novel,

Thurman nonetheless penned tales just as "conventional" in "manner" as well as "theme." Chief among them, needless to say, is *The Blacker the Berry* itself.

Of course, Thurman is the first to expose this contradiction between the conception and the execution of his own work. In "Notes on a Stepchild," in reference to himself in the third person, Thurman admits that

> *he had been most surprised to realize that after all his novel had been scorched with propaganda.* True, he had made no mention of the difficulties Negroes experience in a white world. On the contrary he had concerned himself only with Negroes among their own kind, trying to interpret some of the internal phenomena of Negro life in America. His book was interesting to read only because he had lain bare conditions scarcely hinted at before, conditions to which Negroes choose to remain blind and about which white people remain in ignorance. But in doing this *he realized that he had fixed the blame for these conditions on race prejudice, which manifestation of universal perversity hung like a localized cloud over his whole work.*[45]

Curiously, here, Thurman is "most surprised to realize" that *The Blacker the Berry*, "after all," had departed from his "experimental" ideal, from his opposition to the sentimental, the conventional, and the propagandistic. Curiously, Thurman critiques his novel as if it were another's, as if its author were one of the "respectable" authors he dismisses in "This Negro Literary Renaissance." He deprecates the novel as "scorched with propaganda." Thurman is thus criticizing the same propagandistic bent he maligned in Du Bois himself. And yet it is important to note that Thurman writes that the novel's "propaganda" is evident not mainly in its exposing "conditions scarcely hinted at before," which is to say its focus on the Negro as a "sociological problem." Rather, the propaganda stems from the novel's "fixing the blame for these conditions on race prejudice." This declaration surprisingly notes how Thurman had failed to live up to his own aesthetic valorization of the individual instead of the sociological, the experimental instead of the propagandistic. Thurman then writes that "he was determined not to fall into this trap again, determined to free his art from all traces of inter-racial propaganda," even as he promises to "continue writing about Negroes" as his primary inspiration.[46]

The difficulty Thurman faces, in practicing what he preached, is one of the reasons his novel was vulnerable to critiques that mirror his own reviews of the work of his contemporaries. His fiction traffics in the conventions of naturalism and, specifically, adopts sociological and psychological discourses of the time—

including that of the "misfit." Such a compounding of the "New Negro" with the forces that impinge on his "real life," Thurman found, makes an implicit political argument that could be termed "propagandistic." Focusing only on his fiction, both "Cordelia the Crude" and *The Blacker the Berry* circulate the language of naturalism and social determinism, thus bringing a nonce psychological and sociological perspective to bear on "the haunting chimera of intra-racial color prejudice" (72).

The challenge inherent in writing about individuals as social entities was thus, for Thurman, an inescapable byproduct of his interest in writing about the American Negro as he was, and not as he must be. Thurman's *Blacker the Berry*, even more so than "Cordelia the Crude," belies his professed aesthetic values of detachment and "cosmopolitan" impersonality: "He had consciously detached himself from any local considerations, striven artfully for a cosmopolitan perspective."[47] This seeming contradiction haunts Thurman's reputation, as we have briefly seen above, and goes toward explaining the conflict between his fiction and his editorial program. While professing a modernist or "experimental" agenda, informed by traditions of social realism and literary naturalism, his fiction reads as conventional in manner if not in theme. But the combined effect, to Thurman's readership, if not to the author himself, was a novel that seemed more a sociological document than a literary experiment, more an ideological critique than a literary monument.

Ironically, in another review, Thurman writes, "All art is no doubt propaganda, but all propaganda is most certainly not art. And a novel must, to earn the name, be more than a mere social service report, more than a thinly disguised book on racial relationships and racial maladjustment."[48] That Thurman could have been writing this about *The Blacker the Berry* is evident from the reviews cited above. What explains the contradiction that Thurman's differential positions as editor, novelist, and critic represent?

At this point, it would be detrimental to reify a binary ideological distinction between "art" and "propaganda" that animated so much discussion of the Harlem Renaissance and that empowered so much of Thurman's own commentary. Perhaps Thurman the novelist abided not by an aesthetic agenda—whether that of the detached cosmopolitan individualist, as noted in this passage, or that of the "race man"—but by the concerns of his theme and the organic development of his narrative. *The Blacker the Berry*, as Singh and Scott attest, combines elements of both the social realism of the Harlem underworld, which Thurman brought to the stage and the pages of *Fire!!* magazine, and the middle-class "white Negroes" of the blue-vein circle. On the one hand, Thurman's novel, paradoxically, falls short of the aesthetic dream of transcending "the race problem" that he felt was frankly unliterary. On the other, *The Blacker the Berry* transcends the binary limitations of Thurman's purely aesthetic ideal, which dismisses a novel that functions as a sociopolitical document ("social service report").

Further, the novel also displays Thurman's naturalist predilections—an earlier model for socially engaged modernist fiction that later novelists, notably Richard Wright and Ralph Ellison, would take up in force. The standards of racial transcendence and thematic experimentation as the measure of literary value meet in a novel that centers on the sociological and psychological forces that constrain the individual from transcending race. His first novel obviously abandoned this aesthetic dream of racial and social transcendence. The protagonist of his first novel, Emma Lou Morgan, so often linked to his biography, represents the author's double consciousness regarding the modernist aesthetic program he championed and yet departed from in his own fictional and dramatic production. An earlier origin story for black modernist naturalism might be *The Blacker the Berry*.

Thurman could not tell the story of the desire to transcend race except in a story about the social, or *sociological*, impossibility of racial transcendence and, indeed, about the ordinary desire to transcend racial determinism in an ordinary black subject. Emma Lou—primarily seen as a subversive inversion of the "tragic mulatta" sentimental tradition in American fiction, because of her tragedy and dark skin—is, according to the novel, tragically determined to not transcend her coloration because she is ordinary. But this ordinariness is deeply gendered as well as racialized. Emma Lou Morgan's intersectionality—specifically her gender, but also her lower-middle-class status—is the most qualifying feature of her malaise. Hence: "The people who, in Emma Lou's phrase, really mattered, the business men, the doctors, the lawyers, the dentists, the more moneyed Pullman porters . . . , *in fact all of the Negro leaders and members of the Negro upper class*, were either light skinned themselves or else had light-skinned wives. A wife of dark complexion was considered a handicap unless she was particularly charming, wealthy, or beautiful. *An ordinary looking dark woman was no suitable mate for a Negro man of prominence*" (59; emphasis added). And:

> There had been that *searing psychological effect* of that dreadful graduation night, and the lonely embittering three years at college, all of which had tended to make her color more and more a paramount issue and ill. *It was neither fashionable nor good for a girl to be as dark as she, and to be, at the same time, as untalented and undistinguished.* Dark

girls could get along if they were exceptionally talented or handsome or wealthy, but she had nothing to recommend her, save a beautiful head of hair. Despite the fact that she had managed to lead her classes in school, she had to admit that *mentally she was merely mediocre and average. Now, had she been as intelligent as* Mamie Olds Bates, head of a Negro school in Florida, and president of a huge national association of colored woman's clubs, *her darkness would not have mattered. Or had she been as wealthy as* Lillian Saunders, who had inherited the millions her mother had made producing hair straightening commodities, *things might have been different; but here she was, commonplace and poor, ugly and undistinguished.* (221–22; emphasis added)

This passage illustrates the novel's sustained intersectional focus on the psychology of gender and the sociology of race and class as they complicate the alienated existence of Emma Lou Morgan. Note the focus on her intellectual, social, and cultural "ordinariness": it is not necessarily the darkness of her skin but the fact that Emma Lou is "ordinary" that matters. Her "commonplace" and "undistinguished" position relative to the upper echelon of black society—she is neither inventor nor entrepreneur, neither heiress nor bishop's daughter—relegates her to the margins. It is this focus on her ordinary subjectivity that exemplifies the complexity of the novel's discourse about the complexities of racialized class and gender.

In truth, *The Blacker the Berry* transcends Eurocentric notions of literary value that constrain evaluations of the Renaissance's aesthetic production—even or especially Thurman's own. *Pace* its author, *The Blacker the Berry* short-circuits modernist debates about "art" or "propaganda," which influenced Thurman's sense that his own work had "fallen into a trap." Instead, reading the novel as comprising a naturalist idiom of social environment and genetic inheritance, as well as the social "primitivism" of Jazz Age Harlem, allows us to see Thurman's aesthetic of affective realism, which portrays Emma Lou's consciousness as an all-but-real historical phenomenon, a phenomenology, documenting her minoritarian subjectivity.

Daniel Scott reads *The Blacker the Berry* in ways that reinforce this argument.[49] He writes that Thurman juxtaposes aesthetic extremes espoused by Du Bois and Claude McKay, the bourgeois versus the primitivist, in his own amalgam. So Thurman's novel is a way to reconcile irreconcilable aesthetic politics, one of uplift and one of primitivism.[50] Scott and Singh likewise maintain that the novel enables this juxtaposition by "painting all behaviors with the brush of performance. As the novel questions the fixity of race, it situates that blackness in an environment of constructed and performative identity that allows for a diversity of experiences."[51] Yet this reading does not take into account what I consider the narrator's sociological and psychological discourses, nor the theme of social determinism, bedrock of naturalism, that grounds the "experimental" environment of *The Blacker the Berry*. To wit, let us recall that Émile Zola termed the naturalist novel *le roman expérimental*, denoting his vision of a modern, fictional story-world premised on a scientific laboratory, in which true-to-life characters move and behave of their own accord (as if they were creatures in an experiment), observed from above by their author-creator. (It is in this naturalist sense that Thurman's novel is experimental.)

Scott and Singh note the similarities of *The Blacker the Berry* and Theodore Dreiser's *Sister Carrie* as an "exemplar of the young woman adrift in the city."[52] But they do not draw the connection to naturalism; rather, they view the "nonessential" explanations for race and sexuality in the novel as performative. Rather than link Thurman to a contemporary focus on the social construction of race, gender, and sexuality, however, I think the novel cries for a direct connection to Thurman's literary genealogy. This was an aesthetic that evolved out of naturalism in Europe and in the United States, in figures such as Stephen Crane's Maggie and Émile Zola's Nana, and Thurman's own "Cordelia the Crude," another "girl of the streets."

More importantly, the performativity rubric only helps us sidestep the almost unbearable affective weight of the novel. While it is true that *The Blacker the Berry* focuses on the performative elements of racial consciousness—Emma Lou famously calls her skin a dark "mask"—the emotional core of these performances is elided if the notion of performativity remains the endpoint of such analysis. Rather than end with the dissolution of essentialist notions of race and sex in the novel, I begin with the naturalistic idiom of environmental determinism, which is distinguished by an equally prevalent focus on psychic phenomenology, on the representation of Emma Lou's affective states and her double (or triple) consciousness, her "self-consciousness." The idea that all the world's a stage, and that this allows Thurman's novel to see through to the social construction of racialization, does not go far enough into the phenomenology of racialization as depicted in *The Blacker the Berry*. Indeed, it is the toxic presentation of this phenomenon, from the inside out, that constitutes Emma Lou's complex "tragedy." Thus the narrative's insistence on the "tragedy" of Emma Lou's existence bears careful scrutiny. My reading also reformulates the novel as informed by the ethos of social determinism and the idiom of literary naturalism while plumbing the psychological depths of human consciousness—with elements such as interior monologue and free indirect discourse.

Critical work on affect in modernist studies, notably the work of Anne Anlin Cheng, Heather Love, and Sianne Ngai, has been crucial to my understanding of the importance of attending to the negative affects of minoritarian subjectivity and Thurman's negative minoritarian sensibility. In this light, Hughes's description of Thurman bears referencing:

> Wallace Thurman laughed a long bitter laugh. He was a strange kind of fellow, who liked to drink gin, but *didn't* like to drink gin; who liked being a Negro, but felt it a great handicap; who adored bohemianism, but thought it wrong to be bohemian. He liked to waste a lot of time, but he always felt guilty wasting time. He loathed crowds, yet he hated to be alone. He almost always felt bad, yet he didn't write poetry. Once I told him if I could feel as bad as he did *all* the time, I would surely produce wonderful books. But he said you had to know how to *write*, as well as how to feel bad.[53]

It is easy to see why critics have so often conflated the story of Emma Lou with Thurman's own. The biographical details that both Thurman and Emma Lou have in common include being raised in a predominantly white Northwest town (Salt Lake for Thurman, Boise for Emma Lou); attending college in Los Angeles (USC); coming to New York and joining a Renaissance already under way; and having liberated sexual proclivities (including Emma Lou's sensual encounter with a male in a movie theater, and Thurman's own arrest for homosexual solicitation upon arriving in New York City). It is just as easy to provide caveats to this line of inquiry. Novelistic characters are not human persons; it is a mistake to confuse them. Moreover, implying a biographical significance in the Emma Lou figure risks reducing the literary texture of the narrative to a superstructure, an allegorical layer meant to be unmasked and decoded according to the "base" of Thurman's historical existence. This type of hermeneutic operation risks flattening out the novelistic and the historical worlds by effecting their conflation. Such a procedure begs the question of priority and causality, to go beyond correspondence: so what if Thurman's real life inspired many of the details of Emma Lou's? Can we then dismiss the one in favor of the other? If so, which counts as the explanation, and which counts as the symptom, of the autobiographical "truth" that somehow "determines" the narrative?

I use scare quotes to imply that my reading does not follow this well-trodden path. Many critics, following Dorothy West's account, seem to dismiss the tragedy in *The Blacker the Berry* as merely the result of Thurman's own discomfort with having a darker complexion. And yet my reading does not rest on a one-to-one correspondence between authorial and novelistic figure, much less on using this set of correspondences to explain away the significance of the affective orientation of the novel and the centering of the narrative on the "tragedy" of Emma Lou Morgan. Rather, my reading of the correspondence views both as producing a singular affective resonance in a complex socioaesthetic order. As we have seen with the reception of the novel, the author and the novel are identified as interchangeable, usually for the purposes of maligning Thurman's or Emma Lou's stances, ideas, options, and choices. Carter's review infamously conflates Thurman and Emma Lou in decrying how Thurman "simply has created an incredibly stupid character. The moral that evidently is intended to adorn this tale is to the effect that young women who are black are doomed to a rather difficult existence."[54] It is perhaps what Carter calls the "stupidity" of Emma Lou that registers the difficulty of dealing with her story as a tragedy, her story as the "rather difficult existence" that the novel narrates seemingly despite the incredible "stupidity" that such a moral would imply.

What good is this story if it seems that the narrative and the reader—not to mention the critic—seem to know so much more than the protagonist herself does, about how Emma Lou should live her life? Why, indeed, does the novel insist on the "stupid" character of Emma Lou? And what exactly does this "stupidity" consist of? Here, the protagonist's lack of insight points to a dark facet of social subordination and psychic alienation, belied by standpoint theories of minoritarian epistemic privilege. Emma Lou Morgan's ingenue role is Thurman's way to ironically represent incomplete ideas about race. These are ideas prevalent in his own time, including that becoming black grants us special insight into white-dominated society, affording us sight beyond "the Veil," as Du Bois writes in *The Souls of Black Folk*; or that gender may not matter to racial discourse, as seen in the masculine discourse of the New Negro; or that color prejudice is only a problem in white society, as belied by the narrative of the novel. In our time, however, standpoint theories that seem to stand on the shoulders of Du Bois's claims about blackness affording us "second sight" are belied by *The Blacker the Berry*. Emma Lou Morgan lacks any sight at all, symbolically speaking, so "color-blind" is she—or, rather, so color-struck is bourgeois black society and majority-white culture. Does this novel teach us how optimism about transcending oppression is flawed, insofar as such optimism is premised on familial and internal belonging, which in-group ostracism dissolves? Such is the condition of the "total misfit," lacking the consciousness to see through the Veil when that veil is the self-alienating doctrine of the "blue-vein circle," not an oppositional double-consciousness.

The "Lonesomeness" of a "Total Misfit"

It is easy to adopt the normative mind-set that Carter evinces when she decries Thurman for creating such a "stupid" character. Carter is exasperated by Emma Lou's lack of insight. Indeed, it is not until the last few pages of the novel that the protagonist has her epiphany. She then finally experiences the change in perspective that *is expected of the minoritarian subject as autonomous person*, despite the oppressive social conditions that make such autonomy harder to achieve. Carter's exasperation reveals the novel's strategy of presenting Emma Lou's lack of insight for the majority of the narrative. Such an effect, given through the novel's oscillation between free indirect and omniscient narrative discourse, enacts an ironic distancing for the reader vis-à-vis Emma Lou Morgan and her self-alienating blue-vein ideology.

The novel's interesting effect inheres in that seeming incapacity to transcend her upbringing, given her growing isolation. It is this incapacity to become appropriately (or normatively) socialized that defines the "stupidity" that Carter decries in the character and produces interesting resistances and attachments to the novel. Emma Lou simply doesn't "get it." She is herself "a snob" (45). What she doesn't get is that, despite her familial ostracism, Emma Lou must find another route to adaptive socialization. Such socialization is a product of, and the condition of possibility for, transcending the "Negro-white" ideology that oppresses her, partly through her own desires to *become* "Negro-white" (like her mother, and her mother before her). This is the tragic catch-22 that the novel represents quite movingly. And so the odds of racial uplift are against her.

Thus it is Emma Lou's status as a misfit in her own family that haunts her trajectory, beyond the family home in Boise. Emma Lou is ostracized and excluded in every social circle she penetrates, even, or especially, in the "black Mecca": "She had thought Harlem would be different, but things had seemed against her from the beginning, and she had continued to go down, down, down, until she had little respect for herself" (223). Other examples of the world of social exclusion depict how this experience originated in the cold bosom of her family: "Emma Lou had always been the alien member of the family and of the family's social circle. Her grandmother . . . made her feel it. Her mother made her feel it. And her Cousin Buddie made her feel it, *to say nothing of the way she was regarded by outsiders*" (22–23; emphasis added). As these examples show, the novel documents how the feelings of Emma Lou are the product of *her family's* attitude against her black skin.

The chronology traces a reverse teleology ("down, down, down"), recounting a series of futile flights from the racism of the blue-vein circle to the urbane collegiate atmosphere of USC, only for Emma Lou to discover that everywhere is "haunted" by color prejudice: "She had once fled to Los Angeles to escape Boise, then fled to Harlem to escape Los Angeles, but these mere geographical flights had not solved her problems" (255). This reverse movement serves to underscore the protagonist's "tragedy" as inhering in her tragically ironic attachment to black-bourgeois caste distinctions that categorically exclude her.

The novel itself makes this self-abandoning attachment clear. In an aside, Thurman's narrator becomes obtrusive, describing the protagonist in a naturalist idiom, defined by the dual doctrine of cultural and natural determinism: "Emma Lou was essentially a snob. She had *absorbed this trait* from the very people who had sought to exclude her from their presence. *All of her life she had heard talk* of [the] 'right sort of people,' and of 'the people who really mattered,' and *from these phrases she had formed a mental image* of those to whom they applied. . . . Emma Lou was *determined* to become associated only with those people who really mattered, northerners like herself or superior southerners . . . who were different from whites only in so far as skin color was concerned" (46; emphasis added).

But the language of determinism in this passage is ironic on multiple levels. Emma Lou was "determined" can be read two ways: that her will is to only connect with those whom she—aping her family's wrongheaded color and class "snobbery"—deemed "superior," but "determined" can also be read in the opposite sense, as *fated*. "Determined" here could be read as implying a fateful force other than personal will—indeed, the very opposite of will—that is driving Emma Lou "not to go out of her class or else remain to herself" (57). Emma Lou could be "determined" by her social upbringing to be a snob, thus making any question of her own agency or willingness in following her family's "blue-vein" dictates not a matter of choice but a matter of indoctrination and, more starkly, unconscious replication of the doctrine of color prejudice.

The language of determinism recurs a few pages later, once more in relation to Emma Lou's ventriloquizing of her family's "Negro-white" bourgeois ideology of exclusion. In a moment of psycho-narration, the narrator analyzes Emma Lou's "poor psychology": "Emma Lou was possessed of a perverse bitterness . . . she idolized the thing one would naturally expect her to hate. . . . Emma Lou hated her own color and envied the more mellow complexions" (234).[55] Here, in the analytic idiom of psychology rather than sociology, the omniscient narrator again intrudes, again effecting a visible division in ideology as if to reassure readers, to distinguish this ideology from the narrator's own (a reassurance Du

Bois and Carter seem to miss). This narrative report—let's remember Thurman's description of a (bad) novel as a "social service report"—recurs to explain Emma Lou's "perverse" attachment to "the thing one would naturally expect her to hate," namely, the ideology of colorism: "Had any one asked Emma Lou what she meant by 'the right sort of people' *she would have found herself at a loss for a comprehensive answer. She really didn't know. She had a vague idea* that those people on the campus who practically ignored her were the only people with whom she should associate" (58; emphasis added).

The narrator's exterior look into Emma Lou's lack of insight is a resting point from the "wallowing" in the emotional rhythms of desire and hopefulness and disappointment and pessimism that remain the novel's hallmark as a study in character—as well as the social determinants of that character. Emma Lou's lack of "comprehensive answer" signals her lack of insight into the dilemma that defines her experience of being ostracized by her own people, the very ones she thinks were the "only people with whom she should associate." It is this tragic irony that points to Emma Lou's "stupidity," in Carter's words. Here, the narrator gently points to her "vagueness," her not having "any idea" as to what external influences *unknowingly* shape her own character and her own unconsidered prejudices. More importantly, the narrative eschews explanation, focusing instead on the phenomenology of self-abnegation and self-opacity that defines Emma Lou's experiences. She seeks the approbation of the upper black echelons whose values she shares, but, because of these same values, they shun her systematically.

This problematic of Emma Lou's double marginalization—social ostracism and self-exclusion—represents her chimerical quandary, or the "misfit" between her minoritarian subjectivity, which espouses an ideology antithetical to her own embodiment and her experiences of socially circumscribed abnegation. Along with the narrative series of exclusions and ostracisms, it is this existential, experiential misfit between inner values and exterior reality that is responsible for Emma Lou's general affective state, a sort of baseline mood, which the novel calls "lonesome."

"Lonesome"

There are seven instances where the affect of "lonesomeness" is mentioned, most of which describe Emma Lou or other characters that similarly do not socially "fit in." According to the *Dictionary of American Regional English* (2013), *lonesome* in its adjectival form means "plaintive," "melancholy," or "gloomy," its usage tied "chiefly" to the South Midland region, especially prevalent among black speakers.[56]

The first appearance of the descriptor occurs during Emma Lou Morgan's first weeks in Harlem. The narrator writes that Emma Lou "was lonesome and disappointed" during her first days in New York (100). Unsuccessful in securing a "congenial" office secretary position—because "lots of Negro business men have a definite type of girl in mind and will not hire any other" (101), meaning that they seek light-skinned "girls" to fulfill this role—Emma Lou goes to lunch with Mrs. Blake, the employment agency coordinator, who then asks about her college experience. Emma Lou responds, "I was lonesome, I guess." "Weren't there other colored boys and girls?" To which she replies, "Oh yes, quite a number, but I guess I didn't mix well" (100–101). A second confirmation of her "lonesomeness" comes after she first meets and dances with Alva at Small's Paradise, a dance hall catering to a slumming white clientele. Emma Lou has gone out with her new employer, Arline Strange, a white actress playing a "mulatto Carmen," and Arline's brother (115). A few days later, Alva confides to his roommate, Braxton, that the only reason he had danced with "that coal scuttle blond" was because "she looked so lonesome with those ofays [white people]" (128). After this exchange, the narrator echoes Alva's understanding of Emma Lou's racial alienation: "Emma Lou was very lonesome" (129).

The final instance of the word as a descriptor of Emma Lou's mood, or state of being, is in the last section, "Pyrrhic Victory." In this concluding chapter, Emma Lou becomes the primary caretaker for Alva's disabled son, another naturalist element in the story. The product of Alva's alcoholism and promiscuity, Alva Jr. is as "unfit" as Emma Lou is "misfit," by the same logic of determinism, given his physical and developmental deformity (226). Not coincidentally, it is Emma Lou alone who begins to normalize Alva Junior's limbs: "Within six months she had managed to make little Alva Junior take on some of the physical aspects of a normal child" (246). And yet Emma Lou "was lonesome again, cooped up in that solitary room with only Alva Junior for company" (247). Her self-abnegation includes, now, an ethic of care for Alva's unwanted, motherless offspring, who, perversely, "more and more relegated her to the position of a hired nurse girl"; indeed, Emma Lou's self-sacrifice is nearly complete, as she abandons her former friends and mentors to serve the household (247). Her self-abandonment perversely ensures Alva's and Alva Junior's thriving.

"A Total Misfit"

At her lowest point, Emma Lou is described as a "total misfit." Looking back at her former life with Gwendolyn, her former friend, and Campbell Kitchen (a "Negrotarian" modeled on Van Vechten), Emma Lou reconsiders her life's journey:

> Campbell Kitchen had said that every one must find salvation within one's self, that no one in life need be *a total misfit*, and that there was some niche for every peg, whether that peg be round or square. If this were true then surely she could find hers even at this late date. But then hadn't she exhausted all possibilities? Hadn't she explored every province of life and everywhere met the same problem? It was easy for Campbell Kitchen and Gwendolyn to say what they would do had they been she, for they were looking at her problem in the abstract, *while to her it was an empirical reality*. What could they know of the *adjustment proceedings* necessary to make her life more full and more happy? What could they know of her heartaches? (256; emphasis added)

What could they know of her heartaches, indeed? The narrative voice here, in the free indirect style, voices Emma Lou's perspective. In addition, this rendering is sharply contrasted to the idealistic point of view of her well-meaning friends, who view her "problem" merely in the "abstract." Her narrated monologue calls out to her friends as well as the novel's "friends"—the critics and readers who would judge Emma Lou's dilemma of "adjustment" as mere abstraction. Rather, this passage argues for the importance of experiencing the "proceedings" and the "heartaches" in order to appreciate fully the complexity of intraracial colorism and its tragic internalization. This passage marks an affective defense against the facile solution to the problem as an "abstract" exercise.

The narrator seems to say that "it [is] easy" to presume that Emma Lou's "problem" has a solution to begin with. And given Hughes's take on Thurman, and Emma Lou's problematic attachment to the social worlds that exclude her—and her disdain for the social worlds that welcome her—it is "easy" to blame Emma Lou herself, her own prejudices and self-abnegating attachment to these attitudes, as the root of the problem.

Which is precisely what Alva finally tells her. I quote the following passage at length because I think it provides a microcosm of the novel and its depiction of both Emma Lou's "color-consciousness" and how other characters respond to it; how she remains on the outside, hopelessly on the margins of a vibrant modern black culture. Alva hypocritically blames Emma Lou for being "too color-conscious" (210). "Flared up," she responds:

"Color-conscious . . . who wouldn't be color-conscious when everywhere you go people are always talking about color. If it didn't make any difference they wouldn't talk about it, they wouldn't always be poking fun, and laughing and making jokes. . . ."

Alva interrupted her tirade. "You're being silly, Emma Lou. About three-quarters of the people at the Lafayette [theater] tonight were either dark brown or black, and here you are crying and fuming like a ninny over some reference made on the stage to a black person." He was disgusted now. He got up from the bed. Emma Lou looked up.

"But Alva, you don't know."

"I do know," he spoke sharply for the first time, "that you're a damn fool. It's always color, color, color. If I speak to any of my friends on the street you always make some reference to their color and keep plaguing me with—'Don't you know nothing else but light-skinned people?' And you're always beefing about being black. Seems like to me you'd be proud of it. You're not the only black person in the world. There are gangs of them right here in Harlem, and I don't see them going around a-moanin' 'cause they ain't half white." (210–11)

Blaming the victim never seemed so irresistible. This exchange encapsulates the affective energies of the novel: Alva's tirade echoes Carter's dismissal of Emma Lou as a "stupid character." Both Carter and Alva, in this sense, fault Emma Lou for not figuring it out. What is there to figure out? one might ask. The problem she faces, which, according to Alva—if not Carter—is not a problem at all, except that Emma Lou persists in seeing it as one. Hence: "Seems to me like you'd be proud of it." If only, as Gwendolyn and Campbell also advise, Emma Lou could find the right "peg" and the right "hole"; if she could only socialize with her own kind! After all, as Alva exasperatedly reminds her, she's "not the only black person in the world." It is thus all too easy for Alva—and for the reader—to, in Thurman's words, "fix the blame" on her own "color prejudice," her own lack of "pride." Emma Lou's rejoinder, of course, is that it is far from easy to be "proud" of being "*too* black," when the theatrical reviews and literary salons Alva takes her to make a habit of ridiculing blackness.

How then to resolve this social fact and inner contradiction between Emma Lou's aspiration to be (like Alva) "Negro-white" when her own skin color is the impediment she cannot overcome? Put another way, Emma Lou's "lonesomeness" stems from her being unable to transcend her desire to transcend her "race"— here, "race" represents not blackness but "too-blackness," in the parlance of the novel. Figures such as Alva and Gwendolyn successfully navigate the modern black

Mecca of the Harlem Renaissance, given their "Negro-white" skin color and its attendant social and cultural privileges. The novel thus stages the benighted experiences of "how black self-hate, self-rage is created and how black self-love, black empowerment can triumph," in the lyrical language of novelist Shirley Haizlip.[57]

Yet given that the novel's affective realism documents the racial experience of being "a total misfit," the focus of *The Blacker the Berry* is on the first part of this acculturation process. The novel wallows in the "self-hate, self-rage" far more than it explores a context of "black empowerment" or "black self-love." Indeed, in this exchange, it is evident how the narrative discourse seems to argue that it is far too "easy" to find the solution in the "abstract." It is quite another thing to go through the journey, the wallowing in self-rage, lonesomeness, and self-pity that represent the "total misfit" position.

This exchange, therefore, illustrates the double valence of Alva's exasperation with Emma Lou and his ultimate collusion with the racial caste system he pretends does not matter. The theatrical show they attended, a few hours earlier, caused Emma Lou to "burn up with indignation" (205). It is easy to see why. Toward the end of the show, there "followed the usual rigmarole carried out once weekly at the Lafayette concerning the undesirability of black girls. Every one, that is, all the males, let it be known that high browns and 'high yallers' were 'forty' with them, but. . . . They were interrupted by the re-entry of the little black girl riding a mule and singing mournfully as she was being thus transported across the stage: *A yellow gal rides in a limousine, / A brown-skin rides a Ford, / A black gal rides an old jackass / But she gets there, yes my Lord*" (204). It is clear from this cabaret scene, which precedes the heated exchange quoted above, that Emma Lou's understanding of the color prejudice in Harlem is supported by the narrative. Importantly, it is her "snobbish" reaction to this marginalization and social ostracism that the novel calls into question: not the reality of her experience, but what she does with it. Instead of abandoning the toxic values of Negro-white ideology, Emma Lou struggles to reconcile these mutually exclusive regimes. But this is impossible. Instead of abandoning the Negro-white value system, she abandons herself.

That much is clear. And yet, I would argue, Thurman's novel is more interested in showing the impasse—the virtual impossibility of Emma Lou's reconciling a "blue-vein" mentality with a "black-mask" actuality. This is why the determinism is emphasized, I think: to show the weakness of the individual facing forces as large as social systems. An uplifting novel would, instead, stage Emma Lou Morgan's adaptation, her heroic recovery of self-respect by reversing her internalized color prejudice. But just as with Thurman's anecdote about novels about passing versus the real world, in the realism of the novel, it is not so easy to escape embodiment, acculturation, and ostracism by one's own. Feeling pride in the blackness of her skin is thus out of reach given these circumstances. In sum, rather than peddling redemption, Thurman is more interested in documenting the impasse of internal and social subjugation. An immovable object meets an irresistible force—the ineluctable social facts of an anti-black world and the obstinacy of Emma Lou's own anti-blackness. The narrative evolves from Thurman's aesthetic decision not to solve Emma Lou's problem but rather to trace its contours in excruciatingly painful and repetitive detail. Because that's life, he seems to say.

The former passage, staging the break between Alva and Emma Lou, closes the penultimate section of the novel. "Pyrrhic Victory" stages Emma Lou's resolution of her conflict. If Hughes is right, and Thurman "almost always felt bad," the novel shows us why Emma Lou did as well. Indeed, the narrator notes her "doctrine of pessimism," which was momentarily "weakened by the optimism the future seemed to promise," only to render that future as a series of disappointments (237). It is in the final pages of the novel, after reaching the nadir, that she reaches the other side and makes a decisive break with Alva and her experience of abjection.

Thurman's "Pyrrhic Victory"

So far, the argument has foregrounded the painfully negative affective dimension of Emma Lou's narrative itinerary. One way to contain the excess of such a reading would be to systematically theorize it by explaining it—or rather, by explaining it away. I argued that some critics have done just this, referring to Gaither's focus on the satirical dimension of the novel. Scott recuperates the negative affective dimension by focusing on the novel's presentation of race, gender, and sexuality as performative and thus nonessential to the core of being. In this manner, these two critics, among others, sidestep what I consider the novel's main achievement: that is, to focus on the "adjustment proceedings" of Emma Lou's "heartaches" rather than staging their transcendence. The novel does not, as I have argued, seek such victories; it is more interested in plumbing the depths, in wallowing in defeat. Fittingly, the only victory available in such a narrative is pyrrhic.

Part of the problem, as I briefly noted, is what Carter dismisses as Emma Lou Morgan's "stupidity." For the remainder of this chapter, I sketch out a few examples that demonstrate this naïveté in terms of Emma Lou's lack of insight and social intelligence. These are moments when, for instance, the narrator comments that Emma Lou "made little effort to make friends among" her new colleagues after becoming a public-school teacher (247–48). Why she makes "so little effort" the narrator explains by positing not stupidity, exactly, but insufficient social intelligence: "She didn't know how. She was too shy to make an approach and too suspicious to thaw out immediately when some one approached her" (248). By this point in the story, Emma Lou Morgan is primed to ascribe suspicious motives to friendly overtures, given her history of being ostracized and being blamed as the author of her own problems (232). As we see in the following interior monologue, Emma Lou "tr[ied] to fasten the blame for her extreme color-consciousness on herself as Alva had done," but

> she was unable to make a good case of it. Surely, it had not been her color-consciousness which had excluded her from the only Negro sorority in her college, nor had it been her color-consciousness that had caused her to spend such an isolated three years in Southern California. The people she naturally felt at home with had, some-how or other, managed to keep her at a distance. It was no fun going to social affairs and being neglected throughout the entire evening. There was no need in forcing one's self into a certain milieu only to be frozen out. Hence, she had stayed to herself, had had very few friends, and had become more and more resentful of her blackness of skin. (222–23; emphasis added)

With its recapitulation of Emma Lou's trajectory, the free indirect discourse *reasons out* her increasing isolation, her becoming "more and more resentful" of herself and enduring "tortuous periods of self-pity and hatred" (234). All of this, despite her financial independence as a public-school teacher. Indeed, we are told, "now that she had found economic independence she found herself more enslaved and more miserable than ever" (251). The monologue contin-ues to recapitulate early life stages, beginning with "the searing psychological effect of that dreadful graduation night" (221). The phrase "psychological effect" indicates the narrator's objectivity regarding the protagonist's "empirical real-ity" (256). Reference to "empirical reality" underscores the affective realism of the novel, exfoliated through a naturalist discourse of determinism in contrast to the uplifting promise of the New Negro Renaissance.

Emma Lou's lack of insight continues to haunt her as much as the cause of this lack of insight itself does—her isolated and stunted upbringing. Hence, even as she finds a "congenial" profession in teaching, she is ironically incapa-ble of socializing with her black colleagues. The alienation and ostracism are due to Emma Lou's excessive use of makeup to mask the color of her skin. But this failure to connect is also a result of Emma Lou's being unable to read the social cues that others, less marginalized and better socialized, would have been able to pick up on: "several times upon passing groups of [her colleagues], she imagined she was being pointed out. In most cases what she thought was true, but she was being discussed and pointed out, not because of her dark skin, but because of the obvious traces of an excess of rouge and powder which she insisted on using" (248). And: "It had been suggested, in a private council among the Negro members of the teaching staff, that some one speak to Emma Lou about this rather ludicrous habit of making up. But no one had the nerve. She appeared so distant and so ready to take offense at the slightest suggestion even of friendship that they were wary of her" (248). The narrator, again obtruding, explains that "*it never occurred to her* that the note told the truth and that she looked twice as bad with paint and powder as she would without it. *She interpreted it as* being a means of making fun of her because she was darker than any one of the other colored girls. She grew more haughty, more acid, and more distant than ever. She never spoke to anyone except as a matter of business" (249; added emphasis).

Given *the world's* color-consciousness, its affective aftermath on the protagonist—a state of lonesomeness elevated to a "doctrine of pessimism"—Emma Lou Morgan becomes a mask of antisociality. An off-putting "haughty demeanor" plunges her into a downward spiral of impersonal relations with her colleagues and antisocial anomie. Her own lack of insight redoubles this phenomenon of ostracism; her paranoid suspicion ("She interpreted it as a means of making fun of her") is her biggest stumbling block toward social rehabilitation. Emma Lou embraces a mind-set that precludes friendship. In this sense, her lifelong internalization of a Negro-white ideology that itself excludes and oppresses her, renders her subjectivity aloof and impersonal, and her social relations strictly functional. Consequently, and perversely, Emma Lou is unable to rescue herself from this dilemma. Her lack of insight dooms her to a solitary existence; her solitary existence dooms her to a lack of insight. And unlike Du Bois's uplifting theory of double consciousness (as the "gift of second sight"), as well as standpoint theories of epistemic privilege, Thurman explores a limit case: What of the cases of those who don't belong even to the circle of their own community and are therefore set adrift, at the mercy of the forces of subjugation with no recourse to resilience, much less resistance? The result is less insight, not more; the need for consciousness-raising, in the lingo of the sixties, stems from this logic of prerevolutionary consciousness. But consciousness-raising is a collective effort. Thurman's novel explores the individual subjectivity lacking access to the grace of collectivity, and how this double marginalization—internal as well as external; minoritarian as well as majoritarian—results in epistemic oppression.

Conclusion: Wallowing with Wallace

This reading of *The Blacker the Berry* productively explores, as I said at the outset, a representative critical claim, such as Jarraway's, that Emma Lou Morgan exists in a "perpetual state of victimhood" and Scott's helpful notion that Emma Lou "signifies" on—revises, riffs on, transforms—the sentimental genre of the "tragic mulatta." Another critical conversation that sheds light on Thurman's novel is the work on minoritarian melancholia by Anne Cheng, David Eng, and Judith Butler, among others. But theoretically diagnosing Emma Lou Morgan through the Freudian rubric of melancholia, we would contain, dignify, and even redeem, Thurman's deterministic outlook and his chronicle of affective realism and self-divesting minoritarian subjectivity. The interpretive approach I suggest, *immanent reading*, resists institutional theoretical rubrics as much as possible. To call Emma Lou Morgan a racial melancholic would reframe the novel's affective resonance through an institutional theoretical construct. Indeed, Thurman's novel resists gestures of defense and recuperation. Like Emma Lou Morgan, *The Blacker the Berry* might inspire our sympathy but then reject it as an officious overture ("She grew more haughty, more acid, and more distant than ever").

Instead of rescue through formal theory and a recuperative impulse of optimism, I argue for the importance of attending to "wallowing" in this narrative world of negative affects and incapacities for uplift and reintegration into community. What Sianne Ngai terms the "blocked agency" of weak affects is useful. Just as with Helga Crane, Emma Lou Morgan is a blocked agent experiencing a range of affects—notably "lonesomeness"—that, rather than enabling a movement toward solidarity, frustrates it. Instead, Emma Lou's commitment to a "Negro-white" ideology internally oppresses her and leads her to a self-sacrificial ethic of care. In the final scenes of the novel, she is reduced to being a stereotypical "mammy" for her former lover's disabled son.

And yet Alva Junior is all the better for it. Emma Lou reaches this nadir of self-abnegation, the extremity of which leads to her final break with the dynamic of internalized oppression—though not with the negative affects that reinforce this state of being. Emma Lou Morgan finds the way out of her downward spiral in the final moments of the novel, as if Thurman could not finally allow her total self-abnegation to reign over the narrative. Although, as I have been arguing, it is precisely this sovereignty of the negative and the incapacitating, of the antisocial and the uninsightful, that makes this novel worth reading.

While admitting my own sympathetic reactions to Emma Lou's narrative of abjection, I have also tried to show how the novel has produced the opposite mood in readers' reactions. The novel itself, like Emma Lou, has been "reviled," in Thurman's words, or read as "self-despising," to call back to Du Bois. According to theater critic Theophilus Lewis, *The Blacker the Berry* is a novel of which Thurman "ought to be proud, but isn't."[58] While for me the novel evokes sympathy, for many readers, it evokes the opposite. As with Emma Lou herself, and perhaps with Thurman himself, the negativity of their sensibility promotes an equal negativity in their social interlocutors. To use the dual strategies of reading proposed by Eve Kosofsky Sedgwick, the mimesis in this sense is negative, instead of duplicative; paranoid, instead of reparative.[59] The work that Thurman's tarrying with the negative performs, both as a novelist and as a critic, I think, is essential in representing the "heartaches" and "proceedings" of minoritarian subjects whose dilemmas of disidentification are at an impasse, unresolved, and, perhaps, irresolvable.

Thurman sought to represent affective reality, while seeking to attain modernist literary achievement. My argument is that Thurman succeeded in both, by partially failing in both. By constructing a novel whose affective realism invokes the language and pessimism of naturalism, Thurman defies the uplifting aesthetic that the "damned" writers of the Renaissance resisted. By wallowing in the negative affective dimension of Emma Lou Morgan and resisting facile resolutions to her deeply entrenched social problems, Thurman also impugned a systematic social structure as determining. Thurman tracks the realities of double marginalization—family and community, "to say nothing of the way she was regarded by outsiders"—by staging Emma Lou's existential negation of her own personhood, reducing herself to a "mask" of "despised" ("self-despising"?) blackness. Thurman shows the suffering of those who are excluded, who remain the ethical residuum, in Michael Warner's terms, as an oppressed minority begins the march toward normalization and progress ("from the pantry to the parlor").[60]

Beyond the pathos that Thurman's novel documents, there are political implications of such a representational strategy. What might those political implications be? As noted, one implication runs counter to the progressive notion that social subordination grants greater social insight in standpoint theories. The complication of narrative form, however, qualifies this finding: Thurman's omniscient narrator does convey epistemic privilege, especially when commenting on so many "truths" that Emma Lou Morgan did not know. Nevertheless, Thurman's realistic approach to narration, centered on the subjectivity of his protagonist, seeks to demonstrate that minoritized subjects—especially those who carry conflicting identity formations, such as Emma Lou's self-immolating snobbery—are blinded by the prejudice internalized from their social environment. The interest of the novel, writ large, is when Emma Lou Morgan will have the scales fall from her eyes. This position, Thurman implicitly argues, is definitive for a "total misfit"—that is, one who finds herself displaced within white majority spaces and black blue-vein circles, losing herself in a social vacuum.

Another political implication of Thurman's affective realism is the turn away from the model of sovereign individualism that secretly subtends the political dimension itself. Even while *The Blacker the Berry* wallows in the affective world of negativity and impasse, some of these emotional correlatives, such as Emma Lou's "self-hate," seem unlikely to yield effective political momentum. Indeed, the novel stages how these affective states in fact disable the possibility of recuperation and rehabilitation; they are disabling of what Berlant calls sovereign agency. Instead, Emma Lou represents lateral agency, which, as noted in chapter 5, does not look like agency at all. She finally does escape the self-collusive fate of nonpersonhood and walks out into a new vision of herself and of life itself: "She was tired of running up blind alleys all of which seemed to converge and lead her ultimately to the same blank wall. . . . Life was most kind to those who were judicious in their selections, and she, *weakling that she now realized* she was, had not been a *connoisseur*" (258; emphasis added).

The narrator then goes on to talk of Emma Lou's determination to "fight future battles." But it is this instance that I would like to end with. Here, the narrator again intrudes with the language of naturalism (Emma Lou as a social *"weakling"*), ironically implying an epiphany of self-transcendence, thus marking the "pyrrhic victory" of the protagonist. The narrative of uplift requires that the minoritarian subject transcend somehow, or die trying, even if she had no concept or wherewithal for achieving such self-transcendence ("had not been a connoisseur"). The late epiphany rescues Emma Lou from her self-oppression as well as from, presumably, a *no future* comprised of more of the same: the "blank wall" of total self-diminution and antisocial isolation.

But it is Thurman's focus on the "pyrrhic" that is instructive. This novel illustrates the catch-22 of liberal selfhood: premised on a preexisting web of belonging that, when it is nonexistent, as in the experience of a "total misfit," exposes how normative ideals of self-possession and agency ask too much of certain minoritarian subjects. This novel traces the burdens of "self-respect" entailed in normative personhood as well as the unlikely path from "self-hate" to "self-empowerment" that is blocked by double marginalization. Both the burden of personhood and the burden of representation are suspended, in an impersonal impasse that often avoids social attachment altogether, for fear of further ostracism or humiliation. The "total misfit" the novel depicts is reduced to the bare minimum of agency and represents an existence of self-alterity and self-abandonment. To cross over from this impasse, from the sense of being stuck to the promised land of social integration, is not a linear movement but a "tortuous" set of "adjustment proceedings" shrouded by lonesomeness, self-hate, and self-pity: above all, guided by a doctrine of pessimism belying uplifting fables about the ready availability of collective solidarity. Thurman instead investigates how available solidarity is within marginalized communities. He, like other authors in this study, finds the redoubling of oppressive socialization, rather than its reprieve, in these tales of double marginalization.

Thurman shows us the odds that modernist misfits struggled against. Even if only in Thurman's time, but not in ours, we might appreciate the significance that such haunting tales produce. The burden of representation may not be quite as heavy for contemporary intersectional individuals as it was for Thurman's protagonist, or for Thurman himself. But that is due to the groundbreaking affective realism of novels such as this one. Thurman himself, in an unpublished review of his second novel, *Infants of the Spring*, writes about the agency of the aesthetic that "impelled [him] to write": "The characters and their problems cried out for release. They intruded themselves into his every alien thought. And assumed an importance which blinded him to their true value. The faults and virtues of the novel, then, are the direct result of this inescapable compulsion."[61] With hindsight, we can appreciate the faults better than the virtues of Thurman's narrative, insofar as they illuminate modernist misfits barred from the "rosy castles" of majority culture and minoritarian elites.

4.

Narrating the Mood of the Underdog in Rhys's *Quartet*

If I said I was English they at once contradicted me—or implied a contradiction—no you're a colonial—you're not English—an inferior being. . . . If on the other hand I'd say exasperated I'm not English as a matter of fact I'm not a bit. I would rather be French or Spanish they'd get even more annoyed at that. I was a traitor. You're British—neither one thing nor the other. Heads you win tails I lose.

—**Jean Rhys, "The Black Exercise Notebook"**

It was astonishing how significant, coherent and understandable it all became after a glass of wine on an empty stomach. . . . The Place Blanche, Paris, Life itself. One realized all sorts of things. The value of an illusion, for instance, and that the shadow can be more important than the substance.

—**Jean Rhys,** *Quartet*

Out of her fidelity to her experience, and her purity as a novelist, Jean Rhys thirty to forty years ago identified many of the themes that engage us today: isolation, an absence of society or community, the sense of things falling apart, dependence, loss. . . . Her books may serve current causes, but she is above causes. What she has written she has endured, over a long life; and what a stoic thing she makes the act of writing appear.

—**V. S. Naipaul, 1972**

Introducing a "Passion for Stating the Case of the Underdog"

While now canonized as the author of *Wide Sargasso Sea* (1966), Jean Rhys first made her mark as a Left-Bank bohemian fiction writer. Her Caribbean heritage was mostly deemphasized in her early fiction. Her prewar novels, far better than the postcolonial feminist revenge plot of *Wide Sargasso Sea*, illustrate Rhys's cultural-outsider or misfit sensibility. Ford Madox Ford described it, in his preface to Rhys's first story collection, *The Left Bank* (1927), as a "terrific—an almost lurid!—passion for stating the case of the underdog."[1] From the beginning, Rhys's oeuvre is defined by this harrowing focus on socially marginal, mostly female characters, "underdogs" set adrift as cultural misfits, uneasy in their gendered subordination no less than in their national origin or louche class background. (The early novels' protagonists work in the demimonde, as chorus girls or mannequins, at times lapsing into sex work.) Like Rhys herself, these figures may be nominally British, but are certainly "not English": they often see themselves, and are seen by nativist English characters, as "inferior beings." These antiheroines are marginalized by intersecting strata of national, racial, economic, and gender hierarchies governing the social world of early twentieth-century London, Paris, and other cosmopolitan metropoles.

Rhys's "Vienne," an early story first published in *The Left Bank*, famously describes the author's underdog sensibility as feeling "like a doormat in a world of boots."[2] This sensibility reflects Rhys's real-life experiences of exile from English imperial culture and, as a diasporic self-exile, from her own white-Creole Caribbean heritage and its ancestral slave-owning past. Rhys's novels focus on the feelings of displacement attendant on rootless characters who devolve under personal and political entailments linked to the power imbalances of colonialism and modernity, as lived in the metropolitan class-gender system of the pre–Second World War era. The complexities of Rhys's multiple cultural positions make her, more than any other novelist in this study, an important site for the literary representation of the culturally complex misfit figure in the early twentieth century.

Rhys's early novels examine "vaguely English" (or even "not English") female underdogs. Some of their protagonists, according to Mary Lou Emery, have a "confused national identity," one that is only "'vaguely' English," as in the case of protagonist Marya Zelli (née Hughes) of *Quartet* (1929).[3] Depicting Rhys's "case for the underdog," novels like *Quartet* register the politically conflicting and intense forms such intersectional and marginal lives experience. Rhys's perennial underdogs are deracinated characters who become "fallen women" due to the systemic social, political, and economic forces of cosmopolitan modernity in late colonial decline.

As A. Alvarez writes, "This sense of being an outsider unwillingly involved in the intricate social games the British play is constant" in Rhys's work."[4] Such consistent focus on what she herself called feeling like an "inferior being" distinguishes Rhys's fiction, particularly the early novels. Her limning of feelings of negative social existence showcases her refusal to adhere to an uplifting aesthetic. Instead, Rhys's fiction destabilizes conventions and norms of belonging and social cohesion. These norms are defined by the patriarchal values of late-colonial English majority culture and impact modern colonial subjects as well. In particular, Rhys's focus on underdogs shatters social norms of the autonomous liberal subject and the conventions of social caste and proper social status. In *Quartet*, one line that sums up the underdog's point of view invokes the animal metaphor quite starkly, referring to Marya and Heidler toward the end of their toxic romance: "She was quivering and abject in his arms, *like some unfortunate dog abasing itself before its master*" (131; emphasis added). Here, the underdog is cowed by the incommensurable superiority of "its master"— who occupies an order of being greater than her.

The second dimension of Rhys's "stating the case of the underdog," beyond a critique of colonial racism, sexism, and middle-class respectability, is the early novels' unrelenting focus on negative feelings and the puzzling unavailability of community resources of cultural belonging, optimism, and uplift—including church, family, and nation. The refusal to find succor in the holy trinity of matrimony, motherhood, and religion distinguishes Rhys's early modernist fiction as much as her "lurid" "passion for stating the case of underdog." The case of the author herself mirrors this boundary crossing in the fictions she created.

Rhys as a "Crossroads Figure"

There is a long history of sexist—and even feminist—readings of Rhys's novels that stigmatize the psychological suffering experienced by the main characters. As Emery notes, the pathetic female protagonists in the early novels "can be read sympathetically as victims of the social structure," particularly of "patriarchal oppression."[5] Emery adds, however, that "their apparent complicity in their own oppression remains to disturb readers, and psychological diagnoses of passivity, masochism, and even schizophrenia have become a critical commonplace."[6] It is easy to see arguments for the novels' positive feminist politics *or* for the very opposite: for their protagonists' "apparent complicity in their own oppression." Emery sidesteps this reductive, binary mode of thinking by stressing the importance of "reading Rhys's fiction as West Indian literature," as postcolonial *avant la lettre* (her island home, Dominica, won national independence in 1976). Emery thus resituates Rhys within a "cultural and historical context outside of the strictly European," which she claims "offers possibilities of interpretation that go *beyond the psychological*," which is how many critics read the early novels: as narratives of perverse feminine psychopathology.[7]

Rhys is seemingly always being rescued by sympathetic readers, and she fits uneasily within contemporary ideologies of feminism or postcolonialism. Emery even uses the term "misfit" to describe the ambiguities of Rhys's intersectional cultural positioning, both in the life and in the fictions of the novelist: "*A crossroads figure*, Jean Rhys appears in critical discussions of Caribbean, modernist, postcolonial and women's literature, yet, in each case, remains marginal to the field. This *'mis-fit'* speaks to the eccentricity of her fiction yet also to its power, located at the intersections of significant literary traditions, critical approaches, and historical transformations."[8]

Emery does not develop the notion of Rhys's legacy as a "mis-fit" within existing categories of cultural politics. But this passage illustrates the elision of Rhys's novels and her biographical author-function. Rhys is defined as a "crossroads figure" based on "the eccentricity of her fiction," a "mis-fit" body of work that Emery "locate[s] at the intersections of significant literary traditions"—such as modernism, feminism, and postcolonialism—"yet, in each case," Emery argues, Rhys "remains marginal to the field." Emery locates the categorical "mis-fit" in the *intersectionality* of Rhys—both the author and the work. Early on in Rhys's reception, as Emery notes, readers focused on the novels' intense narrative exploration of female subjectivity, highlighting the brutality of English patriarchal norms toward women who were of the "lower classes." Emery's recuperation of the postcolonial in Rhys, even in the earliest fiction, is based on early readers' penchant for ignoring the importance of colonized, racialized minority identification in her work. To gauge that work strictly through a psychological lens, Emery argues, is to misunderstand the challenging and contradictory ways the fiction represents racialized difference as a function of reverse migration and colonial legacy—well before the Windrush generation of postwar British immigrant writers to which V. S. Naipul belonged. The minimizing of single-identity gender politics as the heart of the early Rhys work, in favor of an intersectional postcolonial feminist approach, has its own problems but at least allows readers to view the complexities of these intersections without eliding a significant aspect of them.[9]

The "Composite Heroine": Modernist Fictions of "Inferior Being"

The Rhys archive was once defined (some would say distorted) by the "composite heroine," a construct for interpreting Rhys's oeuvre introduced by her longtime editor Francis Wyndham in the introduction to Rhys's work he published in 1963. (This introduction still appears in the current Norton paperback edition of *Wide Sargasso Sea* [1992], showing its lasting influence.) The early novels—published between 1928 and 1939—are conventionally linked together in a thematic and anthropomorphic cycle, centered on the so-called composite Rhys heroine: a composite character known as passive, self-abnegating, and self-destructive, if not masochistic. As in Naipaul's comment in the epigraph, the history of Rhys's critical reception often turns on the question of how to interpret the persistent negativity, passivity, and penchant for self-defeat that define Rhys's fictional heroines.

I use the category of the *modernist misfit* as a way to understand Rhys's representation of underdogs, defined by their social subordination and cultural nonconformism, in the context of the complex politics of gender, race, class, and Rhys's prescient focus on what one might call the *pre-postcolonial* condition. Her female protagonists are "not English" and are often intersectionally racialized. Critic Jed Esty describes Anna Morgan, of *Voyage in the Dark*, as "subwhite."[10] And, like Anna, many Rhys protagonists are not just lowly underdogs but personify complex (or intersectional) identities. This is a consistent pattern in the Rhys archive, from the early stories in *The Left Bank* (such as "Mixing Cocktails" or "Again the Antilles") to *Voyage in the Dark* and, later, *Wide Sargasso Sea*.

Rhys's modernist fiction thus focuses on cultural misfits as social underdogs, but their underdog status is keyed to their displacement from rigid gender, class, and national categories and norms. These underdogs transgress such social and cultural boundaries in the intersections of their "creolized" positioning. They are at times figures of the colonized plantation class, racialized by the British colonial class-gender system, as in *Voyage in the Dark*. What defines them most is their "mis-fit" with available Eurocentric cultural models of female subjectivity. Marya Zelli, Julia Martin, Anna Morgan, and Sasha Jansen become emotionally and financially dependent on their male lovers and later become "tarts" or "kept women," in the four early novels: *Quartet* (1929); *After Leaving Mr. Mackenzie* (1931); *Voyage in the Dark* (1934); and *Good Morning, Midnight* (1939).[11] These fictions—shockingly for their time, as Naipaul suggests in the epigraph—resist late-colonial sex-gender norms of respectable English femininity and even of respectable Anglo-Caribbean womanhood. They embrace the "dark" worlds of bohemia and the demimonde, while others also hearken back to island memories and the complex racial politics of a West Indian home-world ruled by the colonial caste system.

The Trouble with Masochism

Much of the debate about the significance of the misery borne by the "Rhys heroine" turns on whether to understand the fictions in terms of oppositional politics, where they illuminate the gender, class, racial, and colonial power structures that symbolically strangle her protagonists. By symbolically strangle them, I mean metaphorically, but also through the medium of language and rhetorical mastery of social situations. Rhys's first novel, *Quartet*, centers on how social control is achieved via rhetorical aplomb—weighted with the freight of lucre and epistemological power. *Quartet* homes in on the power that *top dogs* wield over *underdogs* via discursive means. Sadistic epistemology becomes the antagonistic system that thwarts *Quartet*'s protagonist. The novel calls out the "mania for classification" employed by the Heidlers—the novel's antagonists, a rich English married couple—as a form of epistemological domination. That, perhaps, is the crux of Rhys's tales of "inferior being": that Rhys's fiction dares the reader to confront and live within the contours of negative affects and conditions that have no repair, no transcendent significance. Her early novels refuse any of these redemptive gestures. (The postcolonial "madwoman in the attic's" setting fire to Rochester's manor is what distinguishes *Wide Sargasso Sea* as an eminently political and, from a certain vantage point, a less problematic novel.) Instead, Rhys constructs a world of hurt, which readers and critics alike seem drawn to yet forced for the same reason to explain it—or explain it away.

Quartet is a roman à clef about the affair between Rhys and Ford Madox Ford, which unavoidably involved their respective partners, Jean Lenglet and Stella Bowen. Despite its real-life inspiration, however, *Quartet* has an aesthetic life of its own. Marya Zelli is the protagonist and center of consciousness of the novel. The other central characters are H. J. (Hugh) and Lois Heidler, a wealthy English art dealer and his wife, who is a painter, and Stephan Zelli, Marya's husband, an art dealer of sorts himself. The Heidlers rule the British expatriate scene in 1920s Paris. Stephan is arrested soon after the story begins for trafficking in stolen artifacts. Stephan's imprisonment is the impetus for Marya's accepting the Heidlers' offer to move in with them (48). Soon after, Heidler announces his love for Madame Zelli. At first, Marya resists Heidler's overtures, but Lois—of all people—convinces her to stay and give in to him. Marya eventually becomes Heidler's mistress, while Stephan languishes in prison. A year later, before Stephan is released, Heidler tells Marya that she must leave her husband or the affair is over. Torn, Marya confesses to Stephan that she and Heidler are lovers. The novel ends when, "numbed by misery, Marya mismanages the situation and loses both men," in the words of Wyndham. It is the nature of this "misery" that is in contention, then as now.[12]

Some have read the misery of Rhys's heroines through the psychoanalytic lens of masochism. In a recent essay, Jennifer Mitchell builds on the plentiful readings of masochism in Rhys and *Quartet*.[13] Mitchell's intervention draws on Gilles Deleuze and rehabilitates masochism by applying a feminist standpoint, seeing it as empowering.[14] Rather than proposing another version of the "Rhys heroine" as *victim*, Mitchell argues that Marya's affair with Heidler—and her tortured dynamic with his wife—constitutes a scenario of masochism for all three participants.[15] "The impulse to *diagnose* Marya's masochism as self-destructive and, therefore, victimizing undercuts the ways in which Marya accesses autonomy and satisfaction," Mitchell writes.[16] She explains that Marya "begins to relish the torturous position that she occupies."[17] Mitchell thus recuperates Marya's seeming weakness as a position of strength, albeit one vexed by the definition of masochism as self-induced suffering. The novel is rescued through the agency of psychoanalytic discourse—a systematic mode of knowing fortified by institutional power, premised on categorical classification. Yet it is this form of externally validated, institutionalized knowledge that the novel itself challenges.

I cite this example because it engages in the psychoanalysis of literary characters and even of literary style. And while there is much vibrant work on the intersection of modernism and masochism, especially on Rhys, this chapter opens a space for methodological questions about the use of psychopathological categorization in the context of literary interpretation. My argument, however, is not against psychological interpretations of literary characters per se. Rather, I am more interested in the reading practice that I think Rhys's novel itself invites us to adopt, in its narrative technique as well as in its content. Such a practice, which I term *immanent reading* and discuss at length in the introduction, focuses on the narrative discourse as the key to interpretation, instead of relying on extrinsic frameworks—such as psychoanalysis or other hermeneutics of suspicion—that tend to impose an institutionally validated worldview. Rhys's novel thematizes the oppressive authority of institutional epistemologies, including the authority of psychoanalysis, whose pathologizing labels—such as "hysteric" or, indeed, "masochist"—are symbolically oppressive toward the female protagonist.

Resisting the "Mania for Classification"

Quartet is narrated largely from the protagonist's point of view, or internally focalized. Given the predominance of Marya's focalization, it is important that in the first two chapters there are certain passages that depart from this pattern, where the narrator addresses the reader directly and sketches Marya's background: "Marya, *you must understand*, had not been suddenly and ruthlessly transplanted from solid comfort to the hazards of Montmartre. Nothing like that. Truth to say, she was used to *a lack of solidity and of fixed backgrounds*" (15; emphasis added). The direct address to the reader, in "you must understand," frames Marya Zelli as a deracinated figure before the affair even begins, foreshadowing her sense of feeling like a "ghost walking in a *vague, shadowy world*" (57; emphasis added). What the reader "must understand" is that Marya was already "used to" living in the half-lit world of the demimonde; she is a former chorus girl, and her husband Stephan sells art works of uncertain provenance. This passage echoes one in the previous chapter, which also characterizes Marya as not only transient but undefined: "there were moments when she realized that her existence, though delightful, was haphazard. It lacked, as it were, solidity; it lacked the necessary fixed background" (8).

These two passages, linked by their common language and their external view of the protagonist, serve as framing devices. What is more, the singularity of the direct address suggests something about the overall *mood* of the narrative. The mood of Rhys's novel is almost palpable as an atmosphere that sustains hazy perception, epistemological uncertainty, and emotional instability in the not-so-transparent minds of the characters and in the narrative discourse that envelops and instantiates them. *Quartet* forms a story world made of various shadings of light and dark, a dynamic chiaroscuro of shadow and illusion. Another narrative frame that situates Marya in a world of "shadow" and "illusion" occurs at the end of chapter 2: "It was astonishing how significant, coherent and understandable it all became after a glass of wine on an empty stomach. . . . The Place Blanche, Paris, Life itself. One realized all sorts of things. *The value of an illusion, for instance, and that the shadow can be more important than the substance*" (23; emphasis added).

In this chapter, I argue that this preliminary framing of the protagonist can also help us understand the novel as a whole. In particular, I focus on a narrative technique—the technique of focalization—which, I argue, models for the reader how to understand the novel itself as a "vague, shadowy world." It is this world of shadow and illusion that the novel wants readers to value, to view the "shadow" as "more important than the substance." This direct address to the reader thus signals an important moment, one that solicits the reader's understanding of Marya. Note, however, that the narrator does not ask us to diagnose—or classify—her.

As the reading of masochism in Rhys indicates, many critics use formal classification or psychoanalytic diagnosis to interpret the novel. Yet, in so doing, such critics mirror the Heidlers' way of "reading," their mode of knowing, what the novel calls the "mania for classification" (60, 118). This "mania for classification" is linked to institutional forms of knowledge: normative discourses, like psychoanalysis, that function as heavy instruments of power. Marya claims that Heidler "crushed her. He bore [her] down," at one point, noting how "he had everything on his side. . . . Everything. Including Logic and Common Sense" (119). The Heidlers stand for this powerful way of knowing, a logical and commonsensical mode of putting people into categories, and, in so doing, exerting discursive control over social reality.

By contrast, the narrator's language of understanding introduces a mode of knowing based on *affective* connection with social experience by attending to subjective accounts of that experience. As Stephan, Marya's husband, notes, "You don't know what it is, *la misère*. Nobody knows what it is till it's got them" (172). The only way to know his misery, Stephan claims, is to experience it ("Nobody knows what it is *till it's got them*"). Barring firsthand experience of *la misère*, the narration proposes a secondary way of knowing: *the underdog's*, what the narrator simply calls "understanding." Another example of the "mania for classification" as an oppressive mode of knowing occurs when Marya critiques the Heidlers for "imagining they *know a thing* when they *know its name*" (130; emphasis added). She adds that "Lois and he [Hugh] pretended to be fair and were hard as hell underneath. . . . [T]hey couldn't feel anything and pretended that nobody else could" (130). Here, Marya challenges the Heidlers' propensity for labeling or classifying a thing ("knowing its name") by suggesting that it is a form of *mistaken* understanding—a self-deluding mode of oppressive logic, hallmark of *top dogs* who answer to no one but themselves. She adds that they share a rigid incapacity to "feel" and, by the same token, the Heidlers "pretend nobody else could" feel as well. The Heidlers are thus faulted for callousness, for a lack of sympathy. Their lack of feeling is self-serving and ensures a studied lack of curiosity about others' feelings: as powerful as they project themselves to be, they need not take into account others' points of view. Especially not the point of view of those, like Stephan, marked by *misery*—not unlike that of Rhys herself, with her life's work of centering on the "case of the underdog" and narratively—technically—evolving this "case" through the medium of narrative point of view.

More importantly, in their (self-serving) lack of empathy and sympathy, the Heidlers project an objectifying, classifying gaze: knowing the "name" of something, they falsely "imagine" they know *the thing itself*. Empathy and sympathy are both ways of *emotionally* understanding another's situation. Sympathy, as I use it, is based on a certain social distance and asymmetry between self and others—that between top dogs and underdogs, perhaps—where one feels compassion (or sympathy) for them. In this regard, it is ironic that Marya, in the novel, worries about Heidler's treatment of his wife, Lois. "I shouldn't worry too much about Lois, if I were you," he cautions her, underscoring how "unintelligent" it is for her to worry about his wife, who has probably seen countless "Maryas" come and go (107, 130). Empathy, on the other hand, entails the proverbial "putting oneself in another's shoes," or being able to connect across social distance to see the world through the other's eyes. This ability is a survival mechanism for social or cultural underdogs—to see and understand the world through the aggressor's eyes in order to protect against them. (Another version of this idea is the postpositivist-realist notion of *epistemic privilege*: the oppressed have greater insight into social reality because they encounter its toxic oppressive forces firsthand, while members of the social and cultural majority can afford to ignore that minefield, gliding past in their helicopter of privilege.[18]) And so Marya accuses the Heidlers of being incapable or uninterested in empathy and of spurious sympathy. Their taking up Marya during her time of distress is manifestly self-interested. They are not Good Samaritans but are rather scheming to use Marya for their own purposes: Heidler to have her as his mistress, and Lois to keep an eye on Marya and thus retain a modicum of control over the trying situation. This is what the narration calls the Heidlers' "mania for classification."

The "mania for classification" comes across as the self-satisfied conviction of always being right. Such conviction makes others fall in line with the Heidlers' chauvinistic, self-authorizing point of view—one described as "without pity" (64). Heidler is a veritable "autocrat," per his wife (65). These examples of the Heidlers' power to assert their own point of view are contrasted with Marya's powerlessness: her "longing to assert her point of view" (60) is repeatedly thwarted by the social authority of the Heidlers and their cronies. The tension in the narrative, then, consists of two ways of being in—and knowing—the world. In the words of the novel, one way of being in the world is that which is demanded by the powerful and the elite, by the normative forces of society, as represented by the respectable Heidlers. They rule the British Montparnos while the Zellis live a "haphazard" existence in the "hazards of Montmartre"; they are disreputable vagabonds (8, 15, 60). As opposed to authoritative classification, which is the *modus operandi* of the Heidlers, understanding requires a capacity for feeling and respect for others' feelings—a suspension of prejudgment and a desire to connect through empathy.

We can profitably read *Quartet* by seeking to understand it as a cautionary tale against the "mania for classification" that dooms Marya at the hands of the Heidlers. The moral of this modernist novel, if there is one, is to resist this urge to classify, to try a different approach, one less beholden to existing norms and institutionally validated systems of knowing: to take the underdog's point of view, rather than the top dog's (personified as the Heidlers). To "understand," in my reading, means to read immanently, sympathetically, and empathetically by going along with the experiences of the "underdog" protagonist, even as she descends into misery during her romantic obsession. To coolly objectify these experiences by externally classifying or "diagnosing" them violates *the mood* of the novel and its focus on the cultural underdog's experience of being labeled, and thereby controlled, by the powerful. Understanding that misery, rather than classifying it, is ultimately the point. Not to classify but to understand: this hermeneutic practice is represented not only by the experiences of the protagonist but also in the way they are narrated in the discourse of the novel itself. In other words, we are meant to understand a "lack of solidity and of fixed backgrounds" as the novel's aesthetic principle. The novel's style of presentation values shadow and illusion rather than schemes of classification.

The formal paths of the novel turn on two ways of knowing: either "classifying" or "understanding" the experience—and point of view—of the underdogs in the narrative. Hence, the meaning of *Quartet* is partially about how to read it, or how to understand the stories that people tell of themselves and others and of their complex social situations. One can know the name of a thing without understanding it. Or one can understand the thing itself, but only by living through it, as Stephan warns, or by the capacity to feel and understand others' feelings, their affective reality. In sum, the narrative's injunction to understand functions as a counterpoint to the classifying moves made by two of the story's central characters, which are, in turn, mirrored in critical approaches to Rhys. The text responds to the false certainty of naming, classification, or even clinical diagnosis with the ambiguities of subjective viewpoints and their limited purchase on social reality, including the reality of other viewpoints.

While classification is not synonymous with diagnosis, the two modes of knowing assert a normative purchase on reality, a systematic and categorical knowledge. Understanding, in this novel, is hazy, intuitive, affective, and unsystematic—as, one might say, befits the hazy, "shadowy" mood of *Quartet* and its heroine. Such a shadowy form of knowing as understanding leads to over- or misinterpretation. The problem of knowing and perceiving through the haziness of understanding, as insight into others whose motivations are unknown to us, is the subject of the next section.

The narrative elevates the problem of how to understand accurately without classifying or pathologizing the object of one's interest—the object of one's "nonce taxonomy," to quote Eve Kosofsky Sedgwick.[19] In *Epistemology of the Closet*, Sedgwick coins the phrase to indicate ways of knowing that ordinary people perform as they go about their lives, as opposed to modes of knowing that bend to the force field of institutional power. Such systems of knowledge are what Foucault termed *power-knowledge*, linked to modern discourses of sexology and psychoanalysis, such as masochism and hysteria, which oppressively construct as much as they classify the object of their potent epistemology. A similar idea to Foucault's—that knowledge is a form of power and control, deployed as a mode of social domination—is played out at the level of *Quartet*'s formal concerns with focalization and thematic concerns with intersubjective conflict. Such conflicts are the "obsessions of love and hate" that beset *Quartet*'s central characters (97). The novel employs subtle techniques of focalization in the service of representing fraught dynamics, in contrast to what could be called the "sadism of epistemology" inherent in the Heidlers' "mania for classification."[20]

As narratologist Monika Fludernik claims, in many fictional narratives, "we come across a strategy of repeating keywords and word fields for structuring purposes. . . . In [certain] texts . . . certain key words keep recurring, like leitmotifs. Because of the associations which they conjure up in the context of characters and plot, they become symbols which suggest connections and arguments at a higher level."[21] "To the best of my knowledge," Fludernik adds, "there is no technical term for this."[22] As discussed in the book's introduction, I call this mode of interpretation *immanent reading*, for the reading process it inspires.

Ménage à trois

At the end of the affair, recapitulating the leitmotif of "backgrounds," Marya waits for Heidler at a café—cafés being "the unvarying background" of their romantic rendezvous (177). This phrasing ("unvarying background") echoes the "solid" or "fixed" backgrounds that we are told Marya lacks. In the passage about the pernicious impact of the "mania for classification," Marya's free indirect thought views Heidler as "forcing her to be nothing but the little woman who lived in the Hôtel du Bosphore for the express purpose of being made love to. A *petite femme*. It was, of course, part of his *mania for classification*. But he did it with such conviction that she, miserable weakling that she was, found herself trying to live up to his idea of her" (118; second emphasis added). Beware of such fixity, such solidity, the novel argues. Such reward comes at a steep price: it reduces Marya to whatever category the Heidlers impose upon her—here, a *petite femme*, "the little woman who lived in" dingy hotels "for the express purpose of being made love to." Indeed, Heidler always seeks to control her, often admonishing her not to get "hysterical" during their quarrels (103, 148, 149, 161).

A more expansive example of the Heidlers' "mania for classification" occurs soon after Marya moves in. Lois begins to paint Marya's portrait, Lois's "chest well out, her round, brown eyes travelling rapidly from the sitter to the canvas and back again" (59). The reference to Marya as "the sitter" precludes Marya as the focal point, for Marya would not perceive herself as "the sitter," or the object captured by the painter's gaze. Such an alienated perspective properly belongs to the painter or the narrator, or both. Indeed, if there is a focalizing subject, it turns out to be Lois herself: "The movement of her [Lois's] head was oddly like that of a bird picking up crumbs. She talked volubly. She would often stop painting to talk, and it was evident that she took Montparnasse very seriously indeed. She thought of it as a possible stepping-stone to higher things and she liked explaining, classifying, fitting the inhabitants (that is to say, of course, the Anglo-Saxon inhabitants) into their proper places in the scheme of things. The Beautiful Young Men, the Dazzlers, the Middle Westerners, the Down-and-Outs, the Freaks who never would do anything, the Freaks who just possibly might" (60).

Focalization in this scene is marked by the shift to free indirect discourse, which does not simply report Lois's perspective but also uses her idiom (as in her use of social labels such as "Freaks"). Lois's free indirect speech, however, is ironically parroted, as suggested by the simile of her head's movement "oddly" resembling "that of a bird." In addition to what Brian McHale calls the "lyric fusion" between narrator and character that occurs in free indirect discourse, there is also an *ironic* fusion effected through the free indirect style, anticipated by the deflating description of Lois speaking "volubly" and the "bird" simile.[23] Even as Lois's beliefs and expressions are faithfully represented as tonally imperious, she is meant to seem ridiculous, as when admitting she "took Montparnasse very seriously indeed"—but only as a project to advance the Heidlers' social ambition. But the key signal of the narrator's ironic portrayal of Lois in this passage is the sardonic parenthetical phrase ("of course, the Anglo-Saxon inhabitants"). The free indirect narration doubles down on Lois's penchant to "explain . . .

classify . . . and fit" their Anglo-Saxon brethren as if exercising godlike powers (putting them in their "proper places . . . in the scheme of things"). The Heidlers' ironically pathetic arrogance and naked social ambition are exposed from the inside out, as the contents of Lois's mind—discursive and ideological—are laid bare in brazenly categorical, opportunistic terms, terms that echo the "stepping-stone" notion that ends the free indirect report ("the Freaks who never would do anything, the Freaks who just possibly might").

Lois's classifying of their social milieu is a means to world domination—the Anglo-Saxon inhabitants' world, of course. Ironically, the narrator's ventriloquism of her point of view performs the same classifying operation it deprecates. By parroting Lois's penchant for classifying, the narrator is "explaining," "classifying," and "fitting" Lois into *her* "proper place in the scheme of things." What is more, the syntax of the free indirect report mirrors the taxonomical impulse—a "mania for classification"—that is the subject of the passage. After the paratactic parallel series of "explaining, classifying, fitting" the inhabitants into their "proper place," the next sentence presents another parallel series, that of the "Anglo-Saxon inhabitants" living in Montparnasse, the parallelism mirrored in the lack of a final conjunction ("the Freaks who never would do anything, the Freaks who just possibly might"). Hence, the double parallel series frames Lois with taxonomical precision, "fitting" Lois herself into her "proper place," and then in turn enumerates the social types that her taxonomy fits into their proper places.

By contrast, Marya is described in the very next sentence as "longing to assert her point of view" (60). Lois's ironic detachment is contrasted with the warmth of Marya's longing. Mrs. Heidler exerts a powerful benefactor's control, manifested through a classifying gaze (much more than a painter's). As opposed to Lois, Marya has trouble "asserting" her own point of view while caught in the harsh light of the Heidlers' social gaze. While Marya struggles to describe her life with Stephan, Lois characterizes it coolly and crisply, in contrast to the sentimental effusions that characterize Marya's speech.

> Sometimes she [Lois] would ask questions, and Marya, longing to assert her point of view, would try to describe the charm of her life with Stephan. The vagabond nights, the fresh mornings, the long sleepy afternoons spent behind drawn curtains.
>
> "Stephan's a—vivid sort of person, you see. What a stupid word! I mean natural. Natural as an animal. He made me come alive; he taught me everything. I was happy. Sometimes just the way the light fell would make me unutterably happy."

"Yes, of course," Lois would say intelligently. "I can quite see how he got hold of you. Quite." (60)

The contrast in worldviews could not be more evident, nor the rhetorical precision that characterizes Lois's curt reply from Marya's rambling, vague, and emotional speech. On the one hand, Marya struggles to explain the "charm of her life with Stephan," using abstract diction to describe him, such as "vivid," a word that she realizes is too vague to describe a person ("What a stupid word!"). In contrast, Lois is presented, again, as a shrewd, calculating observer, a social climber who sees life in Montparnasse only as a "stepping-stone to higher things." In a related passage, Marya grants that Lois is "extremely intelligent," insofar as she banks on conventional opinion to legitimize her viewpoint: "She expressed well-read opinions about every subject under the sun . . . and was so perfectly sure of all she said that it would have been a waste of time to contradict her" (60).

In fact, to describe Stephan as "natural as an animal" is telling. Stephan is the antithesis—in Marya's mind—of what the Heidlers stand for. He represents a "natural," "vagabond" life, seemingly free from bourgeois hierarchies of social value. This is why Marya can think only of intrinsic, experiential, inarticulate attributes to describe Stephan and their life together: he is "vivid," he "made [Marya] come alive," "taught [her] everything," he made Marya "unutterably happy." No wonder she struggles to explain the charm of their former life! Their charming existence was, precisely, "unutterable," and thus incalculable by any measure of social hierarchy or material value. (Not least because such charm led only to Stephan's imprisonment and Marya's dependency on the Heidlers.) The Heidlers' point of view dominates this scene, which takes place just after Marya has moved in. Lois coolly responds to Marya's rhapsodic account of her former life: "'Yes, of course,' Lois would say intelligently. 'I can quite see how he got hold of you. Quite'" (60). Lois's repeated "quite" is as cutting as it sounds, as she coldly translates Marya's vague, shadowy web of emotion into a rational social calculus, with winners and losers. Lois implies that Stephan's charm was nothing but a ruse to "get hold of" Marya, a conquest and a trap that Marya fell for. Lois coldly deflates Marya's description of true happiness with her husband into the transaction of a predator marking his prey—to view Marya's animal metaphor from Lois's perspective. What Lois sees is not exactly what Marya says, but how she says it—how she struggles to say it, and then how her words are vague and abstract, vainly trying to convey the sense of being "unutterably happy." Such ineffable qualities as "unutterable," "happy," and "vivid" prevent Lois's taking Marya's point of view seriously; they speak different languages of social value, of what counts as a valuable existence.

They cannot communicate across this ideological divide, which is presented as a tension between incommensurable points of view, each with its own language and rhetorical style. It is thus impossible for Marya to persuade Lois of the value or even the truth of Marya's experience, for such truth cannot be expressed except as ineffable and fleeting ("vagabond"). Lois does not understand feeling and the unutterable, but rationality and the calculable: the classifiable. It is no wonder that after this scene, Lois thinks of Marya as "excitable," an emotional creature naïve enough to fall for whatever pretty story Stephan told her. Even Stephan has a "mania for order," indicating how Marya stands apart as overly emotional, which the Heidlers view as a weakness (77, 87, 178). Marya is even dismissively diagnosed by a minor character as a "neurasthenic" and admonished by Heidler's calling her "hysterical." By contrast, the Heidlers have a "sense of proportion" (77), a phrase identical to the baleful mantra of Sir William Bradshaw, the psychiatrist in Virginia Woolf's *Mrs. Dalloway* (1925). Readers of *Mrs. Dalloway* will recognize Rhys's allusion to that novel and how Sir Bradshaw's "sense of proportion" espouses an institutional, doctrinaire point of view—one whose toxic influence precipitates the suicide of his patient, Septimus Warren Smith.[24] Bradshaw's "sense of proportion" is thus of a piece with the Heidlers', and together they represent the antithesis of the sympathetic viewpoint of Smith, Clarissa Dalloway, and Marya herself.

Finally, note that Marya's rhapsody about her former life with Stephan returns us to the motifs of light, shadow, and illusion associated with the attitude that finds such conditions salutary, rather than alarming: "the long sleepy afternoons spent behind drawn curtains"; "the way the light fell would make me unutterably happy." Marya's rhapsody echoes when the narrator explains "the value of an illusion," that "the shadow can be more important than the substance." My point is not just that this example aligns the narrator's sensibility with Marya's. This passage represents a moment when the narrative discourse itself dramatizes the deep desire ("longing") to present this point of view to an impassive interlocutor. Lois, in turn, sees only what she wants to see: "I can quite see how he [Stephan] got hold of you. Quite," thereby nullifying the value of the life being described, transforming it into a vision of Stephan's exploiting Marya's naïveté in order to control her. Such control over others begins with the rhetorical act of classifying them according to one's own "scheme of things." That scheme defines the Heidlers' worldview as focused on scheming, and classifying others in order to advance those schemes.

The Narrative Mood of *Quartet*

One aspect of the main argument in this chapter is that the narrative design of the novel anticipates the difficulties of interpretation, the reading of other people and social gestures. The novel's key terms highlight why it might be better to understand, rather than to classify (or diagnose, for that matter).

In Gérard Genette's oft-cited *Narrative Discourse*, he claims a distinction between narrative *voice* ("who speaks") and *mode* (originally translated as *mood*), or the "regulation of narrative information," the ways the narrator influences how we interpret that information.[25] "Indeed," Genette writes, "one can tell *more* or tell *less* what one tells, and can tell it *according to one point of view or another*; and this capacity, and the modalities of its use, are . . . what our category of *narrative mood* aims at."[26] Chief among these modalities is point of view—what Genette famously terms *focalization*.[27] In "regulating [narrative] information" by filtering it through focalizing characters, the figural narrative offers the illusion of maximum closeness and maximum partiality. This filtering is subjective—and subject to the distortions of individual perspectives. (A famous case in point is the unnamed governess in Henry James's *The Turn of the Screw* [1898], whose accounts of supernatural phenomena can be construed as mere hallucination.)

Situating narration in subjectivity through focalization, and thus creating a narrative with a characteristically shadowy mood, is the point of departure for my reading of *Quartet*. This novel is a triumph of mood, chiefly through Rhys's experiments in focalization, related by a third-person narrator "who is not one of the characters but who adopts" their point of view.[28] Genette indicates that narrative mood is a function of perspective and ideology, while the structural hermeneutic distinction between understanding and classification in *Quartet* is mapped by Rhys's handling of the narrative mood, which adopts extensive focalization in ways that are hard to describe within existing narrative theory.[29]

Indeed, in his theory of mood, Genette seems to be hypostasizing the narrative discourse itself as having a certain texture, an overall quality that perhaps cannot be reduced to discrete technical categories that help constitute it.[30] The story of *Quartet*, Marya's love affair with Heidler, is similarly imbued with a palpable mood. The novel is as much about *how* it relates the story as about the events that compose the story itself. The narration's overall effect, or what Genette calls its mood, is achieved through its close contact with the "transparent minds" of its central characters, chiefly Marya.[31] But focalized narration is only the beginning of how Rhys achieves the shadowy mood of *Quartet*—a mood that the narrator seems to describe, in relation to Marya's backstory, as "a lack of solidity and of fixed backgrounds."

In a sense, I am equivocating on the definition of narrative *mood* as mode— as technique—and *mood* as affect, a quality or intensity of feeling that pervades, much as climate does, a narrative space. A moody painting or musical composition might be tonally colored in varying shades of blue. Rhys, I am arguing, creates a moody book, mood-as-affect, by way of manipulating the narrative discourse in various ways (mood-as-mode). Ultimately, mood-as-affect and mood-as-mode are one and the same (call it mood-effect). This means that the study of affect in aesthetic forms like literature could benefit from Genette's notion of narrative mood. His theory of mood helps us describe how fiction formulates affect, how it generates and regulates it, through devices and choices in narrative form.

Quartet's characteristic mood is created primarily through the mode of focalization. The (third-person) narrator filters most of the information through the consciousness of Marya. (Most, but not all.) In this regard, Rhys is doing nothing new. But the mood of the narrative permeates the story world, rendering a world of "shadow" and "illusion." The story itself is not as original—indeed, Ford, Bowen, and Lenglet each wrote their own versions.[32] But what is innovative is how the novel produces this narrative climate of uncertainty and instability. And, I argue, Rhys does this by various means. But for the remainder of this essay, I focus on how the novel regularly registers a distinctive form of focalization: one that reflects hypothetical points of view.

The narration adopts focalization and various modes of presenting figural consciousness—including extensive use of free indirect discourse, psycho-narration, and dialogue.[33] But the most peculiar technique is what David Herman calls hypothetical focalization. Briefly, hypothetical focalization (HF), which I define below, is Herman's term for narrative information presented "as if": as in, if there were someone to observe event x, this is what she would see. But there is no one there—only the invocation of that possibility by the narrator. HF also describes the possibility of an actual observer who perceives event x but is not quite sure the event happened as it seemed to. Hypothetical focalization thus creates a story world of uncertainty and instability, a shadowy register of social space peopled with illusions and with illusions about people.

This technique helps imbue the narrative with its characteristic mood and represents the hermeneutics of understanding versus classification that the novel champions.[34] But my reading of Rhys's novel as employing the technique of hypothetical focalization depends on extending this concept from Herman's original description to encompass the way it helps to define the novel's mood.

The hypothetical quality of numerous focalized passages also underscores the narrator's gesture toward subjective understanding as opposed to objective classification. Hypothetical focalization at the character level, which is how it most often appears in *Quartet*, entails that individual figures become narrators of other characters' inner lives. Or they project themselves as such, as in a major scene in a railcar described below.

Before understanding the employment of hypothetical focalization in *Quartet*, I should explain how my account extends Herman's definition. Herman defines hypothetical focalization as the "use of hypotheses . . . about what might be or have been seen or perceived."[35] Herman defines focalization itself as a "perceptual and conceptual frame . . . more or less inclusive or restricted, through which situations and events are presented in a narrative." So, for Herman, "Ways of focalizing a story can thus be redescribed as the narrative representation of propositional attitudes, i.e., modes of focalization encode into narrative form various kinds of epistemic stances that can be adopted towards what is being represented in the narrative. . . . [W]hat I am calling HF is the formal marker of a peculiar epistemic modality, in which . . . the *expressed world* counterfactualizes or virtualizes the *reference world* of the text."[36]

What Herman calls the "expressed world" exists only in *the mind* of the narrator, that is, its reality is "propositional." The expressed world differs from the real world (or "reference world") as it exists in the narrative. This means that hypothetical focalization is legible in narrative statements invoking a probabilistic perspective, grammatically marked by the conditional or subjunctive mood. If we tie his discussion to Genette's notion of mood, we can see that Herman doubles down on the grammatical metaphor of Genette's narratology, where narrative discourse is structured like a language into *tense, voice,* and *mood.* But now we can include in our account of focalization hypothetical statements that invoke a subjective or conditional perspective that "counterfactualizes or virtualizes" the world of the story.

Yet Herman qualifies his definition of hypothetical focalization: HF involves statements of "what might be or have been perceived—if only there were someone who could have adopted the requisite perspective on the situations and events at issue."[37] Herman's examples involve instances that invoke nonexistent or "counterfactual" focalizing agents—such as the narrator's interpolation of a hypothetical witness to Poe's "Fall of the House of Usher": "Perhaps the eye of a scrutinizing observer might have discovered a barely perceptible fissure, which . . . made its way down the wall."[38] Herman notes two grammatical signs that "encode . . . hypotheticality": the adverbial operator *perhaps*, and the subjunctive mood expressed in the modal auxiliary *might*, which, Herman claims, "implies a lack of commitment to the truth of the expressed world relative to the reference world of the story."[39] There is no actual "scrutinizing observer," in other words— only a hypothetical one who, also hypothetically, "might have discovered" the famous crack in the House of Usher. Herman also adduces other forms of HF, instances where, unlike Poe's virtual observer, the focalizor does exist, but only their function as focalizor is hypothetical. In other words, rather than positing an imaginary character who might witness the crack in the House of Usher, a narrative might impute a real character who possibly might function as focalizor, but only provisionally.

Indeed, characters who function as hypothetical focalizors abound in *Quartet*. Thus, when Herman defines HF as "what might be or have been perceived—if only there were someone who could have adopted the requisite perspective," he underestimates instances where hypothetical focalization occurs *between char-acters*—what so-and-so "might be or have been perceiv[ing]," not according to the narrator, but according to another character.[40] As such, I extend Herman's notion of hypothetical focalization to include instances of narrative encoding of hypotheticality that involve *character-based* suppositions about what another character is thinking or perceiving, which also destabilize the reference world by projecting an expressed world that "counterfactualizes or virtualizes" it.

Hypothetical Focalization in *Quartet*

There are at least fifteen significant instances of hypothetical focalization in the novel. Ten of these adopt Marya's point of view, presenting Marya's insight into another character. Normally, the adoption of a character's point of view is an instance of what Mieke Bal calls double focalization, "in which [the exter-nal narrator] 'looks over the shoulder'" of a character whose point of view is adopted.[41] Thus, for Bal, double focalization usually entails the overlay of narra-tor and focalizor. In *Quartet*, however, double focalization—one actual, the other virtual—often occurs under the nose of the narrator, as it were. In these instances, the point of view is Marya's, while she, in turn, adopts the point of view of another character. These instances depict Marya's free indirect thought, in which she presumes to understand another's perspective. Often this double perspective is marked as a supposition that can be proven right or wrong.

A key passage occurs in the opening chapter, when Marya meets the Heidlers for the first time. At dinner, Marya observes Lois's eyes, finding them to be "beau-tiful, clearly brown, the long lashes curving upwards, but there was a suspicious, almost deadened look in them. 'I'm a well-behaved young woman,' they said, 'and you're not going to catch me out, so don't think it.' Or perhaps, thought Marya, she's just thoroughly enjoying her pilaf" (11). Here, the free indirect report presents Marya's perception of Mrs. Heidler: first, Marya thinks that Lois's eyes are physically "beautiful." But, in the same sentence, they also seem to have a "suspicious, almost deadened look in them." Next comes Marya's hypothetical focalization of Lois, presented as imaginary discourse: "'I'm a well-behaved young woman,' they said, 'and you're not going to catch me out, so don't think it.'" But the following sentence returns to simple focalization, with the narrator's bird's-eye view clearly demarcated: "Or perhaps, thought Marya, she's just thoroughly enjoying" her dinner. Thus the passage includes different kinds of discourse and different kinds and levels of focalization.

But, more importantly, the passage encodes conjectures about Mrs. Heidler's personality, based on Marya's perception of the look in Lois's eyes. These conjectures are formulated as a hypothetical statement representing Lois's point of view, imagined as direct discourse. But Marya's hypothetical focalization is immediately qualified, if not canceled, by her next thought—also presented as conjectural, with the word "perhaps" "indicating possibility and doubt," as Herman understands the "alethic and epistemic functions" of hypothetical focalization.[42] Thus there is an ironic double valence in presenting a hypothetical perspective through direct discourse. To speak what "Lois' eyes . . . said" mimes the indicative mood ("they said"), which is contradicted by the conjecture entailed in one character's knowing what another is thinking. Even if "eyes" were able to "speak," Marya's perception is indicative only of her own vision of Lois, her own "expressed world," even if it is presented, grammatically, in the indicative mood. The mere probability of this "expressed world" is emphasized by the sentence, beginning with "perhaps," which casts doubt on this first impression.

Marya's hypothetical focalization of Lois is thus immediately placed under erasure, proven to be fallible, perhaps even mistaken. But the indicative and conditional moods are not so much canceling as balancing each other: just as the first impression of Lois's eyes are that they are "beautiful but . . . ," so is the point of view of Lois as "suspicious" balanced by a much more mundane explanation. This oscillation between darker and lighter impressions of Lois's perspective is mirrored by other instances and, in fact, are structurally indicative of the narrative theme, that of the hermeneutic uncertainty of understanding others' points of view. Marya catches herself getting carried away with Lois's first impression, and, although she sets the conjecture aside for a less suspicious explanation, it nonetheless foreshadows Lois's personality.

Quartet contains several more instances of character-level hypothetical focalization. They involve characters imagining other characters' inner lives.

Such cases of hypothetical focalization employ grammatical signals that a character is imagining what another character *would* say or *would be* thinking. These are signals that indicate an epistemic shift from the reference world of the story to a counterfactual expressed world of the character.

A related instance bears mentioning, because it shows how a similar technique is employed to depict character-level focalization that is not at all hypothetical. In this case, the exception proves the rule. The moment involves Heidler focalizing Marya. Given the surrounding narrative context, double focalization would be the most apt description, narrated as Heidler's free indirect thought: "'I'm still fond of her,' he told himself. 'If only she'd leave it at that.' But no. She took her hands away from her face and started to talk again. What a bore! Now, of course, she was quite incoherent. 'The most utter nonsense,' thought Heidler. Utter nonsense about (of all things) the visiting cards stuck into the looking-glass over Lois' damned mantelpiece, about Lois' damned smug pictures and Lois' damned smug voice" (129–30). In this moment of focalization, Heidler is mentally processing what Marya is saying: trivial complaints about Lois. His interior monologue is quoted directly ("'The most utter nonsense,' thought Heidler") or narrated free indirectly ("What a bore!"). But Heidler silently begins to narrate Marya's speech, which he views as "utter nonsense." There is a reinforcement of this reading, since Marya ends by complaining about "Lois' smug voice," summing up the novel's obsession with voice, with the way characters express their points of view. The free indirect report ventriloquizes Marya but is focalized through Heidler. It is a feat of narratorial engineering, and it stands in contrast to most of the novel's doubly focalized passages, which reveal an expressive, rather than referential, status. Thus most of the novel's character-level focalizations are not factual; they destabilize the "reference world" of the story by marking the distortions of subjectivity, achieved by attempts at intersubjectivity.

Perhaps the most interesting moment of character-based hypothetical focalization occurs at the midpoint of the book. The Heidlers and Marya are riding the train to a fictional town in the south of France, the Heidlers' weekend getaway. For the first time, Marya goes with them. As a consequence, and also for the first time, Marya skips visiting her husband in prison. She chooses Heidler.

> They sat facing her in the railway carriage and she looked at them with calmness, clear-sightedly, freed for one moment from her obsessions of love and hatred. They were so obviously husband and wife, so suited to each other, they were even in some strange way alike. . . .

Lois sat sturdily, with her knees, as usual, a little apart: her ungloved hands were folded over a huge leather handbag; *on her dark face was the expression of the woman who is wondering how she is going to manage about the extra person to dinner. She probably was wondering just that.* (97; emphasis added)

"Freed for one moment from her obsessions of love and hatred," Marya, we are told, sees the Heidlers "clear-sightedly," as if objectively. The shift from psycho-narration to free indirect thought tracks the deepening of perception, from external to internal; from describing how Lois sat, Marya then contemplates what Lois thought. But the final sentence underlines that her image of Lois's consciousness was not necessarily accurate: "She *probably* was wondering just that" signals Marya's personal point of view and colloquial idiom and underscores its hypothetical quality, as an observation that may or may not be true. It most likely is, for Marya is seeing "clear-sightedly." When they reach Brunoy, Marya's supposition is confirmed, as is the source of the double focalization: "Lois said, exactly as Marya had known she would say: 'I must stop on the way because there's not much to eat in the house'" (98).

In this instance, Marya's hypothetical focalization is proven correct. But its suspension as merely subjective is the important point; the reader does not know yet whether Marya is right. The narrator confirms that it was Marya's point of view all along and that this point of view is ultimately correct ("exactly as Marya had known she would say"). She was the source of the narrative insight into Lois and Lois's interior thoughts. In this case, Marya does so with a satirical, dismissive bent: the passage focalizing what Lois was "probably" thinking ends with the dismissal of Lois as "obviously of the species wife" (97).

But perhaps the most interesting dimension of the scene is how Marya's hypothetical focalization continues and becomes more affectively charged. Lois becomes weaponized in Marya's eyes: "There she [Lois] was: formidable, an instrument made, exactly shaped and sharpened for one purpose. She didn't analyse; she didn't react violently; she didn't go in for absurd generosities or pities. Her motto was: 'I don't think women ought to make nuisances of themselves. I don't make a nuisance of myself; I grin and bear it, and I think that other women ought to grin and bear it too'" (97). Transforming Lois into a "sharpened" "instrument" is Marya's doing, through her focalization of Lois's motto no less than her idea about what Lois was probably thinking. In this case, the description conveys intense emotion: note the series that renders Lois, in implicit opposition to Marya, as a cool, rational, self-controlled, and powerful—and powerfully masculinized—figure. The vehicle of the metaphor connotes a phallic object—a knife, or, better yet, a scalpel; the word "instrument" invokes a vision of Mrs. Heidler as scientifically classifying, and then penetrating, the object of her interest ("sharpened for one purpose"). Rather than wounding, as Marya does, with "tears . . . futile rages . . . [and] extravagant abandon," Lois cuts clinically with discursive aplomb (117). The clear aggression in the metaphor, however, marks it as less clear-sighted than Marya's previous insight. But both descriptions are presented as of a piece, as Lois appears to Marya. Whether this instance of character-level focalization is objective or simply a fabrication on her rival's part is partially answered by the narrator's corroboration about what "Lois said," which was "exactly as Marya had known she would say."

But the meaning of the passage rests on the "probably" more than on the "exactly"; the "shadow," not the substance. After Lois, Marya turns to Heidler, who appears

> like the same chord repeated in a lower key, sitting with his hands clasped in exactly the same posture as hers. Only his eyes were different. He could dream, that one. But his dreams *would not be* many-colored, or dark shot with flame like Marya's. No, *they'd be cold, she thought*, or gross at moments. *Almost certainly gross* with those pale blue, secretive eyes. *It seemed to her* that, staring at the couple, *she had hypnotized herself into thinking, as they did, that her mind was part of their minds* and that she understood why they both so often said in exactly the same tone of puzzled bewilderment: "I don't see what you're making such a fuss about." Of course! And then they wanted to be excessively modern, and *then they'd think*: "After all, we're in Paris." (98; emphasis added)

The italicized portions indicate the partiality or conditionality of Marya's perception of the wealthy married couple. Again, the lens of double focalization projects onto the Heidlers while never leaving Marya's side in their "three-cornered fight" (117). Formally, this moment of hypothetical focalization recapitulates the content of the scene. The form of the narration corroborates the idea that Marya's mind *is* a part of the Heidlers'—or, at least, she thinks so, since she can peer into them. She has "hypnotized herself into thinking" just "as they did"; they seem to share one mind too. But do they *really* think so? Marya's focalization—one actual ("It seemed to her"), the other virtual (Heidler's eyes "would not be" like hers)—highlights the self-referentiality, the subjectivity, of these impressions, including the impression that one can enter another's mind.

The formal analysis of the passage should also consider the grammatical. There is a shift from the indicative ("there he was") to the conditional mood ("would not be"; "they'd be"; "they'd think"). Such grammatical signs indicate the hiatus between a narrator's access versus a character's access to fictional minds, access that can be proven wrong. The novel's narrative interest turns on the subjectivity of Marya's account, especially while this subjectivity is itself narrating what it presumes is going on in other minds. The narration thus indicates when objectivity falls and subjectivity reigns, but also when that distinction is blurred, in intersubjective moments when social reality becomes more like a shadow than a substance.

Resisting the "Sadisms of Epistemology"

Marya's (hypothetical) focalizations, marked as they are in the previous passage with the conditional mood of doubt and probability, create an interesting "modulation of intimacy and distance," in McHale's terms.[43] When one character seems to focalize another, is it an attempt at empathy? Or, on the contrary, as in the "species wife" episode quoted above, is it a bit of parodic focalization? Focalization is usually reserved for external narration. *Quartet*'s character-level use of hypothetical focalization, however, rhetorically reinforces the thematic obsession of the narrative with narration itself. Specifically, hypothetical focalization allegorizes how narration, or storytelling, is the central theme of the novel. Not storytelling *tout court* (Rhys is too canny for that) but storytelling from a particular point of view. Whose point of view is it? How fallible is that account?[44] These are the kinds of questions the novel poses to the reader. It plunges the reader into the shadow, the illusion, the "lack of solidity and of fixed backgrounds" of subjective accounts, which seem accurate, even objective, but may prove otherwise.

I began this essay with the well-trod background of *Quartet*: as a roman à clef, it represents a partial account, one inconsistent with those written by the other principals. The real "Stephan," Jean Lenglet, wrote one of these, *Sous les verrous*.[45] Rhys translated Lenglet's novel as *Barred*, cutting approximately seven thousand words from the original French because it seemed to paint her in a very harsh light.[46] But what interests me is not the veracity of *Quartet*, measured against the other accounts of the affair. Rather, what interests me is how Rhys formally incorporates the thematic preoccupation—the obsession— with point of view and with the limits that point of view places on the veracity, even the verifiability, of any story. Members of "l'affaire Ford" projected their perspective with varying degrees of success.

But it was Rhys who formulated the mood of the story by foregrounding the ethical and romantic shadows cast by the four central characters. These shadows are cast most of all by the narrative technique of *Quartet*: one is the extensive use of hypothetical focalization and the self-referential narrative focus on this act as a problem, perhaps the main problem, of the story. The seduction of Marya by Heidler is rendered, as Carole Angier argues, without shedding light on Marya's own culpability and motivations.[47] But the narrative techniques of the novel, especially hypothetical focalization, indicate how the psychological drama of the story lies in its telling and may indeed be a lie in its telling—one can never be too sure. The novel, then, while siding with Marya, also engages other aspects of narration that trouble the reference world of the story as seen by the protagonist. Rhys's narrator largely sustains Marya's point of view while complicating the ruse of focalization itself. This narrative focus on narrative focus at a technical level corresponds to how the narrator describes Marya's background as the lack of a (fixed) background, indicating the radical doubt that permeates even the objective narrator's accounts—and indicating the radical instability of an underdog's social existence when social reality is defined by the top dogs of the world.

An interesting example of hypothetical focalization at the narrator level encapsulates this existential "lack of solidity" as definitive of *Quartet*'s narrative mood. Monsieur Hautchamp, a minor character, reads the newspaper. With "an expression of disapproval," the narrator notes, "he continued his article which . . . began thus: '*Le mélange des races est à la base de l'évolution humaine vers le type parfait.*' ['*Racial mixing is the basis for human evolution toward the perfection of the species.*'] 'I don't think,' thought Monsieur Hautchamp—or something to that effect" (32–33; my translation). The "something to that effect" casts a shadow over this moment of focalization. Here, the omniscient narrator is not sure what this character thought (ironically, is not sure that Hautchamp thought "I don't think"). The probability that language gets in the way—for Hautchamp did not think in English—melts into the probability that fictional minds are not so transparent after all.

One could say that this chapter oversymptomatizes one instance of verb choice ("diagnosed") in the secondary literature on Rhys. But my focus enables metacritical questions that may remain unasked if we elide the category crossing of clinical and critical domains in the study of literature. Some of these questions include: What does it mean when we "diagnose" literary characters as masochistic? What does it mean when a literary novel, or corpus, as in the case with Rhys, impels us to read it as masochistic or, more broadly, as "diagnosable," in some vaguely clinical sense, which can then be transformed into an aesthetic principle?

Among other techniques, *Quartet* employs hypothetical focalization to unsettle the fixity of rational objectivity and systematic judgment—the top dog's self-authorizing point of view. This moody book dims the lights in its reference world, refusing to provide the reader with a narratorial "fixed background," in the terms of the novel. Put another way, the use of counterfactual glimpses into other minds, rendered in complex forms of focalization, combines to create a story defined by its narrative mood, antithetical to the mania for classification.

Given *Quartet*'s figural narration, its reliance on key instances of hypothetical focalization does not merely provide multiple perspectives but also emphasizes how these perspectives are often suspended. Such multiplicity, and virtuality, of focus renders subjective judgments illusory and susceptible to contradicting views—not only Marya's versus the Heidlers' but also, by extension, the reader's. The theme encoded in the title *Quartet* and the character system that it references alerts the reader to the variability of these perspectives. Hypothetical focalizations trouble the actual world of the story by providing competing, conjectural, at times self-canceling perspectives on the true narrative situation. There is no true narrative situation, in other words: at least not "true" in the objective sense.

The ending of the novel, for example, leaves Marya behind after an altercation with Stephan. After telling him the truth about her involvement with Heidler, Marya threatens to call the police when Stephan plans to kill Heidler (179–84). But surprisingly, the end of Marya's story is not the end of the novel. Stephan leaves his wife splayed on the floor: "*Voilà pour toi*," he says, obscenely indifferent (185). We don't know what else happens with her. The story continues with Stephan and his new "girl," who becomes Marya's ostensible replacement on the last page of the novel (186). Marya is left behind, unconscious or dead, the reader doesn't know which. Marya becomes Schrödinger's protagonist, neither living nor dead. Her end is ambiguous and thus open-ended.

Narrative instability strategically weakens the reader's grasp of the ethical and psychological truth of the situation. This instability only deepens as the story goes on, as Marya cannot explain to herself why she continues in the affair despite her deep ambivalence. More importantly, the narrator does not fully explain, choosing only to foreground the absence of comprehensive explanation. The novel includes some perspectives, as we have seen, that psychopathologize the protagonist as "neurasthenic" (174) or "hysterical" (149), while others objectify and belittle her: "this type of woman" (177), "*petite femme*" (118). But nowhere in the novel does the term "masochism" appear. Rather, other clinical terms, such as "mania," "hysteria," and "neurasthenia," are used to stigmatize the protagonist. By contrast, the narrator's focus on Marya establishes the partiality of the story from the outset and provides the reader with an alternative principle for "understanding" her existence by gauging what it lacks, or by suggesting that what Marya's experience consists of *is* a lack. Readers, too, are presented with a discourse that lacks narrative solidity and fixed backgrounds.

As noted, the social space that the Heidlers occupy is a well-ordered bourgeois existence, one held together by their "mania for classification." Ironically, the novel's use of a psychopathological term ("mania") to describe the Heidlers impugns them as misguided for doing the same thing the narrator does: using diagnostic language to classify *them* as classifying others, a reflection of its focus on focalization itself. Nevertheless, the narrative seems to condemn this practice, even given the irony. Rhys's novel rests on such ambiguities of judgment, foregrounding the (lack of) background, transmuting the solidity and fixity of the reference world of the story into shadow and illusion. In doing so, *Quartet* exposes the "mania for classification" that is at the root of the Heidlers' power, which seeks to stabilize and control others through the "sadisms of epistemology." I'm tempted to say that the novel ironically (sadomasochistically?) invites this "mania for classification" on the part of the reader, even as it denigrates such an operation in its least sympathetic characters.

One curious piece of evidence for the instability of the novel's world, due to its focus on the virtuality, or partiality, of perspectives and on subverting systems of power-knowledge—*and one that is missed if we focus on classical psychological categorization*—is the question of how to pronounce Marya's name. "Marya" is an ambiguous spelling for this virginal name—and she is ironically named, of course—though the ambiguity, not the irony, is the main point. Marya's nickname, "Mado," also ironically invokes the virginal trope. When I last taught this novel, the class asked me how to pronounce Marya's name. Typically, the novel leaves the question hanging, until it quasi-reveals the answer. In their first outing together as a trio, the following scene between Marya and the Heidlers occurs, again representing the hypothetical focalization of one character by another: "Lois began: 'There was a young woman called Marya. *Who thought,* "But I must have a *caree—er*"'" (88; emphasis added). There we have an answer. But it is a passive-aggressive, even sadomasochistic, response; it pretends to speak for Marya only to humiliate her. Notably, the answer is belated, elliptical, and easy to miss. The point, however, is that such a fundamental question seems to need answering at all. While this scene provides ample fodder for the (sado-)masochistic reading, the importance of the name of the protagonist suggests something more fundamental is at stake. And that is the aesthetic principle that "the shadow can be more important than the substance." Marya is forever a somewhat unpronounceable ("unutterable"?) character: a shadow, if you will. And no analysis can get beyond this fact, even if the illusion of an answer—Lois's miming Marya's voice, rhyming Marya's name—shows that (sado-) masochism, as well as complex modes of focalization, inform its intersubjective dynamics. Even without diagnostic certainty, we can certainly feel the novel's mood.

Conclusion: Immanent Reading, Immanent Writing

The example of Rhys's *Quartet* indicates, at the level of narrative form as well as thematic concerns, that to tell a story about underdogs, one needs to think like an underdog. As an aesthetic principle, immanent reading responds to what could be called *immanent writing*. Rhys's first published novel adopts this general principle of narrative representation as a way through the maze of intersubjective conflict and its warping of social reality according to self-interest. *Quartet*'s narrative discourse, consistent with general understandings of the modern novel as focused on exploration of interiority, exploits character-based focalization in order to highlight these thematic ends: the modal nature of reality, when seen from "below," and how this noninstitutionally supported perspective is relatively undervalued in social milieus devoted to the pseudoclinical labeling of those who don't fit in: "the Freaks who never would do anything, the Freaks who just possibly might." When Lois uses this example of nonce taxonomy—"Freaks"—she is rhetorically slumming with the true bohemians among whom the Heidlers desperately want to belong. And Marya's labeling of Lois Heidler as "of the species wife" is endowed with the reverse-snobbery of a true bohemian like Marya herself, married in name only to a man she barely knew.

What separates these labels—or their deployment—from each other? If this chapter's argument is sound, then Lois, too, employs a nonce taxonomy ("Freaks"), and Marya, too, adopts the language of power epistemologies in order to attack Lois, cleverly conflating scientistic and normative labels ("species wife"). The difference is not so much rhetorical as it is institutional. Lois's use of "Freaks" encodes a social scene under her appraising glare—not all the Freaks will "do anything"—and she does so while "talking volubly," whereas Marya's "species wife" epithet against Lois occurs in her own mind, and in the reader's, as a moment of focalization. And not just focalization, but hypothetical focalization—which, as I have argued, serves to destabilize the certainty of social reality by turbo-charging the partiality of individual point of view with the added fuel of emotion, wish, and volition: the conditional mood. It is telling that Lois's "Freaks who just possibly might" moment is itself cast in this conditional, shadowy light: these Freaks aren't all going to make it, and not even Lois knows which of them it will be. But for the Lois and Hugh Heidlers of the world, such moments are rare. The majority of their interactions and social labeling carry the weight of fact—debatable facts, for sure, but socially ratified as "*well-read opinions* about every subject under the sun." Lois, for one, "was so perfectly sure of all she said *that it would have been* a waste of time to contradict her," Marya says (60; emphasis added).

Note, again, the seeming ubiquity of the conditional mood. Rhys's novel spends much time on what *might* happen, what someone *would* be thinking, what *could* be the case. To explore the case of the underdog, in modernist narrative form, entails in part creating the social reality or mood of being an underdog through the use of nonindicative moods. What is an underdog if not someone whose view of reality is reliably *not* ratified by the rest? The use of the underdog—or, to borrow Rhys's own idiom, "doormat in a world of boots"—is telling, as it divulges the importance of societal power in the discourse of the modernist misfit. Rhys is special partly through her exploration of various states of being not only a misfit due to cultural intersectionality—above all gender, nationality, and class—but being treated as an underdog, or seeing oneself as an underdog, besides. Rhys's stating the case of the underdog, in *Quartet*, happens not simply through the "top-dog" antagonism of Lois and Hugh Heidler but, more importantly, through the very narrative infrastructure of the novel. Its deployment of focalization within third-person narration is the key to understanding the theme of intersubjectivity, and of the third-rail political dimension of the intersubjectivity between "top dogs" and "underdogs" in "this three-cornered fight."

My immanent reading of *Quartet*, as with the Thurman chapter, indicates how misfit modernism is defined partially through immanent writing: recapitulating the thematic in formal terms. Such an aesthetic procedure is perhaps the only thing all modernisms have in common. But in misfit modernist novels, there is formalization of themes of nonbelonging, even as the narrative story centers on a specific trope of the cultural outsider who is doubly displaced. Like Marya, Rhys's other protagonists have no home to speak of and find no succor from majority culture, despite the "Good Samaritans" who come to their aid. Instead, these underdogs—or "doormats"—find themselves in a "world of boots," a singularly pessimistic vision of social reality. The underdog's vision—her point of view—is warranted by that underdog's culturally marginal, intersecting identities.

5.

Isherwood's Impersonality

"Nonconformist" Queer Relationality in *A Single Man*

Isherwood suffered reputational damage for his metaphysical interests,
and was deemed an unfulfilled talent.

—Murray, "Coleridge, Isherwood, and Hindu Light"

Introduction: "Too Much Fiction and Too Little Frankness"

Christopher Isherwood's early sixties novel *A Single Man* portrays an ordinary gay man as an ordinary human being.[1] For its time, the novel's depiction of homosexuality as a legitimate social identity, rather than individual pathology, was a radical political gesture. Given this context, literary critics—particularly self-identified gay critics, who have always been Isherwood's most passionate readers within the academy—see the novel as anticipating gay liberation. One of these critics, Claude Summers, declares, "The minority consciousness of homosexuals and their oppression are crucial themes of *A Single Man*."[2]

Summers adds, however, that these issues are "balanced and qualified" by Isherwood's "transcendent religious vision," invoking Isherwood's forty-year faith in Vedanta Hinduism and a devotion to its principles of ascetic spirituality.[3] Indeed, the key concepts at work in this chapter—asceticism, impersonal detachment, and divestment of the ego—are reminiscent of the spiritual system and ritual tradition of Vedanta. Isherwood was a faithful disciple of Vedanta. He studied under Swami Prabhavananda and even intended to become a Hindu monk (while he lived in California during and after the Second World War) in the Pasadena-based Vedanta Society of Southern California, which was part of the Ramakrishna Order in India. Isherwood was introduced to Hinduism by another British expatriate, noted intellectual and spiritualist Gerald Heard (and close associate of Isherwood's friend Aldous Huxley). Notably, this Westernized vision of Vedanta promulgated the insignificance of the self and the equivalence of all living things. Isherwood describes Heard's and Prabhavananda's influence on him—as usual, referring to himself in the third person, which is a signature of his impersonal narrative persona—in this fashion: "As the result of his talks with Gerald [Heard] and Gerald's friend and teacher, the Hindu monk Prabhavananda, Christopher found himself able to believe—as a possibility, at least—that an eternal impersonal presence (call it 'the soul' if you like) exists within all creatures and is other than the mutable non-eternal 'person.'"[4] However, in what follows, I frame Isherwood's allegiance to an impersonal ascetic ideal as establishing the precedent for his later dedication to Vedanta ritual and religious practice. Isherwood's penchant for self-distancing ("he" and not "I"; "an eternal impersonal presence") came before Vedanta ever appealed to him; it was, perhaps, the reason Hinduism appealed to Isherwood in the first place.

And, notwithstanding this spiritual dimension—which is part of my reading of Isherwood's novel—Summers's claim that *A Single Man* is a quintessentially gay-liberationist novel is emblematic of the critical commonplace, which underscores the novel's identity politics. *A Single Man* champions an ordinary gay man as synecdoche for a burgeoning gay community, representing the political consciousness of homosexuality as a legitimate minority.

As my argument will demonstrate, however, *A Single Man* endorses an ethos of ascetic queer impersonality, which pervades the majority of the novel's scenes of sociability and attachment. That impersonal asceticism severely qualifies the notion that *A Single Man* celebrates identity politics as the primary strategic weapon of literary-cultural gay activism. More broadly, my argument is that Isherwood's ethos of impersonality is evident in a broader conception of the Isherwood archive, from *The Berlin Stories* to *My Guru and His Disciple*. Of course, *The Berlin Stories* are known for their aesthetic of impersonal detachment—personified in the narrator's famous line, "I am a camera," which begins *Goodbye to Berlin*.[5]

The detached, impersonal narrative ethos of *The Berlin Stories*—easily linked to the contemporaneous German arts movement of the *new objectivity*—also personifies Georg Simmel's sociological figure of the outsider, *the stranger*. Both in real life and in his "autofiction,"[6] Christopher Isherwood was a prototypical *stranger* in Weimar-era Berlin, a figure that Simmel memorably defines as someone who "comes today and *stays* tomorrow."[7] (Isherwood lived in Berlin from 1929 until the rise of the Nazis in 1933. He expatriated to the United States at the start of the Second World War in January 1939.) Simmel theorized the *stranger* as a personified concept that describes individuals who mediate between social worlds given their own position as cultural outsiders to the blood-and-soil community (or *Gemeinschaft*) they live in, but do not belong to, territorially or genealogically. The cosmopolitan stranger personae in the early fiction are the eponymous narrators in *Goodbye to Berlin* ("Christopher Isherwood") and *The Last of Mr. Norris* ("William Bradshaw," Isherwood's middle names), respectively. In both cases, the impersonal and detached observations of Isherwood's reserved English narrator illustrate the insight a stranger has while looking into the maelstrom of political and cultural changes taking place in a foreign society, such as Isherwood with regard to Berlin in the Weimar era. According to Simmel, the stranger can view his social surroundings "objectively" because "he is not bound by roots to the particular constituents and partisan dispositions of the group."[8] Isherwood's allegiance to an aesthetic doctrine of impersonality and ego-divesting ascetic ideal underscores the virtues of the stranger as privileged social observer. But this aesthetic of impersonal objectivity and social detachment goes well beyond Isherwood's *Berlin* writings, as I argue in the remainder of this chapter.

Despite Isherwood's earlier autobiographical fictions being seen as exemplifying an impersonal and detached queer ethos, in the wake of gay liberation, engaged gay critics—and Isherwood himself—recontextualized his career as a gradual coming-out process, culminating with the liberated modernist day-in-the-life novel, *A Single Man*, considered his masterpiece. The "American Isherwood," to borrow James Berg's phrase, became a visible and voluble advocate for gay liberation in the United States. Isherwood's later autobiographical writings depict homosexual themes and scenes openly, which makes the 1930s writings seem quaintly closeted by comparison. At least, this is the dominant critical view of Isherwood's career.

I do not dispute that Isherwood evolved into an outspoken author on behalf of what he himself called the gay male tribe.[9] As other critics can attest, the "tribe" concept is key to Isherwood's worldview of homosexuality as an oppressed cultural identity or "minority," on par with socioeconomic class, since his earliest days in Berlin. The difference between "tribe" and "kind," however, is subtle: "kind" entails a solidarity with other minority groups, as my reading of *A Single Man* makes clear. Thus even in *Christopher and His Kind*, usually taken to be his gay manifesto, Isherwood argues for cross-identitarian (or minoritarian) solidarity.[10]

Decades after the fact—well after Stonewall, in fact[11]—Isherwood's rememorializing of the 1930s, in *Christopher and His Kind* (1976), recapitulates the Berlin years not in *autofictional* but in *nonfictional* autobiographical form. And for once Isherwood holds tight to that distinction. Isherwood's expressed agenda in this memoir is disclosing what he had veiled before. Isherwood, along with his gay critics, viewed his prewar writings as exercises in detachment motivated primarily by the desire to stay closeted, to self-censor. Cue the famous answer to the question of why his narrative alter ego does not avow his homosexuality in *Goodbye to Berlin*: because it would draw too much attention to him at the expense of the story itself, a story in which the homosexuality is displaced onto another Englishman, a double for "Christopher," who has an affair with Otto Nowak. In *Christopher and His Kind*, Isherwood also lays into his 1920s memoir, *Lions and Shadows*, for being "*not truly* autobiographical," as "the author conceals important facts about himself."[12] This serves as a summary judgment, considering that *Christopher and His Kind* is dedicated to divulging the secrets of the Berlin years, starting with why Isherwood went to Berlin to begin with. He adds, "when *Lions and Shadows* suggests [what] Christopher's chief motive for going to Berlin was . . . it is avoiding the truth."[13] And the truth was that "Christopher was then unwilling to discuss [the] sexual significance" of his move to Berlin—namely, and now famously, that "Berlin meant Boys."[14] Isherwood thus critiques his prewar autofiction as "too much fiction and too little frankness."[15] *Christopher and His Kind* is a post-Stonewall memoir framed as the account of Isherwood's sexual emancipation: in 1976, Isherwood seemed dedicated to the "frankness" of autobiography and the politics of visibility of gay liberation, at the expense of the autonomy of his fictional lives.

But the standard readings of Isherwood fall victim to the notion, critiqued by Michel Foucault, that the truth of the self is a sexual truth—a tendency still rampant in accounts of the 1960s, an era defined in hindsight by the cultural logic of gay liberation and the sexual revolution. Perhaps coincidentally, the original French edition of *The History of Sexuality* and *Christopher and His Kind* were published the same year, occupying seemingly opposite poles in the cultural politics of gay liberation. Foucault's is a demystification of the abiding truth-claims of sexual (including homosexual) cultural politics, whereas Isherwood's is a qualified deployment of this very logic of identity.

I take *Christopher and His Kind* to be a qualified deployment of the visibility discourse of gay liberation because, given Isherwood's artistic investment in impersonality as a queer modernist aesthetic doctrine, his use of memoir in the latter stages of his career is in tension with this doctrine.[16] So even as *Christopher and His Kind* is dedicated to divulging the sexual secrets of the Berlin years in an ideological deployment of Isherwood's gay politics, Isherwood's queer sensibility of detachment and impersonality ("he," not "I") is legible in this memoir as well, though less so than in ego-diminishing autofictions such as *The Berlin Stories* and, as I argue, *A Single Man.* Isherwood subscribed to a distinction between the aesthetic orders of fiction and nonfiction, legible in the first clause of his curt dismissal of *Lions and Shadows* ("*too much fiction* and too little frankness"). Even so, *Christopher and His Kind* maintains formal if not political allegiance to Isherwood's aesthetic doctrine of impersonality, a queer modernist principle that is a permanent feature of his oeuvre. In *Christopher and His Kind*, for instance, Isherwood's reliance on the third-person "Christopher" (or even "Isherwood") when speaking of his past selves *grammatically* insists on the impersonal distance between authorial persona and its past instantiations. You could say that in *Christopher and His Kind*, Isherwood mobilizes impersonal form on behalf of the politics of identity, his "frankness" operating as an ideological stance missing in earlier, "too fictional" memoirs (and autofictions), which eschew the burden of directly representing a burgeoning gay consciousness in the first person.

Given this introduction, the argument that follows revises the dominant narrative of Isherwood's career and his queer modernist masterpiece. Rather than read *A Single Man* as laying the groundwork for his sixties autobiographical writings, which embrace the cause of gay self-representation as a legitimate minority, I argue for Isherwood's sustained modernist aesthetic commitment to an ascetic ideal of impersonality, a *queer* ideal in a non-self-possessive, nonidentitarian sense.[17]

It is the representational function of the novel that engaged critics cite as *A Single Man*'s significance as a liberated gay text, insofar as it represents the individual experience of a homosexual as a politically dignified experience of alienation and marginalization, rather than of individual pathology, as homosexuality was normatively considered at the time. (Homosexuality was famously depathologized in 1973 by the American Psychiatric Association when the board of directors decided to remove it from the *Diagnostic and Statistical Manual of Mental Disorders* [DSM].)[18] Isherwood's novella is rightfully at the vanguard of anti-homophobic politics, but the political subjectivity and ethics of relationality Isherwood develops in *A Single Man* are more complex, as my argument demonstrates.

The novel normalizes an ascetic impersonal ideal, an ideal of divesting from the ego, or the idea of self-possessed personhood, in terms that implicitly question the foundations of self-representation—as personal or as collective, identity-based interests. With the aid of the anti-identitarian theoretical frameworks of Leo Bersani and Lauren Berlant, I read *A Single Man* as projecting an impersonal queer ethos. For my purposes, Bersani encapsulates this mode of queer impersonality as the "ascesis of an ego-divesting discipline."[19] Impersonal asceticism involves the urge to suspend or violate the self's personal integrity, to transcend the self, even evacuate personality, through means such as ritual. Such rituals can be as simple as performative displays of self-abnegation, as we will see in *A Single Man*, which stages scenes that serve the protagonist's desire for negative self-transcendence in the service of an impersonal ascetic ideal.

My main contention is that *A Single Man* champions an impersonal queer ascesis, narratively staged in scenes depicting George, the protagonist, engaged in self-abnegating gestures. Thus the novel represents Isherwood's impersonal ascetic ideal and queer ethics of relationality. One form of ascetic escape from the self is disidentification from cultural (or subcultural) identity. Another register of queer impersonality is the escape from the personal, as opposed to the cultural, self. The boundary between the two, of course, is not at all clear: the personal and the political bleed into each other, especially in a novel that foregrounds the importance of being a "minority" and largely set in a college classroom in the multiethnic milieu of Cold War Los Angeles.

My argument isolates four main thematic representations of ascetic self-divestiture and queer impersonality in the novel, which also tend to bleed into one another: (1) what I am calling *detached attachment* to others, often mediated by negative affects, such as envy or hate; (2) performativity and role-playing; (3) political disidentification from one's prescribed social identity; and, most worryingly, (4) self-inflicted injury. Ultimately, the significance of *A Single Man*'s valorization of ascetic self-divestiture and queer impersonality, in scenes that divest the ego of significance, lies in transcending the normative claims of the personal and the political. Such a queer impersonal aesthetic is ideologically inconsistent with the post-Stonewall aura of gay visibility in *Christopher and His Kind*.

In this sense, Isherwood's modernist novel is more queer than gay. George may represent a single gay man, but the novel's ascetic ideal and ethos of queer impersonality argues against reading the narrative as an aesthetic instrument for gay representation. The impersonal ascetic ideal argues against possessive investment in essentialized political identity. Indeed, I argue that the ascetic impersonality in *A Single Man* is in direct tension with the novel's representation of gay identity as a legitimate minoritarian consciousness.

By contrast, *A Single Man* articulates a *misfit* vision of cross-cultural as well as intersubjective solidarity: the novel calls George and others of his kind "nonconformists." This vision clearly departs from the novel's farcical presentation of George's rage as a grotesquely violent passion keyed in his consciousness as a gay "minority-sister," in the novel's famous formulation. The novel instead stages departures from the liberal principles of possessive personhood, as well as token versions of tolerance and equality, in favor of a queer modernist ethos of ascetic impersonality. At the same time, the diction of "minority-sister" in the classroom scene is in tension with this queer impersonal and ascetic ideal.

I am using the term "queer" in the strategically nonspecific sense of forms of being and belonging that are opposed to all regimes of normativity, as articulated by Michael Warner in the introduction to *Fear of a Queer Planet*.[20] Warner writes against the "dominant concept" of "gay and lesbian community" as "a notion generated in the tactics of Anglo-American identity politics and its liberal-national environment": "in the liberal-pluralist frame [the notion of lesbian and gay community] predisposes that political demands will be treated as demands for the toleration and representation of a minority constituency," Warner argues.[21] Isherwood's novella resists this reduction of the political model of sexual dissidence to a community model of discrete identities under a liberal umbrella. Indeed, *A Single Man* criticizes what it calls the "pseudoliberal sentimentality" of "tolerance," a value of the liberal sensibility that the novel considers a tacit form of annihilation through social ghettoization.

Isherwood's relationship to queer history is a vexed one. *Pace* his own increasingly vocal advocacy in the sixties, it would behoove us to analyze the fiction to glean Isherwood's concerted stance toward the aesthetic politics of gay liberation. Here, generic distinctions are decisive. Isherwood's derogation of *Lions and Shadows* as "too much fiction and too little frankness" lays bare his queer modernist aesthetic. Isherwood's *fiction* adheres to an aesthetic doctrine defined by an ethos of queer impersonality and a self-dissolving ascetic ideal. This literary aesthetic exemplifies the cultural trope of the modernist misfit, even in the face of a paradigm shift in cultural politics with gay liberation. In an important sense, Isherwood's late-career turn to *nonfiction* memoir is explained by his modernist doctrine of fictional representation. Art could never function for Isherwood as mere propaganda, which is why he revisits Berlin not in fictional *Stories*, but in factual autobiography, in order to better effect a turn toward identity politics that his modernist approach to fictional representation did not allow. By his own admission, *Lions and Shadows* fails the test of "frankness" of nonfictional autobiography that Isherwood's later memoirs take up. Isherwood's novels follow this logic of generic distinction, which distances fiction from the claims of real-life factuality or frankness, which Isherwood maintains was properly the province of nonfictional autobiography.

I use the term "nonfictional autobiography" to stress the generic ambiguity of texts like *Lions and Shadows*. As Isherwood reminds us in a "Note to the reader," that memoir "is not, in the ordinary journalistic sense of the word, an autobiography . . . it is not even entirely 'true.'"[22] Thus Isherwood presents *Lions and Shadows* as a curious mixture of fiction and autobiography, a fictionalized, if not wholly fictional, autobiography, in contrast to the scrupulous "journalistic" adherence to facts—especially regarding his sexuality—that characterizes his later *Christopher and His Kind*. The latter thus stands as a political correction of the former. However, even in the mode of memoir, Isherwood formally maintains an impersonal remainder not subsumed under the aegis of pure political advocacy. His reliance on third-person narration even in the mode of political autobiography signals his continued skepticism toward the entailments of identity even as he paradoxically mobilized impersonal form to advance a liberationist agenda.

The next section develops Bersani's ideal of ascetic impersonality and Berlant's notion of lateral agency to establish a theoretical framework for my reading of *A Single Man*'s *misfit* (or "nonconformist," in the novel's parlance) modernist aesthetic of ascetic self-divestiture and queer detachment. Then, I consider important moments from the novel that stage this ideal and practice. In the conclusion, I return to the issue of Isherwood's political investments in gay representation and "minority-sister" consciousness, arguing that the theme of ascetic impersonality in *A Single Man* helps us reconceive Isherwood's oeuvre as developing an aesthetic politics of principled detachment from personal and collective projects.

Ultimately, I am arguing for a broader recuperation of Isherwood's pre-Stonewall queer poetics and politics, including the use of the impersonal *Berlin* narrator, denigrated as "sexless" by Edmund White, among others.[23] Rather than read Isherwood's long career as divided thematically by the event of Stonewall, as many critics do, I maintain that his modernist aesthetic practice values impersonality and ascetic self-divestiture, and that his literary positioning does not ultimately conform to the claims of identity politics in the Stonewall narrative of modern gay liberation. His outspoken advocacy as an author on behalf of gay rights must not overshadow his literary valorization of ascetic impersonality and nonconformist queer consciousness. *A Single Man* projects a political spirituality divested of possessive personhood and what poet Reginald Shepherd calls the prescriptive and restrictive burdens of minority identity.[24]

As I do, Joseph Bristow argues that *A Single Man* does not anticipate gay liberation, but rather is continuous with Isherwood's earlier novels, which in many critics' eyes "tactful[ly] silenc[ed] his [narrators'] gayness."[25] I agree with

Bristow that the novel "extends Isherwood's sustained interest in representing homosexuality in some of his earlier novels."[26] Yet Bristow's larger argument regards Isherwood's writings as primarily "backward-looking," which sidesteps Isherwood's evolution as a politically aware writer constantly adapting to his time and place—the world war in continental Europe (as well as the Pacific), the Cold War in the United States.[27] It is just that Isherwood resisted the normative claims of politics, especially if these stigmatized homosexuality—but especially, as I argue, *if these claims threatened to usurp the relative autonomy of liter-ary practice.* Not simply a key member of the Auden generation, Isherwood also saw himself as card-carrying member of the modernist "cult of the Artist," predicated on precepts such as aesthetic autonomy and impersonality or detach-ment.[28] For another example, see Isherwood's "Unused Chapter" to *Christopher and His Kind*, in which he writes maxims such as "the artist stands alone," and in which he credits his mentor Edward Upward, who "had read Baudelaire to Christopher and who had initiated him into the cult of the Artist."[29]

Indeed, I think Isherwood protected his fiction from devolving into "political propaganda," to borrow the vocabulary of the modernist era, to which Isherwood, despite surviving into the 1980s, belonged. Throughout his career, Isherwood sustained an identification with the modernist ideal of the autonomy of art. This modernist ideal, I argue, explains his Sixties turn away from literary fiction to nonfiction autobiography: his embrace of gay liberation entailed a different genre of writing practice. So his fictional works remain ambivalent about the claims of homosexuality as a political identity.

My argument reintegrates the twentieth-century-spanning Isherwood archive, finding continuities in his writing before and after Stonewall, whereas most critics find a break with the prewar writings.[30] It is only if we measure Isherwood according to the dictates of our own contemporary frame of Stonewall that the majority of his prewar writings seem closeted by comparison. I think we should celebrate the *Berlin Stories* and Isherwood's ego-attenuating and impersonal queerness, an ethos of the modernist misfits—or "nonconform-ists"—represented in early and later novels alike.

"Ascetic Self-Divestiture" and "Lateral Agency"

Bersani and Phillips's *Intimacies* names a form of queer impersonality predi-cated on self-attenuation that I find articulated in *A Single Man*.[31] They locate the cultural practice of ascetic self-divestiture in a particular form of seven-teenth-century mysticism, a form of radical submission to an impersonal divine being that invades and annihilates the self. Isherwood's novel exemplifies this form of self-annihilating impersonality. While George masturbates in the penultimate scene of the novel—before his presumable death—the remainder of the narrative is oddly chaste. (There are scenes of George's erotic appreciation for male bodies, however.) Isherwood's ascetic ideal is thus evident in the novel's subtle treatment of erotic desire. This ascetic ideal arguably explains the narrative's sublimation of sexual desires and elevation of nonsexual desires for detached or impersonal attachment.

In a sense, the opposite of self-divestiture that Bersani and Phillips—and, I argue, Isherwood—represent is the conventional conception of identity. In the same chapter in which they elaborate the impersonal ascetic ideal, Bersani and Phillips recapitulate Bersani's well-known notion of queerness as a mode of self-shattering in relation to sexual *jouissance*, as Bersani famously formulates it in "Is the Rectum a Grave?" *Intimacies* touches on the "at once violently aggressive and self-shattering ego-hyperbolizing of racial, national, ethnic, and gendered identities."[32] This phrase implies that social identity is consolidated at the expense of openness to the other.[33] By contrast, Bersani and Phillips analyze the mystics' surrender to an inhuman anonymous other, to whom one grants affective, cognitive, and perhaps sexual access, to the point of self-erasure. The "pure love" mystics in *Intimacies* exemplify the self-shattering embrace of alterity.[34] These ascetics represent the opposite of autonomous liberal personhood or what Lauren Berlant terms sovereign subjectivity in her essay "Slow Death."[35]

Berlant's notion of *lateral* agency is helpful here. Berlant's lateral agent shrinks from the sovereign mode of subjectivity. The latter is linked to the self-obsessed power wielded by an "ego-hyperbolizing" subject. Berlant cites as an ordinary example of sovereign subjectivity the impulse to go to the gym. The subject's investment in futurity and development—bettering one's physical form by regular exercise—is an effective strategy or a strategy of being effective. This example illustrates what psychologist Roy Baumeister considers high-level self-awareness—of oneself as the agent of bildung, the teleological, or theological, self.[36] Sovereign personhood, and its extension as sovereign agency, is anathema to self-divesting subjects, among which I count *A Single Man's* idealizing of social "nonconformists." They remain at the margins of scenes of collective triumph, even minoritarian collectives. According to Berlant, lateral self-management occurs when people stop trying to build personal monuments to themselves. In these moments of lateral, as opposed to vertical, self-extension, the subject thinks in terms of inertia, impasse, and immediate if ephemeral satisfaction. In some ways, "thinking" is the wrong term for these self-suspending scenes of inhabiting oneself without building one's life as a narrative of development. Sovereign subjects negotiate what Baumeister calls the "burden of selfhood."[37] The ascetic subject spreads himself laterally to escape this burden, in what Berlant calls "small vacations from the will."[38]

Berlant's concept of the lateral agent seems, on the surface, to have little to do with what counts as agency proper. Socially symbolic forms of action—such as wearing shoes that match and other ordinary practices of self-management—represent a burden that individuals sometimes put aside. Certain individuals adopt lateral moves rather than vertical trajectories of self-extension, remaining stuck. Her social phenomenology seeks to articulate the many ways in which individuals are engaged in nonsovereign forms of being themselves, of being ordinary, of lacking "effective" agency, thereby evincing "desires not to be an inflated ego deploying and manifesting power."[39]

Bersani and Berlant share the sense that certain modes of living entail an alternative aesthetics of existence.[40] My interest in this critical framework is how it illuminates minoritarian negotiations with the double burden of normative personhood and minoritarian uplift. In ordinary habits of impersonal self-suspension, these lateral investments represent a queer way of being in the world. Rather than centering oneself on personal interest, the lateral agent, or Bersani's impersonal ascetic, looks to self-divestiture as a means of acceding to otherness—including the otherness within—and inhabiting the world in a nonconformist or queer ethical relation. The forms of political possibility that such anti-imperial self-elaboration allows is a key question for me and for Bersani and Berlant, who valorize queerness not as an identity free from the constraints of power, but as an impersonal mode of relationality that dissipates rather than consolidates authority over others and the self.

As my reading of *A Single Man* illustrates, Isherwood's aesthetic is devoted to such an impersonal ascetic ideal and queer ethos, without reducing queerness to sexual identity. The novel dramatizes and epitomizes the "nonconformist"—or misfit—point of view, in scenes of impersonal negotiation and self-abnegation. These scenes suggest that *A Single Man* should not be filtered through a retrofitted lens of gay liberation, at least not primarily. Rather, the novel explores queer impersonality through the suspension of personality and political identity in decidedly unheroic ways.

"I Am with You, Little Minority-Sister": Pedagogy of the Oppressed

The novel's central instance representing homosexuality as a legitimate, shared minoritarian identity—being "minority-sister[s]"—occurs during George's turn at the podium in the lecture hall, when he discusses Aldous Huxley's *After Many a Summer Dies the Swan* (1939). The classroom scene turns on George's impassioned critique of "pseudoliberal sentimentality" (71). More specifically, the discussion is sparked by a question raised by Huxley's novel. A student asks whether Huxley was an anti-Semite for declaring the stupidity of the biblical text, "they hated me without cause" (69). This is a central theme in the novel: multiculturalism in Los Angeles and the relationship between minorities and the US liberal state during the Cold War. Isherwood's novella identifies the hegemony of liberal thought with George's neighbors, Mr. and Mrs. Strunk, who function as the personification of this "blandly annihilating" US liberal majority: "Mrs. Strunk . . . is trained in the new tolerance, the technique of annihilation by blandness" (27). The Strunks represent liberal tolerance toward minorities, a political category that in Isherwood's novel clearly includes homosexuals. Such tolerance, however, as we will see from George's lecture, is a form of domesticating the strangeness—or otherness—that minoritarian subjects represent. So, while integration into the polity is a chief political goal, such integration carries its risks.

Now, Isherwood knew this as a lifelong thinker regarding the challenges that cultural identity posed to large-scale political systems such as democratic liberalism in Britain and the Communisms and fascisms of an earlier era. For example, in the "Unused Chapter" of *Christopher and His Kind*, writing in the 1930s, Isherwood termed British society and its liberal governance a "British heterosexual dictatorship."[41] In the same section, Isherwood scorns the "so-called democracies" of the West, whom he saw in the 1930s as no better than the totalitarian states of Germany and Russian Soviets. He writes, "Only the anarchists of Spain would seem to have affirmed the homosexual's right to live."[42]

The classroom scene foregrounds some of Isherwood's pessimism about politics in general, as well as George's perspective about political struggle. Some of the insights turn on the darkness that oppression visits upon the oppressed. Another insight is that micropolitical or situational dialogues are never between, say, absolutely privileged and absolutely disenfranchised subjects. Rather, Isherwood's narrative presents, in principle, the social contingency and relativity of power—its reversibility, in a sense—thus echoing Foucault's notion of reverse discourse over ten years before Foucault's notion of reverse discourse as a resource for the oppressed, in volume one of *The History of Sexuality*, appeared.

Indeed, one aspect of the argument this chapter is making about Isherwood's seriousness as a political thinker is his problematizing of the stale binaries of liberation and oppression, which Foucault similarly did. Except Isherwood came to these insights a decade before, if not more, the celebrated French philosopher. This is one reason Isherwood's entire oeuvre deserves reexamination in terms that recognize his considerable insights as an analyst of social power and histories of the oppressed—beyond members of his "tribe"—which is one aim of this monograph as a whole: how to think through a focus on "nonconformists" (Isherwood), "total misfits" ("Thurman"), the "inferior being" of "underdogs" (Rhys), or "unconformity" in general (Larsen). These modernist novelists saw in the figure of the misfit an allegory for social oppression, particularly intersectional oppressions, lacking the sophisticated theoretical terminology that we do today. Thanks to Kimberlé Crenshaw and others, we can theorize the intersections of systemic subordination, but *misfit modernists* like Isherwood sought to think through similar questions in literary-narrative form in the earlier decades of the twentieth century.[43]

Particularly in this scene, the novel notes how power and resistance operate on a sliding scale and vary by context. A privileged British accent helps George deal with a world from which he feels excluded, for instance. The novel shows how relatively privileged and less privileged individuals make use of, or even exploit, the sociocultural assets at their disposal. Hence, *A Single Man's* treatment of the relative nature of class and other institutionalized forms of privilege rejects liberal pressure to ignore social differences in the name of equality. Since the novel implies that paying lip service to equality is a way of avoiding the reality of oppression and resistance, George argues against this facile solution: "Minorities are people—people, not angels. Sure, they're like us—but not exactly like us. . . . It's better if we admit to disliking and hating them than if we try to smear our feelings over with pseudo-liberal sentimentality. If we're frank about our feelings, we have a safety valve; and if we have a safety valve, we're actually less likely to start persecuting" (71).

The heart of the scene rests in disputing the liberal notion that majorities persecute the other without cause and, relatedly, that minoritarian subjects are paragons of virtue ("angels"), innocent of all hate. By contrast, George lectures his students that there is always a cause for hate. He asserts that the cause for hate is the majority's perception of the other as a threat, even if this hate is imaginary and without merit, regardless of what liberal sentimentality says (70). George describes a world where hate begets hate and aggression begets aggression—no matter how imaginary the causes for the hatred of the other, the hatred exists, and those so disenfranchised by power react in kind with their "own kind of aggression": "A minority has its own kind of aggression. It absolutely dares the majority to attack it. It hates the majority—not without a cause, I grant you. It even hates the other minorities, because all minorities are in competition: each one proclaims that its sufferings are the worst and its wrongs the blackest. And the more they all hate, and the more they're all persecuted, the nastier they become!" (72). This notion resonates as justification for George's own hate of the "Mr. Strunks of the world" and, by synecdoche, of heteronormative society. The novel spends a great deal of time—especially in the driving scene that shortly precedes George's classroom tirade—describing George's rage and detailing his murderous fantasies as "Uncle George," in which he effects a large-scale campaign of terror on the civilized world.

Putting aside the politically untenable posture that George assumes in this rant,[44] his tirade represents a powerful *yet silent* advocacy for including homosexuals as a protected class; he mentally, thus provisionally, claims the shared identity he sees in his gay student, his "minority-sister." George's lecture articulates the political desire to end the persecution of others by allowing democratic subjects to speak the "unspeakable," which is George's term for negative affects repressed by the norms of "pseudoliberal sentimentality." Such a belief in speaking truth to power—confess your sins and you shall be free—follows a 1960s cultural logic against repression. This logic, in the form of the so-called repressive hypothesis, was Foucault's principal target in the first volume of *The History of Sexuality*. Unenlightened by this Foucauldian critique, George expounds the cultural belief that releasing one's social prejudices and blind spots creates, in his terms, a social "safety valve" that dissipates the hate and aggression that we all share. More importantly, George argues that voicing prevailing negative attitudes toward the other prevents the eventual return of the majority's aggression in the political form of persecution ("if we have a safety valve, we're actually less likely to start persecuting"). This line of thinking is a utopian wish for political rapprochement across classes of social and political division following from agonistic democratic dialogue.

And this radical principle of *liberatory de-repression*, in Marcuse's terms in *Eros and Civilization*, is what Foucault attacks as misguided. George imparts this notion of liberation through unfettered personal expression to his students, culminating in a wish-fulfillment fantasy. Expounding on the distinctions that divide the social body—what we would call the nature of identity and difference—George voices the dated and facile example of the difference between "a Negro and a Swede" (71). At once, he regrets his choice. The narrator records George asking himself in interior monologue, "Why, oh why daren't George say 'between Estelle Oxford and Buddy Sorensen'?" (71). (Estelle and Buddy are two of his students, then present in the classroom.) George wonders whether "if he did dare" to use student names, instead of using impersonal identity categories, "there would be a great atomic blast of laughter, and everybody would embrace, and the kingdom of heaven would begin, right here in classroom 278. But then again, maybe it wouldn't" (71). Here we see how George's diatribe against liberal repression of cultural difference expresses a utopian wish for transcending these differences, which divide his students and the social body as a whole.

But George is not so un-Foucauldian as it might appear. He also deflates such a wistful fantasy, admitting how far-fetched such an outcome would be. Despite his utopian motivation, in other words, George does not believe entirely in the efficacy of his own fantasy of liberation, of transcending hierarchical social differences through democratic dialogue and free expression. Rather, George's utopianism is balanced by his sardonic anti-sentimentality, his refusal to romanticize the oppressed, or even oppression. Such a position runs the risk of political relativism ("all minorities are in competition: each one proclaims that its sufferings are the worst"). But George seeks to shock his students out of their complacency—their own pseudoliberal biases—and thus allows himself the role of gadfly. He takes up the modernist injunction to *épater le bourgeois*, typical of a character drawn from another era—the era that Huxley and Isherwood knew firsthand. George's students believe in the fantasy of liberation through the absence of discourse, the refusal to accept the darker emotions and motives of even benighted groups.

His "frankness" in admitting negative emotions, especially that of aggression ("every minority has its own aggression"), reflects George's own aggressive impulses, as noted in his murderous fantasies. *A Single Man* thus represents the aggression of a minoritarian subject, such as George's "murderous rage," even prior to the recognition of the political legitimacy of this rage: the radicalized homosexual, before the moment of Stonewall and modern gay liberation, itself a violent uprising against political repression. It is in this sense that Isherwood's novel functions as cultural weapon against American society's oppression of homosexuals, especially during the Cold War. Dignifying the political anger of George's murderous "Uncle George" fantasies, as we see below, the classroom lecture is a pedagogy of the oppressed to the complacent majority, a counterpoint to the queer ethics of ascetic impersonality that the novel represents.

Given this scene, therefore, it is curious how the rest of the novel champions a self-effacing mode of minoritarian subjectivity, a misfit or nonconformist style of being, distinguished by ascetic self-suspension and impersonal intersubjectivity. Rather than celebrating the minoritarian subject's clamoring for representation and recognition, the novel usually clamors to show an alternative poetics and politics. This alternative queer model has been illegible to Isherwood's critics as a form of agency, a mode of political subjectivity. Yet the classroom scene prepares us for the "aggression of the minority," and I argue that these scenes demonstrate just what such aggression, and other negative affects, might signify in a narrative economy that privileges the impersonal ethos of a self-diminishing minoritarian subject.

Rather than assuming the sovereign mode of subjectivity that George personifies in the classroom scene, he more frequently acts as a self-effacing protagonist, engaging figures to whom he is attached impersonally—his student Kenny, or Doris, his deceased partner's former lover. This alternative ethics of living in self-suspension, in modes counter to aggression and hate and other affects of political extension, informs Isherwood's queer impersonal sensibility. This sensibility is pre-Stonewall, and far from the recognizable political modes of sovereign subjectivity. This is what I consider the novel's aesthetic political agenda—its imagining of an alternative or nonconformist mode of minoritarian subjectivity, marked by affects and postures that embrace impersonal detachment and ascetic self-abstention rather than normative filiation and self-interest. *A Single Man* endorses a self-diminishing, impersonal mode of being in double exile, a *silent* gay "minority-sister" who is also, more radically, a "nonconformist"—not fitting in with majority culture but also ambivalent about vocally claiming that homosexual identity (however limited at the time). This is a position far from the triumphs of Stonewall and the retroactive will-to-power of gay liberation.

I now turn to the novel to analyze more systematically key scenes that project an ascetic ideal of impersonality that is oriented to an ethics of queer relationality.

Ascetic Queer Impersonality

The following scenes track *A Single Man*'s development of queer impersonality and ascetic self-divestiture as a practice. The classroom scene, which precedes the others, laid the theoretical groundwork in touching on the inescapable tensions haunting the social field: the inequities of minority and majority. George's lecture articulates the ordinary realities of social difference and political marginalization and gestures toward a way of reconceiving minoritarian subjectivity, thereby engaging with this political reality in an alternative fashion. The lecture scene also employs the persistent theme of social existence as a series of performances, or as performative being—a theme introduced in the very first passage of the novel (10). Isherwood's protagonist argues against what he terms "pseudoliberal sentimentality," and what such an ideology of idealizing minorities entails for the multicultural world of Cold War Los Angeles. In short, George lectures his students regarding the negative affects and the historical intransigence of social conflict based on structural inequality.

George's classroom lecture thus prepares the reader for the following scenes, which put the theory of social marginality into practice. At the intersubjective level, this theme highlights how social position haunts interpersonal relations and thereby depicts ascetic impersonality as an ideal practice of ethical exchange. These depictions illustrate how the personal impinges on the social, how performativity and negative affects provide a model for impersonal attachments, and how to practice impersonal performativity and self-effacement in moments of recognition of social differences.

Yet beyond the interpersonal domain lies the political and cultural significance of the homosexual as victim of heteronormativity, or what George at another moment calls "the American utopia, the kingdom of the good life upon earth" (126). This is a "kingdom" "owned" by his banal neighbors, Mr. and Mrs. Strunk. George bitterly reflects how they "are proud of their kingdom," one that he feels excludes him (126). In consonance with the minoritarian valence of *A Single Man* that critics focus on, the novel thus depicts moments that register George's cultural-political rage. At one point, George entertains a political fantasy of becoming a homicidal "Uncle George" in response to the fact that a "local newspaper editor has started a campaign against sex deviates" (36). George's political rage is directed at this editor, his neighbors, and the heteronormative "three-quarters" of the world (40) that, symbolically, took Jim away from him. Notable for its hyperbolic—following Bersani, "ego-hyperbolizing"— aspect, George's sadistic revenge fantasy (to "launch a campaign of systematic terror," in his words [38]) is directed against individuals who represent the dominant power structures in society, such as a US senator: "His wife may be kidnapped, garroted [*sic*], embalmed and sealed in the living room to await his return from the office. His children's heads may arrive in cartons in the mail" (39). In Bersani's terms, this mode of identity politics is keyed to hyper self-extension. George admits that his rage stems from a belief that "all are, in the last analysis, responsible for Jim's death; their words, their thoughts, their whole way of life willed it, even though they never knew he existed" (40). Such powerful representations of George's "minority consciousness" extend an expansive sense of cultural politics ("their whole way of life") into the personal arena in ways that we can appreciate as militant; these moments allow Isherwood's critics to identify the novel with a straightforward politics of gay liberation.

Yet, in contrast, the novel gives us disciplined abdications of sovereign self-interest. Such an escape registers the queer subject's ambivalence to fighting for a collective cause, ambivalence toward the "Uncle George" register of a sexual minority's pent-up political rage.[45] It is important, therefore, to recognize the impersonal narrator's self-parodying tone as he ventriloquizes the "Uncle George" fantasy. In such a fantasy, the narrator ironically notes, "Jim hardly matters anymore. Jim is nothing now but an excuse for hating three quarters of the population of America" (40). The narrator continues, "What is George's hate, then? A stimulant, nothing more. . . . Rage, resentment" (40). The free indirect style undercuts George's incendiary homosexual "rage [and] resentment." Now the rage is "but an excuse" and this "hate" "nothing more" than a testament to George's "middle age," an impersonal affect mobilized as political passion. The "middle age" qualifier ("nothing more") ironizes George's passionate political identity, undercutting its murderous seriousness (40). (The words "rage" and "resentment" reappear later in the novel, as we see below.)

In this reading, I am more interested in the novel's ordinary moments of escape from self-aggrandizing identitarian political claims and entailments, the latter of which surface in the self-parodying "Uncle George" fantasy. More common than such hyperbolic fantasies that align pink-baiting newspaper editors and lavender-baiting US senators with modern totalitarian regimes such as the Khmer Rouge (36–37, 37), are moments such as George's self-effacing refusal to go to Jim's funeral, despite being invited by the latter's family. Such resistance conveys George's discipline of self-diminution: his queer, antisocial rejection of inclusion in the "sacred family grief," as the novel sarcastically puts it (126). Indeed, George usually chooses the opposite of sovereign self-extension. He refuses the normative response, which would be to defend his self-interest, indeed his self-respect. George also enacts narcissistic self-injury and abdicates the burden of representation that defending the honor of his gay identity would entail. I like this novel because it champions an alternative queer ideal, the position of the modernist misfit in one of its clearest articulations. In the discourse of the novel, the modernist misfit, or "nonconformist," is distinguished by an ethos of self-abnegation, contrary to contemporary social norms that champion collective self-interest and the reification of minoritarian identity.

"Rage Without Resentment, Abuse Without Venom"

At the Starboard Side, the bar that George visits later in the novel and the place where George first set eyes on Jim, he overhears an old couple arguing drunkenly. The narrator calls their exchange "rage without resentment," "abuse without venom" (150). Echoing George's grammar of impersonality and negative affects, the novel here combines self-contradicting concepts. What *is* rage without resentment or abuse without venom, if not a practice of impersonal intimacy? The performative function of these roles is what renders the rage free of resentment, and the abuse devoid of venom. In this scene, the novel continues to depict a paradoxical practice of impersonal attachment—here based on performativity and distancing, entailed in the use of role-play—one that is laced with negative affects and erotic desire. From George's increasingly inebriated, limited point of view, the narrator describes an older couple rehearsing the vibrant impersonal script of their romance as "*two nonconformists* practicing their way of love: a mild quarrelsome alcoholism which makes it possible for them to live in a play-relationship, like children. You old bag, you old prick, you old bitch, you old bastard: *rage without resentment, abuse without venom.* This is how it will be for them till the end. Let's hope they will never be parted, but die in the same hour of the same night, in their beer-stained bed" (149–50; emphasis added).

This perversely romantic description might bring tears to a reader's eyes. But said reader would have to be a misfit themselves, a "nonconformist" "unhypnotized" by the norms of pseudoliberal sentimentality (149). Such liberal social norms eschew negative intensities because they seem "abusive" and "resentful." But these intensities are, instead, performative utterances cementing a "play-relationship" that constitutes a paradoxical practice of love. To the conformist reader who adheres to strictly affirming models of self-sovereignty and reciprocal relationality, especially the romantic kind, there is no such thing as abuse without venom, rage without resentment. For such conformists, allowing self-diminishment, in a scene embracing insult and self-injury, is anathema to the very idea of interpersonal romance. Here, a queer ethics of impersonality triumphs—note the lack of proper names, and the lack of normative forms of expressing love—which paradoxically enables the couple to continue their romance into middle age and beyond.

This scene epitomizes Isherwood's skewering of the "sacrosanct value of selfhood," a fundamental value of liberal society. Yet this is a value, according to Bersani's formulation, that "may account for human beings' extraordinary willingness to kill in order to protect the seriousness of their statements."[46] This couple's performative interaction underscores the novel's investments in minimizing the "sacrosanct value of selfhood," here dramatized in a self-conscious "play-relationship." Indeed, George's murderous revenge fantasy stands in parodic contrast to the impersonal negativity that mediates the couple's interaction. Their rage has no resentment, their abuse no venom. Here, *A Single Man* makes a case for the importance of such perverse affective relations, which value the discomfiture of impersonal intimacy and abdicate the burden of defending the self against real or perceived narcissistic injury. Indeed, this scene perversely delights in a playful, sadomasochistic exchange of insults and equates it with a durable form of intimacy.

As we see below, *A Single Man* stages various such scenes of dynamic resistance to "pseudoliberal sentimentality," or socially normative models of individuals as sacrosanct entities, and to relationships solely based on liberal tolerance, affirmation, and equality. This resistance is based on the novel's argument that such sentimental norms simply hide the truths of a social reality composed of violence, aggression, injustice, and inequality. Moreover, the novel's critique of what it terms pseudoliberal sentimentality is due to its implicit claim that hypocritical disavowal of such reality serves only to perpetuate that very same status quo. To engage with the terms of this status quo is a form of truth telling of an impersonal sort.

As a detached observer, George seems to champion an impersonal model of romance personified by this couple from a bygone era—they belong to the first colonists who founded the picturesque seaside town George lives in. And this model of romance is beyond Freud's pleasure principle, for the scene represents an alternative, drawn from the combination of both erotic and aggressive forces that underlie a marriage as well as other intimate relations. This reality suggests that impersonal intimacy dramatized in a sadomasochistic "play-relationship" can sustain a lifelong marriage, and even allow the spouses to maintain a "child-like" innocence beyond middle age. Even substance abuse ("mild quarrelsome alcoholism," "beer-stained bed") is valorized in this impersonal attachment, this mutual, performative abnegation of personal sanctity. Their bad romance runs counter to a sentimental vision of social hygiene that disavows the possibility of a "beer-stained bed" without alcoholism—eschewing the stigma of addiction—or of lovers projecting rage without resentment, or abuse without venom.

"Because the Dialogue Is by Its Nature Impersonal . . ."

Perhaps the most important scene of impersonal relationality involves Kenny Potter's entry into George's drunken world. This moment dedicates itself quite openly to a celebration of the value of a queer impersonal dynamic sustaining a self-abnegating, detached intimacy. The tenor of George and Kenny's exchange is pining for a bygone era when, in Kenny's words, "you could call your father sir" (159). In the discourse of the novel, such a desire reads as the longing for a formal mode of attachment. George recognizes Kenny's desire for a hierarchical structure between them, given their respective power imbalance and age difference. After Kenny longs to be living in a time "when you could call your father sir," George warns Kenny that he will soon forget this. Kenny submissively agrees, "Well if you say so—okay." George: "Okay, sir." Kenny: "Okay, sir!" Kenny "beams" with "pleasure" (159). Such dialogue entails a mode of relating between impersonal, formally hierarchical categories of social identity, such as, in the case of Kenny and George, Youth versus Age (154). The novel implicitly advocates "nonconformist" social and affective intimacies that such hierarchical relations can afford for both minority and, perhaps, majority subject positions. As with the practice of nonconformist intimacy expressed as rage without resentment, here we have another form of self-dispossession that constitutes libidinal, yet formal, ethical contact.

A *Single Man* suggests that there is a salutary function in an ethos of embracing social polarization in order to achieve impersonal intimacy, a form unavailable to politically overdetermined modes of exchange. George notes that in this type of "symbolic dialogue," "what really matters is not what you talk about, but the being together in this particular relationship" (154). The content of the conversation is not as important as the formal relationship being forged— one that lets interlocutors "talk about anything and change the subject as often as [they] like" (154). Implicit in this line of thinking is the fact that seldom do individuals stratified and polarized by social hierarchies engage in dialogue at all, so beholden are they to individual and collective self-interests, especially vis-à-vis the burdens of sustaining them in the face of the other.

George advocates this queer paradigm of impersonal intimacy achieved through detached attachment, as we see in his observation of the couple, and qualified deindividuation, which enables personal engagement with impersonal otherness. For instance, George insists that the symbolic dialogue only works if both "you and your dialogue-partner [are] somehow opposites" (154). This type of formal interaction is based on depersonalization (Kenny calls him "sir" rather than "George"). Suspending one's individuality thus fosters a queerly impersonal attachment, laced with erotic energy, as this scene makes clear. The novel's psycho-narration builds a defense of George's ascetic ideal of queer impersonality, which, in addition to entailing denial of individuality and self-investment, also entails disinterested attachment to one's social (or "symbolic") identity.

Why do the partners have to be opposites? the novel's narrator asks, in George's drunken interior monologue: "Because you have to be symbolic figures—like, in this case, Youth and Age. Why do you have to be symbolic? Because the dialogue is by its nature impersonal. . . . It doesn't involve either party personally" (155). At this moment in the novel, the doctrine of impersonality is rhetorically reinforced as precisely a doctrine of ascesis, or an aesthetics of existence. George argues that one must rely on an impersonal relationship to one's own symbolic identity in order to dialogue across reciprocal yet polarized lines—here, generational, but also national. Ironically, the purpose is not to identify, but to disidentify: to see across the divide, and not to reify that division, as with normatively minoritarian injunctions of self-advocacy and self-representation. The self is suspended in an "abstract" or impersonal intimacy of polar opposites as dialogic equals—an ethical experiment in impersonal intersubjectivity, in the name of an ascetic ideal of deindividuation. Such lateral ascesis momentarily suspends the burden of selfhood and its possessive political entailments.

Among the queer desires George evinces in his intimacy with Kenny is the desire for impersonal mutuality, in which the self is depersonalized and divested, replaced by the ironic performance of a hierarchical role—as the nostalgia for "sir" makes clear. More importantly, such abstract encounters stage the desire to play with social identity in a drama of power exchange. As we have seen, George resists espousing the "pseudoliberal sentiment" of denying social differences in the name of civic equality. In fact, he perversely urges the opposite, the performative intensification of differences as a nonnormative or queer ethical principle for negotiating a salient interaction. But this identification is nonpossessive and nonadversarial: or, in the novel's parlance, without resentment and without venom. The recognition is an effort to bridge across identitarian divisions, rather than emphasizing them as a political form of self-extension. The scene's sadomasochistic energy lends this queer relation an added frisson, which could be claimed as antithetical to a visibility ethos of gay liberation, as George flirts with his student but they never openly address the erotic undertow of their exchanges.

This queer model of interpersonal discourse, as with the couple engaging in a paradoxical, impersonal intimacy, depends on embracing socially determined identities as a performance, a (role-) play, and not as one's "self." That self is too "personal" to be of use in this meeting of cultural personae. Developing an impersonal ascetic ideal of relationality suggests that playing with power differentials and symbolic identities is one form of potentially transforming one's relation to oneself, as well as to the other, by performing a script as a social actor embedded in a hierarchical social world. This queer ethical alternative contrasts a possessive form of political identification, one the novel satirizes in the genocidal fantasies of "Uncle George." Engaging in such symbolic exchanges allows for impersonal understanding, without the sugar-coating or "bland annihilation" that Mrs. Strunk practices with George (27–29). Her "incurious" tolerance betrays a resistance to engage with George as an Other. But beyond allowing the dialogue to take place, the impersonality of playing a social role self-consciously adds a safeguard. One cannot take personally the enactment of a social role; rather, the responsibility now belongs to society for structuring itself along these differential lines to begin with. One's personal culpability fades as the determinism of social roles comes into sharper focus; abdicating burdensome attachment to one's cultural self pays dividends in demonstrating the entailments of identity formation outside an individual purview.

The novel thus stages George's nonconformist subjectivity in impersonal encounters rich in affective and libidinal intensities. These are very retrograde desires represented here: wanting a more impersonal, more hierarchical, relationship. Yet George reaches a rapprochement across social divides. By so doing, he ensures that the novel refuses to ignore these divisions (as "liberals" would) or to relegate them to the collective level of political rage (with resentment, as in the politics of identity). The novel offers escape from the liberal tenet of sovereign agency and the rhetoric of identity. In what I read as *misfit modernist* poetics and politics, the novel stages scenes of self-attenuation, affective and libidinal negativity, antisocial detachment, and impersonal relationality as paradoxical intimacies.

"Cognizing Darkly": The Spiritual Ascetic Ideal

Having seen the ways in which the novel stages ascetic flights from possessive selfhood and identitarian political attachments, it is ironic how, in the words of Lilly, *A Single Man* is easily considered "one of the very earliest novels to give an emphatically positive face to the gay experience."[47] How "emphatically positive" is Isherwood's novel? While Isherwood's Berlin novels depicted homosexuality at one remove, *A Single Man* is single-mindedly dedicated to its portrayal. As we have seen, this focus on male homosexual experience before the Stonewall riots and the modern gay liberation movement makes Isherwood a standard-bearer for this cause.

A Single Man, however, while refusing to recapitulate phobic narratives of tragic homosexuality, also ends with George's death. Hardwick, in a contemporary review, deems the novel "a sad book, with a biological melancholy running through it, a sense of relentless reduction, daily diminishment."[48] What Hardwick conceives as *A Single Man*'s "biological melancholy" is another name for its representation of a self-abnegating impersonal ascetic ideal. She notices the novel's persistent strain of melancholy—calling it "biological" is a way of indicating how fundamental and definitive is Isherwood's thematic treatment of ascetic impersonality. Its integral nature to Isherwood's novel is the key to Hardwick's implication that a novel could conceivably entertain a "biological melancholy" as well as a "sense of relentless reduction" and "daily diminishment." This narrative is motivated by an ascetic ideal of "daily" self-"diminishment" and impersonal relationality.

And yet these elements of the novel coexist with the positive "vitality" that Garnes and other critics praise: "I am alive, [George] says to himself, I am alive!" (104). The narrator continues, "And life-energy surges hotly through him, and delight, and appetite. How good to be in a body—even this old beat-up carcass—that still has warm blood and live semen and rich marrow and wholesome flesh!" (104). This passage culminates a triumphant moment, which occurs right after George visits Doris in the hospital. After his brief and awkward hospital visit, George is sure that Doris is not long for this world. And he feels "proud," "glad," and "indecently gleeful" to "be counted in . . . the ranks of that marvelous minority, The Living" (103). Isherwood's emphasis on the vitality of the body is, at a superficial level, the celebration of "The Living" over the dead: George is ecstatic for being alive even as Jim is dead, and his former rival nearly so. At this moment, George experiences the survivor's euphoria at life's triumphing over death, regardless of what this means emotionally for him: being a single man graying in Los Angeles. This brief exultation in vitality, in contrast to the sense of ascetic "diminishment" in the rest of the novel, invigorates George's sense of his own body, and, by extension, because George can serve a minoritizing function, rehabilitates the politics of male homosexual embodiment as vital rather than moribund.

But it is important to attend to the ways in which *A Single Man* sustains its "biological melancholy," its ascetic sensibility and idealization of impersonal intersubjectivity. The novel centers on a grieving gay widower and, a few hours later, returns to a darker sense of the body as inert, the living dead, or even as a corpse. And even when his body is joyfully alive, George describes it as "an old, beat-up carcass," foregrounding another instance of the novel's many scenes of George's "relentless reduction" and "daily diminishment," which qualify this momentary vitality and revisit *A Single Man*'s ascetic ideal.

Compare this moment to the penultimate scene in the novel. Now, George is asleep, and the significance of his body is indeed less "vital," more "diminished": "Here we have this body known as George's body, asleep on this bed and snoring quite loud. . . . Jim used to kick it awake, turn it over on its side. . . . But *is* all of George altogether present here?" (183; original emphasis). This moment suggests the novel's evacuation of George's self-consciousness, a total escape from self. This description also represents the devitalization of George's body.

As it lies in mindless slumber, the narrator transcends the limited third-person point of view, speaking as if watching George's body from above. And the narrator adopts this quasi-omniscient perspective to raise a number of existential questions, beginning with "But is all of George altogether present here?" Such a metaphysical questioning of the significance of the body "cognizing darkly" signals that the body is reduced to being an appurtenance to a dissociated consciousness (181). While George sleeps, his body might be there, but his consciousness, and therefore the "personal" part of him, his soul, might not be. As such, the narrator refers to George as a mere body, formally reduced to an object devoid of personal significance: "The body on the bed is still snoring"; "Jim used to kick it awake, turn it over on its side" (185, 183). George is now reduced further, to an impersonal object, notably lacking the dignity of personhood altogether.

Hence, the last scene in the novel depicts a reduction of George's body to being just a "body on the bed"—an "it" that can be kicked or, more ominously, a "vehicle" that can malfunction (184, 185). This final section of *A Single Man* portrays how the individual consciousness itself is a "nonentity" (186). And by extension, the significance of being alive is similarly diminished. After positing the existential question—*is* all of George present while his body sleeps?—the narrator contemplates the multiplicity of entities in the world. He uses the metaphor of rock pools, which are found a few miles north up the coast from George's house.

By so doing, the novel sets up the gradual diminishment of individual consciousness, after calling into question the significance of the corporeal form without a conscious agent.

> Each pool is separate and different, and you can, if you are fanciful, give them names, such as George, Charlotte, Kenny, Mrs. Strunk. Just as George and the others are thought of, for convenience, as individual entities, so you may think of a rock pool as an entity; though, of course, it is not. . . . And, just as the waters of the ocean come flooding, darkening over the pools, so over George and the others in sleep come the waters of that other ocean—that consciousness which is no one in particular but which contains everyone and everything, past, present and future, and extends unbroken beyond the uttermost stars. (183–84)

This, the penultimate passage in the novel, stages the decreation of George, rendering him a "nonentity." Whereas he (and the other characters) were hitherto seen as "individual entities," now their most personal emotive experiences—"hunted anxieties, grim-jawed greeds [*sic*], dartingly vivid intuitions" (183)—are rendered indistinguishable, drowned by the ocean, which is "that consciousness which is no one in particular but which contains everyone and everything." Seen from the inhuman perspective of the cosmic ocean, the narrator here subsumes the personal and the individual into an impersonal entity, the ocean that "comes . . . flooding, darkening over the pools." The narrator considers individual consciousness a "fanciful" and "convenient" fiction. As the waters of the pool become one with the waters of the ocean, George's consciousness leaves his body and is submerged in that impersonal entity. The transcendent unity within multiplicity, or unity that dissolves within multiplicity, comprises "everyone and everything," and effaces the singularity and significance of anyone or anything.

This dispassionate discourse is in marked contrast with the romantic cult of the body that George experiences after visiting Doris or swimming on the beach at night with Kenny (161–64). How far the novel has come from George's exultation in his body for being rudely alive ("How good to be in a body . . . that still has warm blood and live semen and rich marrow and wholesome flesh!"). The reason for this spiritual turn is the persistence of the ascetic ideal of impersonality in the narrative. This turn coincides with George's sleep and signals the novel's turn away from matters of the body, individual desire, and social embeddedness to matters of the spirit. George's vitality is represented chiefly as a celebration of his sexual vitality ("live semen," "wholesome flesh"). And it is this vitality that is now subsumed, decreated, within an impersonal cosmic entity. The body is living on borrowed time, and borrowed energy, and at any moment will give way to the quintessence of all things, which also entails any given individual's death.

Indeed, the conclusion to the novel strongly intimates George's death: "if some part of the nonentity we called George has indeed been absent at this moment . . . away out there on the deep waters, then it will return to find itself homeless. For it can associate no longer with what lies here, unsnoring, on the bed. This is now cousin to the garbage in the container on the back porch. Both will have to be carted away and disposed of, before too long" (185). Passages such as these are informed by Isherwood's intensive identification with a Western Vedantic spirituality of transcending the self and the interconnection of every living thing in a universe composed of one form of energy, one God.[49] What I would add is that this spiritual conception of reality decenters and dissolves the individual, representing the impersonal ascetic ideal in extremis. See, for instance, how the narrator compares George's body to "garbage." Hence, our protagonist is now reduced to a mere "nonentity" in the grand scheme of things.

Furthermore, the use of deixis and demonstrative pronouns ("this moment," "what lies here," "this") suggests an immediacy to the now-objective narration, as the narrator and reader enjoy a bird's eye view of George's body as it lies, "unsnoring, on the bed," a description and position that suggest the body's life-lessness. The body is now no longer vital; it is a corpse, "cousin" to mere refuse.

What is more, this passage, the ending of the novel, raises the question of whether George is truly a corpse or simply makes a transcendent spiritual claim for the metaphysical status of all bodies as impersonal "nonentities." The locution "the nonentity we called George" further renders him corpselike, especially in its use of the past tense: what was George is now gone, replaced by a "nonentity," a probably dead body on a bed. And so, the notion that George is a nonentity is ambiguous: was he always a nonentity, as the previously cited passage suggests ("you can, if you are fanciful, give them names, such as George")? Are individuals nonentities to begin with, whether asleep or awake, alive or dead? Or does this conclusion to the novel suggest on the contrary that the "nonentity we called George" was a vital consciousness, the essence of which will be "homeless" once his body dies?

It seems to me that the novel is trying to have it both ways. George is a nonentity at the end of his narrative arc, but a vital embodiment of individual yearnings and consciousness, regardless of the "old beat-up carcass" it is housed in, in the middle of the narrative. Other scenes in the novel convey a similar dissociation of body and consciousness as the last scene, elevating the metaphysical and reducing the physical: the scene of George driving effects an impersonal division of labor, wherein his mind is free to think about import-ant issues, emotional and existential concerns, while his body is a mere servant, subserviently maneuvering the vehicle. By the end of the novel, the body is itself a vehicle, and the spirit or mind—what the narrator consistently calls "conscious-ness"—is what solely renders individuals unique. Then, by a final turn, precisely what renders individual persons unique—their consciousness—is relegated to the unreal status of fiction. What matters in the end is the spiritual over the personal. After me comes the flood.

Conclusion: Ascetically, Impersonally Queer

To be clear, I am arguing that Isherwood's *A Single Man* anticipates, and also critiques, what we now understand to be the cultural logic of identity, well before Stonewall and other triumphs of minoritarian collective actions and the social transformations of the 1960s. My argument is that the novel represents

Isherwood's considered and consistent alternative to the politics of identity, what I call the misfit-modernist aesthetic In this vein, the cultural misfit trope—or the idea of being "nonconformists"—operates in qualified resistance to the siren song of embracing a shared gay social identity (being "minority-sister[s]"). Such robust identitarian claims, *pace* the classroom scene, are too easily recuperated as grandiose self-possessive projects. The impersonal ascetic ideal of queer relationality resists this very call—George never utters the words "minority-sister"; instead, he talks of *minorities*—collectivities that intersect in the multicultural space of his college lecture hall. Ultimately, Isherwood resisted the call to write himself into what Garnes terms the "pantheon of modern gay literature."[50] *A Single Man* conveys a contrary tendency away from prescriptive and restrictive claims of political identity, projecting instead a nonconformist minoritarian model of ascesis, depicting modes of self-divestiture and what I consider Isherwood's quintessential queer ethos of impersonal attachment, which perhaps defines his contribution to Anglophone letters and queers everywhere. In this sense, to call Isherwood a proleptic advocate for an identitarian politics of gay visibility in *A Single Man* is to miss his aesthetic demurral from such prescriptive and restrictive models of relationality and subjectivity. Isherwood deconstructs the very subject he reconstructs, in a literary novel that is politically resonant in a contrary sense to the politics of gay identity he is most known for now.

Isherwood's novel thus represents a particularly resonant, nonconformist minoritarian subjectivity that survived two world wars, expatriation and self-imposed exile, and the multicultural American century. From his wide experience with transnational homosexual politics in the 1930s, Isherwood wrote the modernist impersonality into *A Single Man*, one that engages in flights from liberal norms of minoritarian identity. These are social and affective norms that the novel suspends and that serve as a now-familiar critique of what Sedgwick calls "the strategic banalization of gay and lesbian politics."[51] In our time, I think we ought to consider the lateral agency of Isherwood's literally muted "minority-sister" as a response to the "slow death" that marginalized subjects bear and represent, as Berlant claims.

By "slow death," Berlant indicates an ongoing ordinary experience that "refers to the physical wearing out of a population and the deterioration of people in that population that is very nearly a defining condition of their experience and historical existence."[52] Berlant's focus on "death" is dramatically political, in order to demonstrate that the "general emphasis of the phrase ['slow death'] is on the phenomenon of mass physical attenuation under global/national regimes of capitalist structural subordination and governmentality."[53] One could say that my focus is on "slow life," or the less dramatically inflected phenomenon of ongoing physical and social experiences of marginalization, lack of access to the good life, yet perseverance through affective and social, not to mention aesthetic, means such as ritualized religion, literary and cultural invention and consumption, and so on. To call such ongoing experiences of limited pleasure, limited transcendence of social and political marginalization "slow death" is in some ways to minimize the creative potential for any individual or "population," to use Berlant's term, to enact resistance, however fleeting or weak, to regimes of domination.[54]

We might view the scenes of ascetic enjoyment in a diminished sense of self, as well as the enjoyment of playing impersonal roles within sadomasochistic intensities, as forms of "slow life," or impersonally queer lives. Minoritarian subjects can impersonally enjoy suspending the burden of selfhood, of sovereign agency, and even entertain transcending the claims of the social—if interpellated as the call to aggressive action and violence—altogether.

Coda

Two Forms of Feeling Like a Misfit

Two MCs can't occupy the same space at the same time. It's against the laws of physics.

—Lauryn Hill, 1996

The Contemporary Social Form: Dorothy Dean and "Her Gays"

In Hilton Als's magical book *The Women,* one of the women he discusses is not queer. Or is she? The chapter on Dorothy Dean begins with her funeral, in which the mourners were "white and, for the most part, gay."[1] Als writes that Dean was a cynosure in the influential white gay demimonde of the 1960s and 1970s. She was a member of the "Lavender Brotherhood" of Harvard-educated gay white men, a whip-smart fag hag, back when that term had currency and meaning. Dean herself wasn't gay, but she was queer. In many ways, Dean was queerer than "her" gays; she was a cultural misfit among them. As Als puts it, "They could always go home again; Dorothy wouldn't."[2]

Why *wouldn't* Dean go home again? Als suggests why: "The principal attraction between Dean and the gay men she had begun to seek out in Cambridge was language, but language as a tool to obscure intimacy and enforce distance. ... Dean and her male companions tried to communize their language of isolation through academic study and drinking parties, but at its core this language was noncommunicative, since it had been cultivated in their childhood rooms, where books and an interest in aesthetics supplied the metaphors that approximated their feelings but could not describe them or be made to express them."[3] Als positions Dean and the gay men of Cambridge as members of a community brought together by their shared language—a language that was, paradoxically, "noncommunicative." But, paradoxically or not, it was a language—or, rather, a special relationship to language—that they shared nonetheless, one they "tried to communize," a language based on "isolation" and "aesthetics." They shared and co-constructed a queer social form, in other words. But, notably, Dean was a misfit even within this subcultural space: doubly displaced, but central to the world making of this small queer world.

Hence, the version of Dorothy Dean's life that Als constructs is that of being a cultural misfit among others who today would simply be seen as highly privileged, white, gay cis-men (from Harvard, no less). Dean's queerness, in Als's terms, is routed through her interest in developing a queer social form based on shared isolation and an interest in "aesthetics." Dorothy Dean and "her gays" shared a queer longing for form, which, according to Als, originated in the "childhood rooms" where their queerness was cultivated as a relation to (aesthetic) form. The language of isolation became a paradoxically special bond.

The queer antisocial thesis that Als implies here includes misfits like Dean— nongay but racially and culturally queer subjects who refused the comforts of heteronormativity. Language as noncommunicative indexes the misfit pleasures in aesthetic misconnection within this pre–Stonewall queer world. According to Als, this structure of feeling originated in childhood rooms and ended in "an interest in aesthetics" that paradoxically belied the promise to represent queer longings. Here, aesthetics could neither adequately "describe" nor "express" queer feelings, even as it sublimated them sublimely, sometimes scandalously, as in the story of Dorothy Dean.

According to Als, Dean, more than "her" gays, paid a real price for this refusal to relate to language in the proper (sexual, social, cultural) ways. She never went home again. Her steadfast cross-identification—some would say misidentification, or *misfit identification*—with white gay men is but one aspect of Dorothy Dean as a misfit among queers.

The Counterfactual Form: *Miss Kilman*

Miss Kilman is hiding in plain sight.

If we take seriously the provocations of this book, then modernists like Virginia Woolf—known for queer texts and subtexts—are a potential resource for mining for the semantic figure of the misfit. (Even when such figures are not central to the story.) *Mrs. Dalloway*'s Doris Kilman is just such a figure. Though in a minor key—an abject, lonely, and antisocial minor character—"Miss" Kilman represents the other side of lesbian desire and mannish identification that Woolf's novel holds at bay. Like the titular character, Clarissa, who as a young woman fell in love with the "romantic" Sally Seton, Doris Kilman is also in love with a young woman: Clarissa Dalloway's teenage daughter, Elizabeth. Embedded in this novel are sharply distinct treatments of same-sex intimacies. One, Clarissa's love for Sally, is a memory of the past—from the Gay Nineties, when Clarissa and Sally were discovering love, that halcyon summer spent in Bourton, the Dalloways' country house. The novel is anchored by this love between Clarissa and Sally, even as the story centers on "Mrs." Dalloway, wife of an MP, and a certain Lady Rossetter who comes as an uninvited (but welcome!) guest. Both figures marry well and are absorbed into the heteronormative matrix; Clarissa's memories of first love as lesbian love are touching, yet highly aestheticized, artifacts of sentimental reminiscence for the time when she was *only* Clarissa and *not* Mrs. Dalloway. Sally Seton's libidinal energies are similarly sublimated and ultimately contained by their very nature as past, as merely a phase.

Which, of course, is what Richard tells Clarissa when they discuss their daughter's seeming infatuation with Doris Kilman, her tutor: "It might only be a phase, as Richard said, such as all girls go through. It might be falling in love. But why Miss Kilman?" asks Clarissa Dalloway, in Woolf's free indirect interior monologue.[4] Clarissa sees Kilman as Elizabeth's "seducer" and has a bout of jealousy.[5] That Mrs. Dalloway views her daughter's same-sex intimacy with Doris Kilman as though it "might be falling in love," and also as a phase "such as all girls go through," indicates the compulsory heterosexual viewpoint that Clarissa has internalized: phrases that her husband "Richard [had] said."

Furthermore, the anguish Doris Kilman experiences in her desire for Elizabeth is jarring, when compared to Clarissa's own "falling in love" with Sally. And her anguish is directly related to her abject, overweight, "unlovable body": "No clothes suited her. . . . And for a woman of course, that meant never meeting the opposite sex."[6] The mannishness of Kilman—her surname is obviously emblematic—is thus tied to her inability to secure Elizabeth's love or the proper object love of "the opposite sex." Doris Kilman seems to be a misfit in a very particular way, a "born invert," to cite another lesbian foil—a foil for Woolf herself: John (Radclyffe) Hall. The sartorial origin of the word rearises here, which, as we saw in the introduction, Jack Halberstam ties to Hall's (and her protagonist, Stephen Gordon's) self-fashioning code of female masculinity. The clothes make the trans man, in our terms. And in the terms of Hall and Woolf, and Doris Kilman and Stephen Gordon, the clothes that do not "suit" Doris Kilman do not "fit" her, either; her body resists the accoutrements of femininity that Clarissa Dalloway, in particular, wears so well in her green mermaid's dress.

Woolf herself conjured a counterfactual semantic figure—Shakespeare's Sister—in her landmark feminist essay, *A Room of One's Own* (1929). In the spirit of intersectional revision of Woolf's vision, let us consider the very different novel she might have written about a *real* modernist misfit: *Miss Kilman*. In other words, this structural character typology of *Mrs. Dalloway* generates a binary of homo/*homo*: a feminine, woman-identifying, and ultimately heterosexual protagonist, versus a mannish, feminist-identifying, and ultimately homosexual minor character. The two visions of homosexuality that Sedgwick analyzes in male homosocial representations is, here, extended and problematized. Doris Kilman is the queer "monster" that symbolically haunts Clarissa's heteroflexible incorporations of same-sex desire as an aestheticized memorable "experience," kissing Sally Seton as a "religious feeling!"[7] Meanwhile, the "unlovable" Doris Kilman eats her feelings and pines for Elizabeth *now*, in the novel's present, "this moment of June."[8] What would the novel *Mrs. Dalloway* become if the famous protagonist were Miss Kilman; if "*Miss Kilman* had decided to *eat all the cakes* herself"? Such would be the reversal—or inversion—of the character system and homo/*homo* binary that Woolf deploys to narratively buttress an ultimately satisfying performance of *transcending* homosexuality— and vanquishing its abject avatar, Miss Kilman. Then we would investigate the structure of feeling for which Miss Kilman would be a central semantic figure, one who transcends Woolf's brainy novel, which purges from the halls of the party, the pages of the novel, a real modernist misfit.

Conclusion: Against the Laws of Physics

Lauryn Hill's verse in the Fugees' song "Zealots" encapsulates the impossibility of living two lives at once, or the impossibility of being able to live those lives in the same space: "Two MCs can't occupy the same space at the same time. / It's against the laws of physics." As with Nella Larsen's Helga Crane: "Why couldn't she have two lives, or couldn't she be satisfied in one place?"[9] The tragic irony of Larsen's first novel is the impossibility of a biracial woman, raised by a bourgeois white family, being accepted by that white family—or by the bourgeois black community to which she also belongs. Published the same year as John (Radclyffe) Hall's seminal lesbian novel, *The Well of Loneliness*,

Larsen's *Quicksand* is informed by the double exiles of queer subjectivity. Like the other narratives chronicled in this book, *Quicksand* implicitly adds to the queer modernist archive in ways that exceed the narrow band of sexual and gender nonconformity that has defined queerness to this day. But queerness and trans embodiment are only recently disaggregated from hegemonic whiteness. Being a cultural misfit, like Helga Crane or Marya Zelli—indeed, like most protagonists of the authors collected in this study—entails a queerness that is irreducible to same-gender object choice. A queerness that is as fundamental as physics, as gravity. Only recently have sexuality and gender become "raced," following a revisioning of the modern sex-gender system through the global history of colonialism, with its formulation of racialized gender and sexual categories. But, by parallel logic, only recently have race, caste, ethnicity, and coloniality become gendered and sexualized. The novels in this study explore these intersecting matrices, foreshadowing their mutual imbrication. Not until Kimberlé Crenshaw and black feminism's legal standpoint theory have we begun to speak the language that Lauryn Hill figures as "Two MCs can't occupy the same space at the same time. It's against the laws of physics."

What the Fugees knew in 1996, and what misfit modernists like Larsen, Thurman, Rhys, and Isherwood knew within the first six decades of the twentieth century, was that these multiple selves were incompatible within one "space"—the space of the self. That self is now accepted as intersected, multiply inflected, by n dimensions of difference. But the single-identity categories of modernism and modernity demanded—well, they demanded one MC for every category. And so we read about *The Well of Loneliness*'s Stephen Gordon and her aristocratic English lineage as an "invert," as if being working-class, or from the colonies, would be an impossibility for a queer subject of literary modernism. And it was, if we presume to canonize queer modernism as originating from a white queer standpoint that then gets colored in. But authors like Larsen corresponded with Gertrude Stein, who herself metaphorized same-sex female desiring through the lens of an errant black femininity in "Melanctha" (1909). The history of sexual dissidence, we have come to learn, is written in white ink, by white hands, but its historians often forget the racial makeup of sexuality itself. Queerness wasn't born white; it was whitewashed. Larsen famously wrote to Stein about "Melanctha," praising her story, which she must have known was autobiographical. Larsen paid obeisance to Stein:

> Dear Miss Stein: I have often talked with our friend Carl Van Vechten about you. Particularly about you and Melanctha, which I have read many times. And always I get from it some new thing. A truly great story.

I never cease to wonder how you came to write it and just why you and not some one of us should so accurately have caught the spirit of this race of mine. Carl asked me to send you my poor first book, and I am doing so. Please dont [*sic*] think me too presumptuous. I hope some day to have the great good fortune of seeing and talking with you. Very sincerely yours Nella Larsen Imes February first, 1928. [10]

The letter shows Larsen's characteristic irony. On first reading, her tone sounds obsequious, smarmy: "Carl asked me to send you my poor first book," meaning her novel *Quicksand*. But the double-bladed comment is italicized: "I never cease to wonder how you came to write it ["Melanctha"] and just why you and not some one of us should so accurately have caught the spirit of this race of mine." Larsen pays Stein a big compliment here, but also subtly digs at why a white queer modernist should have mined the material of "Melanctha," rather than "one of us," even though—rather, especially because—Stein "should so accurately have caught the spirit of this race of mine," Larsen adds, twisting the stiletto. Even at her most canny, networking best, paying obeisance to a grande dame of queer modernist letters, Larsen makes the rather obvious point that only "one of us" (like her) could be the judge of Stein's "accuracy" in depicting an African American woman. Larsen "never cease[s] to wonder how [Stein] came to write it," exploiting the semantic ambiguity of a phrase like "cease to wonder," which colloquially reads as at best a backhanded compliment, and at worst, a subtle accusation: *I never cease to wonder how you got away with appropriating this material before any "one of us" had the chance to do so first!*

To paraphrase Larsen's associate, Jessie Fauset, who famously said at the start of the "Negro Renaissance" that Americans were obviously taken with African American vernacular culture and so the Talented Tenth may as well write about it, since they were best poised to do so, before the white writers got there and made a hash of it. And so, the final irony of Larsen's *éloge* to Stein is the adverbial phrase "so accurately." Contemporary readers of "Melanctha"—some of my black students among them—will find the story cringeworthy, chiefly in its almost surreal deployment of African American Vernacular English, Baltimore-style, in the form of the Dada-esque experimental expressionism of Stein's early modernist style. By contrast, Larsen's "poor first book," *Quicksand*, as I show in chapter 2, *is* accurate in its razor-sharp analysis of biracial, if not black, female subjectivity (given its focus on "a despised mulatto," in the novel's ventriloquism of that sentimental racial trope). "Melanctha" is a poor early example of what Fauset (and, in this letter to Stein, Larsen herself) worried about: the plundering of African American cultural uniqueness by modernist experimenters with aesthetic form. There are very clear and systemic reasons why Stein "got there first," and Larsen knew them. But, as Lauryn Hill reminds us, "Two MCs can't occupy the same space at the same time. It's against the laws of physics."

And, in this example, Larsen is decrying the "O.G." "MC," Gertrude Stein, just as in the letter cited below she spies Lord Alfred Douglas but can't bring herself to introduce herself to him. Larsen Imes, as she then styled herself, was a black matron of the Talented Tenth, and Stein already a towering figure in modernism partly because of her primitivist experiments with black English, as in "Melanctha." *I would've done it sooner, and better,* goes Larsen's subtext, *but I'm not a white (queer) modernist myself.* In that letter, writing to Carl Van Vechten from Mallorca during her Guggenheim fellowship, Larsen writes about seeing Lord Alfred Douglas: "There is a Lord Douglas staying here. He has remnants of fine looks. I'm awfully curious about him, but of course one can't go to him and say: 'Pardon me but are you the Lord Douglas who slept with Oscar Wilde?' No more than one can leap into a conversation about the Winston Churchill libel suit."[11] Larsen then says she might never know if it's really him, since there is no polite way to bring up the topic, "not with this man who has his share of the English standoffish manner and a quite ferocious look in his handsome eyes. So, I suppose I will never know."[12] Again, as with her letter to Stein, Larsen bears an uncanny relationship to the queer modernist agent provocateur, though Stein was a much bigger deal, and a much closer cultural figure, than Douglas. She had, after all, written "Melanctha" from personal experience as a medical student in Baltimore. But the point is more that Stein's "Melanctha" was too close for comfort to Larsen's own aesthetic project—limning the modern contents of black or biracial women's subjectivity, in their social contexts. Thus, Stein was easier to approach than Douglas. At least via the written word, and through the mediating connection of Van Vechten, their mutual friend. Lord Alfred Douglas in 1930 was another, queerer than queer, matter. I suppose Larsen wanted to come close to the great Oscar Wilde and not his *homme fatale.*

But the larger point is that proximity can rule out self-expression. Larsen's dialogue with the "O.G." of transatlantic queer modernism reveals how she regretted Stein's being in that "space" first; "Melanctha's" occupying it as early as 1909 meant that *Quicksand* had some queer modernist antecedents, but they were white. Larsen's Helga Crane, described as a "queer, indefinite factor," is thus queer in her racial liminality, her biracial defiance of the color line, not unlike Stein's Melanctha, whose black female mobility (and, by extension, her sexual promiscuity) is a figure for queer desire itself.

Such is perhaps the complexity, and the literary fate, of misfit modernists like Larsen. Unlike clearer, *queerer* modernists, like Stein herself—who appropriated racial tropes and racial discourses to advance formal experiments on the page as a cover or figure for queer desire (or the love that dare not speak its name, to gesture toward Douglas)—authors like Larsen, Thurman, and Rhys are developing a different relation to queerness and to modernism. This different relation is what I call the trope and discourse of the modernist misfit. "Melanctha" is a figure for black female sexuality coded as queer by her mobility and by its author's autobiographical location as a queer modernist invested in sexuality between women. Larsen's *Quicksand* also encodes nonwhite female subjectivity in the terms of the queer, if not queerness per se. This "queer indefinite factor" is more about race and gender than about same-sex desires; but it is also quite about desire, and a biracial woman's desire to occupy the same space at the same time as the "MC" of her own "two lives" (one black, the other white).

In the case of Jean Rhys's *Quartet*, the coded queerness of its modernist experiment in form and misfit alienation rests on the vexed relation between the protagonist, Marya Zelli, and her female antagonist, Lois Heidler, Hugh Heidler's wife. Their sordid *ménage à trois* has only recently been understood as a same-sex triangle with the male as the (traditionally female) go-between. Just as with Larsen, Rhys's sexuality is not readily legible as queer—and certainly not "lesbian"—but Rhys's oeuvre still engages with the codes of queer modernism and the sexual tensions of queer modernity, or relations between the sexes unmoored from the institutions of heteronormative patriarchy. Again, the focus is not on making cultural alienation seem like a cover for queerness, but rather to unpack the universality of queerness to the modernist ethos of literary expression, so heavily weighted and shaped by early queer precursors (like Stein, Wilde, and Hall, among so many others). As Heather K. Love notes in her introduction to a special issue on "Modernism at Night," "Is queer modernism simply another name for modernism" itself?[13] The answer is, yes and no. The queerness of modernists like Rhys, Larsen, and the other authors in this study—Thurman and Isherwood—is inflected by cultural identities beyond the axis of sexuality itself. Even the author most associated with queerness in the Stonewall sense of the term, Isherwood, as I show in chapter 5, was ambivalent about the politics of "gay" self-representation when these politics were projected via a single-identity lens. *A Single Man* is a wonderful instance of Isherwood's expansive notion of queerness, not simply gayness; of the possibility for coalitions of "minorities"—as the novel's dated discourse has it, of bringing together "a Negro and a Swede." And while this dated discourse of transcultural dialogue has its blind spots, Isherwood's novel is not simply a paean to white gay male personhood, as many white gay male critics would have us believe. The gay "minority-sister" of Isherwood's protagonist, George, is a chubby gay student in George's lecture hall, but note that the two gay avatars are *minority*-sisters, not simply *sisters*. Isherwood's long game with sexual dissidence meant not only that he famously included the world's first discussion of Camp in an English novel, nor that E. M. Forster named Isherwood as his literary executor in order to publish *Maurice* posthumously. Isherwood, as I mention in my study of his final modernist novel, was gay before Stonewall, and he turned toward a politics of coalition that we can only call queer, rather than single-identity gay, even in the Isherwood novel most celebrated for projecting a single *gay* man's point of view.

Thurman, by contrast, had a more vexed relationship to the discourse of queerness as well as the legacy of queer modernism and the formal repertoire of literary modernism itself. His debut novel, *The Blacker the Berry*, the subject of chapter 3, famously ends with a scene of male homosexual libertines threatening to put the novel's besotted female protagonist "to rout." But Emma Lou Morgan has the last word and wins that particular skirmish with Alva and his orgy of "effeminate boys." The interesting point, however, is that Thurman, who was known as bisexual if not just gay, deploys a homophobic rhetoric as the final obstacle to Emma Lou's self-liberation from the racist and sexist oppression she is mired in. Mired in thanks to her faithless former lover, Alva, whose sexual licentiousness is the instrument for almost shattering Emma Lou's self-respect. The fact that Thurman mobilizes a scene of male queer camaraderie as the final obstacle to Emma Lou's self-liberation is thus not *only* a mark of internalized homophobia, just as Emma Lou's low self-esteem is not *only* a mark of internalized racism; it is an artifact of systemic racism. Thurman's coding of male queer liberty as libertinism differs greatly from the elaboration of that theme by his associate Richard Bruce Nugent in the latter's "Smoke, Lilies and Jade" (1926). Nugent's famous short story entertains polyamory and bisexuality in a utopian stream-of-consciousness narrative told in the free indirect style. Melva and Adrian (a.k.a. Beauty) are the female and male love interests, respectively, of Alex, the protagonist. In Thurman's novel, Alva has many gay and lesbian associates. The protagonist, Emma Lou, is propositioned by an elderly landlady in a clearly lesbian scene. And she has a sexual tryst with a man in a movie theater—as if Emma Lou, a woman from a middle-class black family, were not constrained by the normative expectations of black bourgeois respectability. In other words, Thurman's *The Blacker the Berry* elaborates the trope of male queerness as distinct from, and even opposite to, the narrative of self-liberation of Emma Lou Morgan as a "total misfit," due to the complex of her gender and her darker skin. (A black man of her complexion and class background, the novel successfully demonstrates, would *not* be socially impeded to the same degree.) Thurman's intersectional meditation on the difference gender-and-skin-color make in the elaboration of modern subjectivity thus routes the narrative through queerness. But in this case (as with Stein?), queerness is a figure for liberty and mobility, rather than race and gender as a complex figure for (self-) oppressive cultural contexts. Many critics have read Thurman's novel as "wearing a female face," in Thadious Davis's famous formulation, and thus elaborating an autobiographical narrative of being "too black" while inhabiting the female gender.[14] Despite competing claims, there is perhaps some truth in the autobiographical valence of Emma Lou Morgan as Thurman's alter ego, but only insofar as the exotic, light-skinned Alva is also an avatar for Thurman's sexual dissidence and cultural sophistication. In short, Thurman explores what it means to be intersectional in its originary sense: "All the women are white, all the Blacks are men, but some of us are brave."[15] Again, the trope of intersectional alienation Thurman's novel calls feeling like a "total misfit" explores that alienation through the discourse and backdrop of Jazz Age libertinism and somewhat-liberated queerness. (At least, relatively liberated compared to the post–Second World War period of the "lavender scare.")

But the moral of Thurman's novel, and in conclusion to this book, is that modern queerness is not simply synonymous with oppressive socialization. At least, not by the time that Larsen is writing to Stein and spotting Lord Alfred Douglas; not by the time Thurman is writing *The Blacker the Berry* and Nugent "Smoke, Lilies and Jade." By the Roaring Twenties, or the "Harlem" Renaissance, black subjectivity under the violent terror of Jim Crow and the Klan was under siege like never before. Queerness by contrast was never so open, public, and free. (Historians like George Chauncey and John D'Emilio have made this case.[16]) Black literary expression, by contrast, was beholden to a *queer* white patronage system personified by Carl Van Vechten (and Gertrude Stein) in the States. It is only in the wake of black feminism that these intersectional insights have become common sense. But in the time periods explored in *Misfit Modernism*, intersectional nuances presented by Thurman's novel—that it was easier to be a light-skinned sexually liberated black male than a dark-skinned, sexually liberated black female—were original. By the early sixties, and Isherwood's *A Single Man*, the same insights held. Hence the argument in that novel for the coalition of multicultural standpoints ("a Negro and a Swede"). But these insights also shed light on the queer career of modernism, and sexuality, itself. The misfit modernists showcase not only how "queer modernism" is synonymous with modernism itself, but also how the queer in modernism was elaborated in intersectional ways, at times salient more so for its racial, ethnic, and regional marginality than that of sexuality itself. Hence the shift to the trope of the "misfit," and the discourse of *Misfit Modernism*, to inflect the legacy of queer modernism with a queerness more queer than sexuality or gender, given the entanglements of both sexuality and gender with race, nationality, and class. These are insights we largely take for granted now—but *without shifting the canonical understandings* of modernism or even queer modernism as hegemonically white, despite the evidence of experience of black feminists in the 1970s and '80s. Or the literary evidence of experience of misfit modernists in the 1920s through the 1960s. These intersectional MCs occupied more than two spaces at the same time, bending the modern laws of cultural physics in ways we need to understand.

NOTES

Preface

1. Thurman, *The Blacker the Berry*, 256.
2. For a literary history of class and intr-aracial politics in African American literature and culture, including phenomena such as the blue-veined society and the brown-paper-bag test, see Williams, *Dividing Lines*.
3. Larsen, *Quicksand*, in *Complete Fiction*, 161.
4. Locke, *New Negro*; Locke, "Enter the New Negro."
5. Love, "Modernism at Night," 744.
6. Quoted in Canning, review of *Isherwood*.
7. Sullivan, "Curses," 13.

Introduction

1. Hardwick, "Sex and the Single Man," 4.
2. Berlant, "Slow Death"; see chapter 4.
3. Davis, *Nella Larsen*, 431; see chapter 2.
4. Nash, *Black Feminism Reimagined*.
5. Ibid., 3.
6. Edelman, *No Future*.
7. Ibid.
8. Musser, "Re-membering Audre."
9. Hill Collins, "Mammies, Matriarchs, and Other Controlling Images."
10. Warner, *Fear of a Queer Planet*, xxvi.
11. Caserio et al., "Antisocial Thesis in Queer Theory."
12. Love, "Rethinking Sex," 6–7.
13. Warner, *Fear of a Queer Planet*, xxvi, xxvii.
14. Rubin, "Thinking Sex."
15. Eng, Halberstam, and Muñoz, "What's Queer About Queer Studies Now?"
16. King, "Transformed Nonconformist," 466–77.
17. Heinlein, "Misfit," 55.
18. Reference to Meursault as on the (autism) spectrum is a provocation; see chapter 3 on the pitfalls of "diagnosing" fictional characters.
19. Booth, *Rhetoric of Fiction*, 327.
20. Joyce, *Ulysses*, 9.
21. Hall, *Your John*, 78; emphasis added.
22. Halberstam, "Writer of Misfits," 145–61; Hall, *Well of Loneliness*.
23. Liggins, "Misfit Lesbian Heroine," 163–206, 182–83.
24. Ibid., 187, 201, 191, 201.
25. Wood, "Misfits, Anarchy, and the Absolute," 37.
26. In addition to Hall, other famed Sapphic modernists include Gertrude Stein, Djuna Barnes, Natalie Barney, and H. D. (Larsen corresponded with Stein early in her career, and was involved with H. D.'s circle toward the end of it; see the coda.) Cf. Doan, *Fashioning Sapphism*; Nair, *Secrecy and Sapphic Modernism*.
27. *Oxford English Dictionary*, 3rd ed. (online, 2002), s.v. "misfit (*n*. and *adj*.)"; emphasis added.
28. Payne, "Program of Educational Sociology," 461.
29. Beer, "Social Psychiatry and the Day Nursery," 209, 210, 214.
30. Sneller provides a chilling account of the racist trope of black children as "grotesque misfits," as seen in the popular fiction of Ruth McEnery Stuart. As, in England, lower-class children were stereo-

typed as having low "intelligence," so, in the late nineteenth-century United States, black children were stereotyped as "grotesque misfits" belonging to a "weak and backward race" (Sneller, "Bad Boys / Black Misfits," 217). Here, we see the oppressive underside of using the term *misfit* as a category of cultural difference. But the concept's liberatory potential, as glimpsed in Hall's letter and Garland-Thompson's essay, is explored throughout this study.

31. Cummings, "First Aid to the Misfit," 403.

32. Ibid.; emphasis added.

33. Ibid.; emphasis added.

34. Ibid.; emphasis added.

35. Tredgold, "Changes in Social Responsibilities," 873.

36. Ibid., 874, 875, 877, 874.

37. Ibid., 874.

38. Roche, "Ordinary Novel," 101.

39. Ibid.

40. Aside from Wood, see Farmer, "Female Misfit"; Desmond, "O'Connor's Misfit and the Mystery of Evil"; and Horner, "Misfit as Metaphor."

41. An essay on Fanon frames him as a "theoretical misfit" because he does not "fit in any of the movements with which he is associated," using the term's general meaning (Mardorossian, "Franz Fanon," 19).

42. Hawkes, *Ford Madox Ford*. Nandrea's *Misfit Forms* invokes the term in its account of "variant forms" of the British novel in the eighteenth and nineteenth centuries. But Nandrea's *Misfit Forms* does not address the term's cultural meanings, especially in regard to social marginalization.

43. Hawkes's book also elides the symbolic significance of the term, not asking what it means to call a modernist a *misfit* to begin with; he, too, takes for granted the transparency of the concept.

44. Garland-Thompson, "Misfits," 592, 591, 592, 594.

45. Ibid., 598; emphasis added.

46. Ibid., 602.

47. Naipaul, "Without a Dog's Chance."

48. West, "Pursuit of Misery."

49. The term *homonationalism* was coined by Puar, *Terrorist Assemblages*.

50. Isherwood, "Unused Chapter [*Christopher and His Kind*]," 79.

51. Love, *Feeling Backward*, 100.

Chapter 1

1. Williams, "Structures of Feeling," 134, 134–35; emphasis added. Further page references to "Structures of Feeling" are embedded parenthetically in the text.

2. Williams, *Marxism and Literature*, 121.

3. The notion of inchoate aesthetic form presides over Aarthi Vadde's *Chimeras of Form*, which practices a critical formalism centered on the concept of the *chimera* to read "modernist internationalist" authors of the long twentieth century.

4. Larsen, *Quicksand*, in *Complete Fiction*, 42.

5. Thompson, "Russian Formalists and New Critics"; Culler, "Closeness of Close Reading," 8.

6. Jin, "Problems of Scale in 'Close' and 'Distant' Reading," 106.

7. For more on "reading" as hegemonic paradigm for literary interpretation, see Goldstone, "Doxa of Reading."

8. Williams, "Structures of Feeling," 133–34.

9. DeKoven, "History, the Twentieth Century, and a Contemporary Novel," 332; emphasis added.

10. Ibid., 333.

11. Jin encapsulates a more familiar version of my model of immanent reading in his claim that close reading is "synecdochic"—a representative part, such as a vibrant narrative scene, stands in for the *social* whole, as in this example: "the gypsy interlude in book 12 of *Tom Jones* metaphorically encapsulates a vast network of political tensions in eighteenth-century England" (Jin,

"Problems of Scale in 'Close' and 'Distant' Reading," 118).

12. Williams, *Reading and Criticism*, 86, 86, 101. Jin's history of close reading shows earlier formulations, such as Williams's remarks about the self-reflexive "structure" of novels, or Watt's notion of "symbolic prefiguring" in "The First Paragraph of *The Ambassadors*." Watt's tour-de-force explication of James's novel posits a method similar to immanent reading. Yet Watt's method ("synecdochic representativeness") focuses only on the novel's *first* paragraph, as a "synchronic introduction" to its themes and preoccupations (Watt, "First Paragraph," 270).

Chapter 2

1. Walker, "Looking for Zora"; Walker, *In Search of Our Mothers' Gardens*.

2. Carby, *Reconstructing Womanhood*.

3. Hutchinson, *In Search of Nella Larsen*, 486.

4. Ibid., 486; emphasis added.

5. McDowell, introduction to *"Quicksand" and "Passing."*

6. Walker, "Nella Larsen Reconsidered," 166.

7. Hutchinson, *In Search of Nella Larsen*, 487.

8. The line goes: "She could neither conform nor be happy in her unconformity." Larsen, *Quicksand*, in *Complete Fiction*, 42. (Further citations to *Quicksand* and *Passing* refer to their republication in *Complete Fiction*.)

9. Larsen Imes, "At Home," letter to Van Vechten. Italicized emphasis added.

10. "Nella Larsen . . . Honor Guest at N.A.A.C.P. Tea," *Amsterdam News*, 5.

11. It is ironic that Van Vechten seemed to better understand the "significance of the literary movement to [the] larger development" of black uplift. For a revisionist account of Van Vechten's role, see

Bernard, *Carl Van Vechten and the Harlem Renaissance*.

12. Having just moved to Harlem, Larsen complains about the inner-city heat in a racist observation: "Right now when I look out at the Harlem streets I feel just like Helga Crane in my novel. Furious at being connected with all these niggers." Larsen Imes, "Tuesday 19th," letter to Peterson.

13. Hutchinson, *In Search of Nella Larsen*, 257; emphasis added.

14. Wertheim, "Nella Larsen, 1891–1964," *New York Times*.

15. For example, note Larsen's self-ironizing tone when apparently discussing her second novel, *Passing*: "this poor coloured child who for some reason or other has been feeling blue over that same old book." Larsen Imes, "At Home," letter to Van Vechten, May 1, 1928. *Quicksand* appeared in late March 1928. But *Passing*'s official publication date, April 26, 1929, may not be accurate. See Kaplan, "Nella Larsen's Erotics of Race," xi n. 6; Hutchinson, *In Search of Nella Larsen*, 272–75, 318.

16. Elmer Imes's affair was with Ethel Gilbert, administrator at Fisk University.

17. Larsen, *Passing*, 181.

18. Larsen's last visit to Peterson was in June 1943, as documented by Peterson in a letter to Van Vechten: "I forgot to tell you on Sunday [June 20] that Nella had been to visit me on Saturday [June 19] and stayed until I had to leave. . . . Sunday she came back to see me again." Peterson never saw Larsen again.

19. Larson, *Invisible Darkness*; Davis, *Nella Larsen*.

20. Davis, *Nella Larsen*, 457, 458.

21. Ibid., 431; emphasis added.

22. Ibid., 432. Davis adds that Peterson "sealed her letters from this period, so that whatever she knew has not yet been revealed" (ibid.). As of the time of this writing, these letters remain sealed.

23. For a journalistic example of this phenomenon, see Jenkins, "Forgotten Work of Jessie Redmon Fauset"; similarly, Helene

Johnson's collected works, *This Waiting for Love*, only appeared in 2006.

24. Indeed, Davis and Hutchinson list several novels Larsen wrote, or was working on, including the manuscript of "Mirage" (or "Fall Fever"), a "white" novel she composed while traveling in western Europe on a Guggenheim fellowship. Larsen's other unpublished novels include "Crowning Mercy," "The Gilded Palm Tree," "The Wingless Hour," and "Adrian and Evadne." Davis, *Nella Larsen*, 456.

25. Hutchinson, *In Search of Nella Larsen*, 465.

26. Davis, *Nella Larsen*, 459, 461.

27. Ibid., 460–61.

28. Esty, *Unseasonable Youth*.

29. Davis, *Nella Larsen*, 461.

30. Larsen, *Quicksand*, 51. Further page references to *Quicksand* are embedded parenthetically in the text.

31. Hutchinson discusses Larsen's unconsummated *ménage à trois* with a lesbian couple: Edna Thomas, cofounder of the Negro Actors Guild, and Olivia Wyndham, a member of the H. D. circle through her friendship with Bryher (Winifred Ellerman), H. D.'s lover. Bryher reassured H. D. that her friendship with Larsen was platonic by "inventing children" for her. Larsen is thus queer in ways that exceed same-sex desire, but also don't rule it out. Her white lovers represent another aspect of her queerness, interracial romance being illegal in her time. Hutchinson, *In Search of Nella Larsen*, 440–51.

32. Josh. 9:21, 9:23, 9:27.

33. Du Bois, "Of Our Spiritual Strivings," 1–8.

34. Hutchinson, *In Search of Nella Larsen*, 63.

35. Quoted in ibid., 62–63.

36. Ibid., 63.

37. Ibid., 354.

38. Cohn, *Transparent Minds*.

39. Bal, *Narratology*, loc. 3037, Kindle.

40. Cohn, *Transparent Minds*, 29; emphasis added.

41. Ibid.

42. The narrator focalizes Helga's view of white people thus: "Sinister folk, she considered them, who had stolen her birthright" (113).

43. Du Bois, "Browsing Reader," 248.

44. McIntire, "Toward a Narratology of *Passing*," 778; emphasis added.

45. Ibid., 779.

46. Cohn, *Transparent Minds*, 14, 12.

47. Ibid., 12.

48. Ibid., 5.

49. Genette, *Narrative Discourse*; Genette, *Narrative Discourse Revisited*.

50. The lower-class status of the congregants, legible in their vernacular speech, is problematically presented in the novel.

51. "Monday," letter from Larsen Imes to Van Vechten.

52. Davis, *Nella Larsen*, 458; emphasis added.

53. Quoted in ibid., 458; emphasis added.

54. Walker, "Nella Larsen Reconsidered."

55. For more on Genette's concept of *mood* in modernist narration, see chapter 4, on Jean Rhys.

Chapter 3

1. Singh and Scott, *Collected Writings*, 232.

2. Thurman, "High, Low, Past, and Present," 219. Some of Thurman's essays appeared in periodicals like the *Messenger*, the *New Republic*, and the *Independent*. Individual citations refer to the archival manuscript, the periodical publication, or *Collected Writings*. Where possible, references note the specific version being cited.

3. Thurman, "High, Low, Past, and Present," 219.

4. Ibid., 218.

5. Dorothy West claims that "there is no other name that typifies that period as does that of Wallace Thurman" and that Thurman

was "perhaps the most symbolic figure of the Literary Renaissance in Harlem." West, "Elephant's Dance," 77, 85.

6. Thurman, "Negro Artists and the Negro," *New Republic*, 37–39.

7. Thurman, "Negro Artists and the Negro," in *Collected Writings*, 198.

8. Ibid.

9. Ibid.; emphasis added.

10. Du Bois, "Criteria of Negro Art," 42.

11. Granville Ganter refers to Thurman's "most challenging characteristic," his "acerbic intractability." Ganter, "Bohemian Vision," 194.

12. Daniel Walker notes that Thurman "believed that artistic concerns outweighed those of the political, social, or personal nature. This posture put him at odds with Harlem's old guard, most notably Du Bois and Locke [and] Charles Johnson." Walker, "Exploding the Canon," 154.

13. West, "Elephant's Dance," 79.

14. Ganter, "Bohemian Vision," 194.

15. Thurman, "Notes on a Stepchild," in *Collected Writings*, 239.

16. Ibid., 238.

17. Ibid., 248; emphasis added.

18. Ibid.; emphasis added.

19. Ganter, "Bohemian Vision," 194–95.

20. Nugent, letter to Dorothy Peterson. Like *Fire!!*, *Harlem* only lasted one issue.

21. Carter, review of *The Blacker the Berry*, 162.

22. Ibid., 163.

23. Thurman, "Notes on a Stepchild," Wallace Thurman Collection, 2–3; emphasis added.

24. Thurman, "Nephews of Uncle Remus," 297–98.

25. Du Bois, "Browsing Reader," 249.

26. Ibid., 250.

27. Ibid., 249.

28. Ibid., 250; emphasis added.

29. Ibid.; emphasis added.

30. Walker, "Exploding the Canon," 155, 156.

31. Thurman, *The Blacker the Berry*, 18. Further page references to *The Blacker the Berry* are embedded parenthetically in the text.

32. For more on aesthetic distancing in Thurman, see Gaither, "Reappraisal of Thurman's Aesthetics."

33. Thurman, "Nephews of Uncle Remus," 297.

34. Davis, "Female Face." On Thurman's queerness beyond the sexual binary, see Ganter, "Bohemian Vision," 194–97.

35. Davis, "Female Face," 99.

36. Gaither, "Reappraisal of Thurman's Aesthetics," 86.

37. Jarraway, "Tales of the City," 47.

38. Thurman and Rapp's play, *Harlem*, premiered on Broadway in 1929.

39. Thurman, "This Negro Literary Renaissance," 243.

40. Ibid., 244.

41. Ibid., 248, 242.

42. Ibid., 242.

43. Ibid.

44. Hughes, *Big Sea: An Autobiography*, 235.

45. Thurman, "Notes on a Stepchild," Wallace Thurman Collection, 7; emphasis added.

46. Ibid., 7–8.

47. Ibid., 6.

48. Thurman, review of *Flight*, in *Collected Writings*, 183.

49. Singh and Scott, *Collected Writings*, 441–44.

50. Scott, "Harlem Shadows," 331.

51. Singh and Scott, *Collected Writings*, 443.

52. Ibid., 443.

53. Hughes, *Big Sea*, 185.

54. Carter, review of *The Blacker the Berry*, 162.

55. For more on psycho-narration, defined as the narrator's discourse on the psychology of the character, see chapter 1, and Dorrit Cohn, *Transparent Minds*.

56. *Dictionary of American Regional English*, s.v. "lonesome (*adj.*)."

57. Haizlip, introduction to *The Blacker the Berry*, 14.

58. Lewis, "Wallace Thurman Is Model Harlemite."

59. Sedgwick, "Paranoid Reading and Reparative Reading."

60. Warner, *Trouble with Normal*.

61. Thurman, review of *Infants of the Spring*, in *Collected Writings*, 226.

Chapter 4

1. Ford, "Rive Gauche," 24.

2. Rhys, "Vienne," *Tigers Are Better Looking*, 207.

3. Emery, "Poetics of Labor," 168; *Quartet* was first published as *Postures* in Britain (1928). Further references to *Quartet* are embedded parenthetically in the text.

4. Alvarez, *New York Times Book Review*, March 17, 1974, 7.

5. Emery, *Jean Rhys at "World's End,"* xv.

6. Ibid., xii.

7. Ibid., xii; emphasis added. For an early instance, see Abel, "Women and Schizophrenia."

8. Emery, "Poetics of Labor," 167; emphasis added.

9. See Savory, *Jean Rhys*, which discusses Edward Braithwaite's critique of Rhys. Braithwaite argues that the canonization of white Creole writers such as Rhys comes at the expense of recognizing black Caribbean authors (quoted in Savory, *Jean Rhys*, 206–7). Cf. Savory, "Jean Rhys, Race and Caribbean/English Criticism," and Braithwaite, "Helen of Our Wars."

10. Esty, *Unseasonable Youth*, 172.

11. Rhys's early novels are set in Paris or London, were published in Britain and the United States, and often translated into French, underscoring Rhys's transnational position in the modernist "world republic of letters." Cf. Casanova, *World Republic of Letters*.

12. Wyndham, introduction to *Wide Sargasso Sea*, 7.

13. Mitchell, "Trouble with 'Victim.'"

14. Mitchell relies on Deleuze's seminal essay on masochism, "Coldness and Cruelty." Rubin argues for the lack of material evidence to support Deleuze's claims in Rubin's "Sexual Traffic."

15. Soskind, in a review of *After Leaving Mr. Mackenzie* (1931), claims that the novel is "a sadistic book" because of the "cruelty and poisonous satisfaction men take in downing an already-beaten woman." There is a growing field on masochism in Jean Rhys and on modernist masochism, including: Dell'Amico, *Colonialism and the Modernist Movement*; Moran, "'A Doormat in a World of Boots'"; and Emery, *Jean Rhys at "World's End."* For the intersection of modernism and masochism, see Sorum, "Masochistic Modernisms"; Howarth, "Housman's Dirty Postcards"; and Carter and Taylor, *Modernism/Masochism*.

16. Mitchell, "Trouble with 'Victim,'" 203–4; emphasis added.

17. Ibid., 204.

18. On epistemic privilege, see Mohanty, "Epistemic Status of Cultural Identity."

19. Sedgwick, *Epistemology of the Closet*, 23.

20. I borrow "sadisms of epistemology" from Kurnick, "Embarrassment and Forms of Redemption," 402.

21. Fludernik, *Introduction to Narratology*, 76–77.

22. Ibid., 77.

23. McHale, "Free Indirect Discourse," 275.

24. Woolf, *Mrs. Dalloway*, 99, 100, 101, 109.

25. Genette, *Narrative Discourse*, 162.

26. Ibid.

27. Ibid., 168. The other modality of *mood* is what Genette calls *distance*, or how mimetic the narrative is: from most mimetic (extensive use of dialogue; the "scenic method") to least mimetic (narrator eclipses the story itself). Genette, *Narrative Discourse Revisited*, 46. For more on narrative mime-

sis, see Cohn, "Signposts of Fictionality," and Martínez-Bonati, *Fictive Discourse*.

28. Genette, *Narrative Discourse*, 168.

29. See Herman, "Hypothetical Focalization."

30. Focalization and free-indirect narration are the chief means by which the first-person narrator of Proust's *À la recherche du temps perdu* tells the stories of multiple characters, including "Swann in Love." Genette bases all of *Narrative Discourse* on Proust's magnum opus.

31. Cohn, *Transparent Minds*.

32. The real Stephan, Jean Lenglet, under the pseudonym Édouard de Nève, published his account in French as *Sous les verrous* and in Dutch as *In de Strik*. The other couple's accounts appear in Ford, *When the Wicked Man*, and Bowen, *Drawn from Life*.

33. *Psycho-narration* is Cohn's term for the narrator's discourse regarding the character's internal cognitive and affective experience, in a more formal and distanced idiom from other styles of focalization, such as interior monologue or free-indirect discourse. Psycho-narration differs from interior monologue (first-person) and free-indirect narration (third person inflected by the character's idiom and emotions). Cohn, *Transparent Minds*, 21–140; cf. chapter 2.

34. Passages of hypothetical focalization can be classified as "ambiguous" or "double" focalization: Bal, *Narratology*, 158–59, and Genette, *Narrative Discourse*, respectively. If focusing on the rhetoric, they can be described as "imaginary," "modalized," or "complex" representations of characters' discourse. See, respectively, Moore, "Focalization and Narrative Voice," 18; Sanders and Redeker, "Speech and Thought in Narrative Discourse," 296; and McHale, "Free Indirect Discourse," 277.

35. Herman, "Hypothetical Focalization," 231.

36. Ibid., 231.

37. Ibid., 231.

38. Quoted in ibid., 237.

39. Ibid., 237.

40. Ibid., 231.

41. Bal, *Narratology*, 159.

42. Herman, "Hypothetical Focalization," 237, 249 n. 17.

43. McHale, "Free Indirect Discourse," 275–76.

44. As opposed to narrators, which can be reliable or unreliable, characters can be more or less fallible. On the distinction, see Fludernik, *Introduction to Narratology*, 28, and Shen, "Unreliability."

45. Cf. Angier, *Jean Rhys*, 129–219; Kappers–den Hollander, "Gloomy Child"; and Latham, *Art of Scandal*.

46. Kappers–den Hollander, "Gloomy Child," 45.

47. Angier, *Jean Rhys*, 183–219.

Chapter 5

1. Isherwood, *Single Man*. Page references to the primary work are embedded parenthetically in the text.

2. Summers, *Isherwood on Writing*, xiii.

3. Ibid.

4. Isherwood, *Christopher and His Kind*, 305–6.

5. For more on Isherwood's queer detachment in the *Berlin Stories* not as "disengagement from or refusal of history," but rather as a mode of queer world making, see Price, "Queer Detachment," 649.

6. For a definition of "autofiction," a term coined by Doubrovsky in 1977, see Vilain, "Autofiction," 5–7. Isherwood's fiction was autobiographical to varying degrees. For another take on Isherwood's early nonfictional autobiographical writings, such as *Lions and Shadows*, see Battershill, "Reticent Autobiography."

7. Simmel, "Stranger," 143.

8. Ibid., 145.

9. In the first draft to *Christopher and His Kind*, for example, Isherwood calls Forster "a great chieftain" of the homosexual "tribe." Isherwood, "First Draft," 55.

10. For a different reading of Isherwood's distinction between *tribe* and *kind*, see Carr, *Queer Times*, 2.

11. The famed Stonewall riots occurred in the last weekend of June 1969, as a violent protest against yet another NYPD raid on the queer bar on Christopher Street, in New York's West Village. The riots are considered the birth of the modern LGBT rights movement, though as we see in this chapter, Isherwood's queer politics were far ahead of his time.

12. Isherwood, *Christopher and His Kind*, 2; emphasis added.

13. Ibid.

14. Ibid., 3, 2.

15. Ibid., 3.

16. Dean draws on the modernist doctrine of impersonality through a Lacanian reading of the Unconscious as the Other within. Dean, "T. S. Eliot, Famous Clairvoyante." For other takes on modernist impersonality, see Ellman, *Poetics of Impersonality*, and Cameron, *Impersonality*. The *locus classicus* for modernist impersonality is Eliot's "Tradition and the Individual Talent."

17. The 1960s in the United States stretched into the 1970s, and thus into the post-Stonewall era, a period of history DeKoven calls "the long sixties." DeKoven, "Psychoanalysis and Sixties Utopianism," 263.

18. See Spitzer's statement for the APA for a concurrent resolution regarding homosexual discrimination as a civil rights issue. Spitzer, "Homosexuality and Civil Rights." Hooker noted no difference in homosexuals' sense of adjustment to society. Though he steadfastly refused to become a subject of her research, Isherwood supported her groundbreaking work. Hooker, "Adjustment of the Male Overt Homosexual."

19. Bersani and Phillips, *Intimacies*, 35.

20. Warner, *Fear of a Queer Planet*. Cf. Warner, *Trouble with Normal*, for an influential account of the march toward social and cultural conformity in the contemporary LGBT movement.

21. Warner, *Fear of a Queer Planet*, xxv–xxvi.

22. Isherwood, *Lions and Shadows*, 7.

23. White, "Tale of Two Kitties," 2.

24. Shepherd, "Interview with Chad Parmenter," 11.

25. Bristow, "'I Am with You, Little Minority Sister,'" 147.

26. Ibid., 147.

27. See Auden and Isherwood's account of their 1938 trip to China before the Sino-Japanese conflict, *Journey to a War*.

28. For more on the Auden–Isherwood friendship, see Hynes, *Auden Generation*.

29. Isherwood, "Unused Chapter," 13.

30. In 1974, Isherwood gave an MLA address on homosexuality and literature that was, according to Berg, the first of its kind for that organization. Berg, "American Isherwood," 9–10.

31. Bersani and Phillips, *Intimacies*, 31–56, 57–88.

32. Ibid., 55.

33. For a treatment of the double burden on a queer, but not *gay*, individual, see Love's chapter on Pater, *Feeling Backward*.

34. Bersani and Phillips, *Intimacies*, 51–55.

35. Berlant, "Slow Death."

36. Baumeister, "Masochism as Escape from Self," 24.

37. Ibid., 29.

38. Berlant, "Slow Death," 779.

39. Ibid., 757.

40. Foucault's *History of Sexuality* popularized the notion of an "aesthetics of existence." Cf. Foucault, *Use of Pleasure* and *Care of the Self*.

41. Isherwood, "Unused Chapter," 5.

42. Ibid., 9.

43. Crenshaw, "Demarginalizing the Intersection of Race and Sex" and "Mapping the Margins."

44. In the classroom, George vocally sides with something called "the majority" and speaks of "minorities" in condescending and reductive terms (71–72).

45. In *Ugly Feelings*, Ngai calls anger one of the "classical political passions," 5.

46. Bersani, *Culture of Redemption*, 4.

47. Lilly, *Gay Men's Literature*, 189. Lilly writes, "The tradition of social realism [in] coming out novels . . . is indebted to the work of Isherwood."

48. Hardwick, "Sex and the Single Man," 4.

49. Much of my analysis of *Single Man*'s Western Vedic spirituality is based on Isherwood's spiritual autobiography, *My Guru and His Disciple*. The critical consensus is summarized by Bucknell and Summers. Bucknell, "Who Is Christopher Isherwood?" For a contemporary account of Isherwood's decades-long engagement with the Vedanta Society of Southern California, see Nagarajan, "Isherwood and the Vedantic Novel." For an unsympathetic take, see Chatterjee, "Guiding Star." For a more sympathetic account, see Murray, "Coleridge, Isherwood and Hindu Light."

50. Garnes, "*Single Man*," 201.

51. Sedgwick, *Touching Feeling*, 13.

52. Berlant, "Slow Death," 754.

53. Ibid.

54. For a classic example of the possibility of cultural vibrancy despite systematic oppression, see Patterson, *Slavery and Social Death*. Like Berlant's emphasis on "slow death," Patterson's focus on "social death" takes into account the potential for agency among the oppressed despite morbid conditions. Such agency bespeaks a form of optimism that might qualify as "cruel," in Berlant's terms (Berlant, *Cruel Optimism*). However, such optimism can also be read as a mode of affirmation. For a contrasting account, see Snediker, *Queer Optimism*.

6. Ibid., 129.

7. Ibid., 126, 36.

8. Ibid., 3.

9. Larsen, *Quicksand* (original 1928 edition), 208.

10. Larsen letter to Gertrude Stein, February 1, 1928; emphasis added.

11. Larsen refers here to Douglas's public defamation of Churchill. As the Douglas Archives tells it: "Douglas had claimed that Churchill had been part of a Jewish conspiracy to kill Lord Kitchener, the British Secretary of State for War. Kitchener had died on June 5, 1916, while on a diplomatic mission to Russia: the ship in which he was travelling, the armored cruiser HMS *Hampshire*, struck a German mine and sank west of the Orkney Islands." Douglas accused Churchill of falsifying a report on the sinking of the ship after the Battle of Jutland to cause a downturn in the market for British securities, so Churchill's Jewish associates could profiteer from buying the stocks at a cheaper price. In 1923, the Crown found Douglas guilty of criminal libel and sentenced him to six months in prison.

12. Larsen letter to Carl Van Vechten, postmarked November 18, 1930.

13. Love, "Modernism at Night," 744.

14. Davis, "Female Face."

15. Quoting the title of Hull, Scott, and Smith, *All the Women Are White, All the Blacks Are Men, But Some of Us Are Brave*; cf. the Combahee River Collective Statement.

16. Chauncey, *Gay New York*; D'Emilio, *Sexual Politics, Sexual Communities*; D'Emilio, "Capitalism and Gay Identity."

Coda

1. Als, *Women*, 67.

2. Ibid., 85.

3. Ibid., 75–76.

4. Woolf, *Mrs. Dalloway*, 11.

5. Ibid., 175.

BIBLIOGRAPHY

Abel, Jessica. "Women and Schizophrenia: The Fiction of Jean Rhys." *Contemporary Literature* 20, no. 2 (1979): 155–77.

Alcoff, Linda Martín, Michael Hames-García, Satya P. Mohanty, and Paula M. L. Moya, eds. *Identity Politics Reconsidered*. New York: Palgrave, 2006.

Als, Hilton. *The Women*. New York: Farrar, Straus & Giroux, 1998.

Alvarez, A. *New York Times Book Review*, March 17, 1974, 6–7. The Jean Rhys Archive. McFarlin Library, University of Tulsa, Oklahoma.

Amin, Kadji. *Disturbing Attachments: Genet, Modern Pederasty, and Queer History*. Durham: Duke University Press, 2017.

Angier, Carole. *Jean Rhys: Life and Work*. New York: Little, Brown, 1990.

Anonymous review of *Quartet*, by Jean Rhys. Newspaper clipping of book reviews of *The Left Bank and Other Stories* and *Quartet*. The Jean Rhys Archive. McFarlin Library, University of Tulsa, Oklahoma.

Auden, W. H., and Christopher Isherwood. *Journey to a War*. London: Faber and Faber, 1939.

Bal, Mieke. *Narratology: Introduction to the Theory of Narrative*. 2nd ed. Toronto: University of Toronto Press, 1997.

———. *Narratology: Introduction to the Theory of Narrative*. 3rd ed. Toronto: University of Toronto Press, 2009. Kindle.

Battershill, Claire. "Reticent Autobiography: Henry Green and Christopher Isherwood at the Hogarth Press." *Journal of Modern Literature* 39, no. 1 (2015): 38–54.

Baumeister, Roy F. *Escaping the Self: Alcoholism, Spirituality, Masochism, and Other Flights from the Burden of Selfhood*. New York: Harper, 1991.

———. "Masochism as Escape from Self." *Journal of Sex Research* 25, no. 1 (1988): 28–59.

Beer, Ethel S. "Social Psychiatry and the Day Nursery." *Journal of Educational Sociology* 10, no. 4 (December 1936): 207–14.

Berg, James J. "Introduction: The American Isherwood." In *Isherwood on Writing*, edited by James J. Berg, 1–33. Minneapolis: University of Minnesota Press, 2007.

Berlant, Lauren. *Cruel Optimism*. Durham: Duke University Press, 2011.

———. "Slow Death (Sovereignty, Obesity, Lateral Agency)." *Critical Inquiry* 33 (2007): 754–80.

Bernard, Emily. *Carl Van Vechten and the Harlem Renaissance*. New Haven: Yale University Press, 2012.

Bersani, Leo. *The Culture of Redemption*. Cambridge: Harvard University Press, 1990.

———. "Is the Rectum a Grave?" In *AIDS: Cultural Analysis, Cultural Activism*, edited by Douglas Crimp, 197–222. Cambridge: MIT Press, 1988. Reprinted in *Is the Rectum a Grave? and Other Essays*, 3–30. Chicago: University of Chicago Press, 2009.

Bersani, Leo, and Adam Phillips. *Intimacies*. Chicago: University of Chicago Press, 2008.

Bewes, Timothy. "Reading with the Grain: A New World in Literary Criticism." *differences* 21, no. 3 (2010): 1–33.

Bonikowski, Wyatt. Review of *Ford Madox Ford and the Misfit Moderns: Edwardian Fiction and the First World War*, by Rob Hawkes. *Modernism/Modernity* 20, no. 3 (September 2013): 614–15.

Booth, Wayne C. *The Rhetoric of Fiction*. 2nd ed. Chicago: University of Chicago Press, 1983.

Bowen, Stella. *Drawn from Life*. London: Virago, 1941.

Braithwaite, Edward Kamau. *Contradictory Omens: Cultural Diversity and Integration in the Caribbean*. Mona, Jamaica: Savacou, 1974.

———. "A Post-Crutionary [*sic*] Tale of the Helen of Our Wars." *Wasafiri* 11, no. 22 (1995): 69–78.

Bristow, Joseph. "'I Am with You, Little Minority Sister': Isherwood's Queer Sixties." In *The Queer Sixties*, edited by Patricia Juliana Smith, 145–63. New York: Routledge, 1999.

Bucknell, Katherine. "Who Is Christopher Isherwood?" In *Isherwood Century*, edited by James J. Berg and Christopher Freeman, 13–30. Madison: University of Wisconsin Press, 2000.

Butler, Judith. Bodies that Matter: On the Discursive Limits of "Sex." New York: Routledge, 1993.

———. *Gender Trouble: Feminism and the Subversion of Identity*. New York: Routledge, 1990.

Cameron, Sharon. *Impersonality: Seven Essays*. Chicago: University of Chicago Press, 2007.

Canning, Richard. Review of *Isherwood: A Life*, by Peter Parker. *Independent*, May 21, 2004. https://www.indepen dent.co.uk/arts-entertainment/books /reviews/isherwood-a-life-by-peter -parker-61347.html.

Carby, Hazel V. *Reconstructing Womanhood: The Emergence of the Afro-American Woman Novelist*. New York: Oxford University Press, 1987.

Carr, Jamie M. *Queer Times: Christopher Isherwood's Modernity*. New York: Routledge, 2006.

Carter, Eunice. Review of *The Blacker the Berry*, by Wallace Thurman. *Opportunity* 7 (May 1929): 162–63.

Carter, Erica, and Jenny Taylor, eds. "Modernism/Masochism." Special issue of *New Formations*, no. 7 (1989).

Casanova, Pascale. *The World Republic of Letters*. Translated by Malcolm DeBevoise. Cambridge, MA: Harvard University Press, 2007.

Caserio, Robert L., et al. "Forum: Conference Debates. The Antisocial Thesis in Queer Theory." *PMLA* 121 no. 3 (2006): 819–28.

Chatterjee, Niladri. "Guiding Star: Christopher Isherwood's Passage to Calcutta's Star Theatre." *ANQ: A Quarterly Journal of Short Articles, Notes, and Reviews* 21, no. 2 (Spring 2008): 61–65.

Chauncey, George. *Gay New York: Gender, Urban Culture, and the Making of the Gay World, 1890–1940*. New York: BasicBooks, 1994.

Cheng, Anne Anlin. *The Melancholy of Race: Psychoanalysis, Assimilation, and Hidden Grief*. New York: Oxford University Press, 2000.

Cohn, Dorrit. "Signposts of Fictionality: A Narratological Perspective." In *The Distinction of Fiction*, 109–31. Baltimore: Johns Hopkins University Press, 1999.

———. *Transparent Minds: Narrative Modes for Presenting Consciousness in Fiction*. Princeton: Princeton University Press, 1978.

Collins, Patricia Hill. "Mammies, Matriarchs, and Other Controlling Images." In *Black Feminist Thought: Knowledge,*

Consciousness, and the Politics of
Empowerment, 69–96. 2nd ed. New
York: Routledge, 2000.

Combahee River Collective. *The Combahee
River Collective Statement: Black
Feminist Organizing in the Seventies
and Eighties*. Albany, NY: Kitchen
Table / Women of Color Press, 1986.

Crenshaw, Kimberlé. "Demarginalizing
the Intersection of Race and Sex:
A Black Feminist Critique of
Antidiscrimination Doctrine, Feminist
Theory, and Antiracist Politics."
University of Chicago Legal Forum 14
(1989): 538–54.

———. "Mapping the Margins:
Intersectionality, Identity Politics, and
Violence Against Women of Color."
Stanford Law Review 43, no. 6 (1991):
1241–99.

Crowley, Mart. *The Boys in the Band*. 1968.
New York: Alyson Books, 2008.

Cullen, Countee. *Countee Cullen: Collected
Poems*. New York: Library of America,
2013.

Culler, Jonathan. "The Closeness of Close
Reading." *ADFL Bulletin* 41, no. 3
(2011): 8–13.

Cummings, Helen. "First Aid to the Misfit."
Journal of Education 120, no. 15
(December 1937): 403–4.

Cycholl, Garin. "'The Peculiar Immediacy of
Image': Formal Disintegration in *The
Misfits*." *Arthur Miller Journal* 10, no.
1 (2015): 18–26.

Davis, Thadious M. "A Female Face: Or,
Masking the Masculine in African
American Fiction Before Richard
Wright." *Teaching African American
Literature: Theory and Practice*,
edited by Maryemma Graham, Sharon
Pineault-Burke, and Marianna White
Davis, 98–131. New York: Routledge,
1998.

———. *Nella Larsen: Novelist of the Harlem
Renaissance: A Woman's Life Unveiled*.

Baton Rouge: Louisiana State
University Press, 1994.

Dean, Tim. "T. S. Eliot, Famous Clairvoyante."
In *Gender, Desire, and Sexuality in
T. S. Eliot*, edited by Cassandra Laity
and Nancy K. Gish, 43–65. New York:
Cambridge University Press, 2004.

———. *Unlimited Intimacy: Reflections on the
Subculture of Barebacking*. Chicago:
University of Chicago Press, 2009.

DeKoven, Marianne. "History, the Twentieth
Century, and a Contemporary Novel."
Novel 42, no. 2 (2009): 332–36.

———. "Psychoanalysis and Sixties
Utopianism." *Journal for the
Psychoanalysis of Culture and Society*
8, no. 2 (2003): 263–72.

Deleuze, Gilles. "Coldness and Cruelty." In
Masochism, translated by Jean McNeil,
9–142. New York: Zone Books, 1999.

Deleuze, Gilles, and Félix Guattari.
*Anti-Oedipus: Capitalism and
Schizophrenia*. 1983. Translated by
Robert Hurley, Mark Seem, and Helen
R. Lane. New York: Penguin, 2009.

———. *A Thousand Plateaus: Capitalism and
Schizophrenia*. Translated by Brian
Massumi. Minneapolis: University of
Minnesota Press, 1987.

Dell'Amico, Carol. *Colonialism and the
Modernist Moment in the Early Novels
of Jean Rhys*. New York: Routledge,
2005.

D'Emilio, John. "Capitalism and Gay
Identity." In *The Lesbian and Gay
Studies Reader*, edited by Henry
Abelove, Michèle Aina Barael, and
David M. Haleperin, 467–76. New
York: Routledge, 1993.

———. *Sexual Politics, Sexual Communities:
The Making of a Homosexual Minority
in the United States, 1940-1970*. 2nd
ed. Chicago: University of Chicago
Press, 1998.

Desmond, John. "Flannery O'Connor's Misfit
and the Mystery of Evil." *Renascence*
56, no. 2 (Winter 2004): 129–37.

Doan, Laura. *Fashioning Sapphism: The Origins of a Modern English Lesbian Culture*. New York: Columbia University Press, 2001.

The Douglas Archives. "Lord Alfred Douglas, 1870–1945." April 21, 2014. http://www.douglashistory.co.uk /history/alfreddouglas.htm.

Du Bois, W. E. B. "The Browsing Reader." Review of *Banjo*, by Claude McKay, *Passing*, by Nella Larsen, and *The Blacker the Berry*, by Wallace Thurman. *Crisis* 36, no. 7 (July 1929): 234, 249–50.

———. "Of Our Spiritual Strivings." 1903. In *The Souls of Black Folk*, 1–8. New York: Bantam, 1989.

———. *The Souls of Black Folk*. 1903. New York: Bantam, 1989.

Edelman, Lee. *No Future: Queer Theory and the Death Drive*. Durham: Duke University Press, 2004.

Eliot, T. S. "Tradition and the Individual Talent." *The Egoist* (1919).

Ellman, Maud. *The Poetics of Impersonality: T. S. Eliot and Pound*. Cambridge: Harvard University Press, 1988.

Emery, Mary Lou. *Jean Rhys at "World's End": Novels of Colonial and Sexual Exile*. Austin: University of Texas Press, 1990.

———. "The Poetics of Labor in Jean Rhys' Global Modernism." *Philological Quarterly* 90, nos. 2–3 (2011): 167–97.

Eng, David L., David Kazanjian, and Judith Butler. *Loss: The Politics of Mourning*. Berkeley, CA: University of California Press, 2002.

Eng, David L., with J. Halberstam and José Muñoz. "Introduction: What's Queer About Queer Studies Now?" Special Issue of *Social Text* 84–85 (2005): 1–17.

Esty, Jed. *Unseasonable Youth: Modernism, Colonialism, and the Fiction of Development*. New York: Oxford University Press, 2012.

Farmer, Joy A. "The Female Misfit: The Enduring Legacy of Flannery O'Connor's Ruby Hill and JoAllen Bradham's Genie Putman." *Flannery O'Connor Review* 2 (2003–2004): 53–62.

Felski, Rita. "Context Stinks!" *New Literary History* 42, no. 4 (Autumn 2011): 573–91.

———. *The Gender of Modernity*. Cambridge: Harvard University Press, 1995.

Fisher, Philip. *The Vehement Passions*. Princeton: Princeton University Press, 2002.

Fisher, Rudolph. "City of Refuge." *Atlantic Monthly* (February 1925).

———. *The Walls of Jericho*. 1928. Salem, N.H.: Ayer, 1992.

Fludernik, Monika. *An Introduction to Narratology*. Translated by Patricia Häusler-Greenfield and Monica Fludernik. New York: Routledge, 2009.

Ford, Ford Madox. "Preface: Rive Gauche." In *The Left Bank and Other Stories*, by Jean Rhys, 7–27. London: Jonathan Cape, 1927.

———. *When the Wicked Man*. London: Jonathan Cape, 1932.

Foucault, Michel. *The Care of the Self*. Vol. 3 of *The History of Sexuality*. Translated by Robert Hurley. New York: Random House, 1986.

———. *An Introduction*. Vol. 1 of *The History of Sexuality*. 1978. Translated by Robert Hurley. New York: Vintage, 1990.

———. *The Use of Pleasure*. Vol. 2 of *The History of Sexuality*. Translated by Robert Hurley. New York: Random House, 1985.

———. *La volonté de savoir*. Vol. 1 of *Histoire de la sexualité*. 1976. Paris: Gallimard, 2014.

Gaither, Renoir W. "The Moment of Revision: A Reappraisal of Wallace Thurman's Aesthetics in *The Blacker the Berry* and *Infants of the Spring.*" *College Language Association Journal* 37, no. 1 (1993): 81–93.

Ganter, Granville. "Decadence, Sexuality, and the Bohemian Vision of Wallace Thurman." In *New Voices of the Harlem Renaissance: Essays on Race, Gender, and Literary Discourse,* edited by Australia Tarver and Paula C. Barnes, 194–213. Madison: Farleigh Dickinson University Press, 2006.

Garland-Thompson, Rosemary. "Misfits: A Feminist Materialist Disability Concept." *Hypatia* 26, no. 3 (Summer 2011): 591–609.

Garnes, David. "*A Single Man,* Then and Now." In *The Isherwood Century: Essays on the Life and Work of Christopher Isherwood,* edited by James J. Berg and Christopher Freeman, 196–202. Madison: University of Wisconsin Press, 2000.

Genette, Gérard. *Narrative Discourse: An Essay in Method.* Translated by Jane E. Lewin. Ithaca: Cornell University Press, 1980.

———. *Narrative Discourse Revisited.* Translated by Jane E. Lewin. Ithaca: Cornell University Press, 1988.

Goffman, Erving. *Stigma: On the Management of Spoiled Identity.* New York: Simon & Schuster, 1963.

Goldstone, Andrew. "The Doxa of Reading." *PMLA* 132, no. 3 (2017): 636–42.

———. *Fictions of Autonomy: Modernism from Wilde to de Man.* New York: Oxford University Press, 2013.

———. "Remarks to the Comparative Modernisms Workshop at Northwestern." January 15, 2013. https://andrewgoldstone.com /blog/2013/01/15/nu-remarks.

Haizlip, Shirlee Taylor. Introduction to *The Blacker the Berry,* by Wallace Thurman, 9–15. New York: Scribner, 1996.

Halberstam, J. (Jack). "'A Writer of Misfits': 'John' Radclyffe Hall and the Discourse of Inversion." In *Palatable Poison: Critical Perspectives on "The Well of Loneliness,"* edited by Laura Doan and Jay Prosser, 145–61. New York: Columbia University Press, 2002.

Hall, Radclyffe ("John"). Letter to Evgenia Souline. October 24, 1934. In *Your John: The Love Letters of Radclyffe Hall,* edited by Joanne Glasgow, 76–79. New York: New York University Press, 1997.

———. *The Well of Loneliness.* 1928. New York: Anchor Books, 1990.

Halley, Janet. *Split Decisions: How and Why to Take a Break from Feminism.* Princeton: Princeton University Press, 2006.

Hames-García, Michael, and Paula M. L. Moya, eds. *Reclaiming Identity: Realist Theory and the Predicament of Postmodernism.* Berkeley: University of California Press, 2000.

Hardwick, Elizabeth. "Sex and the Single Man." Review of *A Single Man,* by Christopher Isherwood. *New York Review of Books* 3, no. 1 (August 1964): 4.

Hawkes, Rob. *Ford Madox Ford and the Misfit Moderns: Edwardian Fiction and the First World War.* Basingstoke: Palgrave Macmillan, 2012.

Heinlein, Robert A. "Misfit." *Astounding Science-Fiction* 24, no. 3 (November 1939): 53–67.

Hemingway, Ernest. *The Sun Also Rises.* 1926. New York: Scribner, 2006.

Herman, David. "Hypothetical Focalization." *Narrative* 2, no. 3 (1994): 230–53.

Holland, Sharon Patricia. *The Erotic Life of Racism.* Durham: Duke University Press, 2012.

Hooker, Evelyn. "The Adjustment of the Male Overt Homosexual." *Journal of Projective Techniques* 21 (1957): 18–31.

Horner, Carl S. "Misfit as Metaphor: The Question and the Contradiction of Lupus in Flannery O'Connor's 'A Good Man Is Hard to Find.'" *Disability Studies Quarterly* 25, no. 4 (Fall 2005).

Howarth, Peter. "Housman's Dirty Postcards: Poetry, Modernism, and Masochism." *PMLA* 124, no. 3 (2009): 764–81.

Hughes, Langston. *Autobiography: The Big Sea.* In *The Collected Works of Langston Hughes*, edited by Joseph McClaren. Vol. 13. Columbia: University of Missouri Press, 2002.

———. *The Big Sea: An Autobiography.* New York: Knopf, 1940.

———. "The Negro Artist and the Racial Mountain." *Nation* (1926).

Hull, Akasha (Gloria T.), Patricia Bell Scott, and Barbara Smith, eds. *All the Women Are White, All the Blacks Are Men, But Some of Us Are Brave: Black Women's Studies.* New York: Feminist Press, 1982.

Hutchinson, George. *In Search of Nella Larsen: A Biography of the Color Line.* Cambridge: Harvard University Press, 2006.

Hynes, Samuel. *The Auden Generation: Literature and Politics in England in the 1930s.* New York: Viking, 1977.

Isherwood, Christopher. *The Berlin Stories.* 1945. New York: New Directions, 2008.

———. *Christopher and His Kind.* 1976. Minneapolis: University of Minnesota Press, 2001.

———. "First Draft [*Christopher and His Kind*]." 1973–1974. TS. Christopher Isherwood Papers CI 1030, Huntington Library, California.

———. *Goodbye to Berlin.* 1939. In *The Berlin Stories.* New York: New Directions, 2008.

———. *Isherwood on Writing.* Edited by James J. Berg. Minneapolis: University of Minnesota Press, 2007.

———. *The Last of Mr. Norris.* 1935. In *The Berlin Stories.* New York: New Directions, 2008.

———. *Lions and Shadows: An Education in the Twenties.* 1938. Norfolk: New Directions, 1947.

———. *My Guru and His Disciple.* New York: Farrar, 1980.

———. *A Single Man.* 1964. Minneapolis: University of Minnesota Press, 2001.

———. "Unused Chapter [*Christopher and His Kind*]." 1973–1974. TS. Christopher Isherwood Papers CI 1029a, Huntington Library, California.

James, Henry. *The Turn of the Screw.* 1898. New York: Dover, 1991.

Jameson, Fredric. *The Political Unconscious: Narrative as a Socially Symbolic Act.* Ithaca: Cornell University Press, 1981.

———. *A Singular Modernity: Essay on the Ontology of the Present.* New York: Verso, 2013.

Jarraway, David. "Tales of the City: Marginality, Community, and the Problem of (Gay) Identity in Wallace Thurman's 'Harlem' Fiction." *College English* 65, no. 1 (2002): 36–52.

Jenkins, Morgan. "The Forgotten Work of Jessie Redmon Fauset." *New Yorker*, February 18, 2017. https://www.new yorker.com/books/page-turner/the -forgotten-work-of-jessie-redmon-fauset.

Jin, Jay. "Problems of Scale in 'Close' and 'Distant' Reading." *Philological Quarterly* 96, no. 1 (2017): 105–29.

Johnson, Helene. *This Waiting For Love: Helene Johnson, Poet of the Harlem Renaissance.* Edited by Verner D. Mitchell. Amherst: University of Massachusetts Press, 2006.

Johnson, James Weldon. *Autobiography of an Ex-Colored Man.* 1912. New York: Knopf, 1927.

Joyce, James. *The Portrait of the Artist as a Young Man.* 1916. New York: Norton, 2007.

———. *Ulysses*. 1922. New York: Random House, 1986.

Kaplan, Carla. "Introduction: Nella Larsen's Erotics of Race." In *Passing*, by Nella Larsen, edited by Carla Kaplan, ix–xxvii. New York: Norton, 2007.

Kappers–den Hollander, Martine. "A Gloomy Child and Its Devoted Godmother: Jean Rhys, *Barred, Sous les Verrous*, and *In de Strik*." In *Critical Perspectives on Jean Rhys*, edited by Pierrette M. Frickey, 44–53. Washington, DC: Three Continents, 1990.

King, Martin Luther, Jr. "Draft of Chapter II, 'Transformed Nonconformist.'" July 1962–March 1963. In *Advocate of the Social Gospel, September 1948–March 1963*, vol. 6, *The Papers of Martin Luther King, Jr.*, edited by Clayborne Carson, Susan Carson, Susan Englander, Troy Jackson, and Gerald Smith, 466–77. Berkeley: University of California Press, 2007. The King Papers, Stanford University. https://kinginstitute.stanford.edu/king-papers/documents/draft-chapter-ii-transformed-nonconformist.

Kurnick, David. "Embarrassment and the Forms of Redemption." *PMLA* 125, no. 2 (2010): 398–403.

Ladani, Zara J. "Robert A. Heinlein in Historical and Cultural Context." In *Critical Insights: Robert A. Heinlein*, edited by Rafeeq O. McGiveron, 27–41. Ipswich, MA: Salem Press, 2005.

Larsen, Nella. *Passing*. New York: Knopf, 1929. Reprinted in *The Complete Fiction of Nella Larsen*, edited by Charles R. Larson, 163–275. New York: Anchor, 2001.

———. *Quicksand*. New York: Knopf, 1928.

———. *Quicksand*. In *The Complete Fiction of Nella Larsen*, edited by Charles R. Larson, 29–162. New York: Anchor, 2001.

———. *"Quicksand" and "Passing."* Edited by Deborah E. McDowell. New Brunswick: Rutgers University Press, 1986.

Larsen Imes, Nella. "At Home." Letter to Carl Van Vechten. Postmarked May 1, 1928. Carl Van Vechten Papers Related to African American Arts and Letters, James Weldon Johnson Collection in the Yale Collection of American Literature, Beinecke Rare Book and Manuscript Library.

———. Letter to Carl Van Vechten. Postmarked March 5, 1930. Carl Van Vechten Papers Related to African American Arts and Letters, James Weldon Johnson Collection in the Yale Collection of American Literature, Beinecke Rare Book and Manuscript Library.

———. Letter to Carl Van Vechten. Postmarked November 18, 1930. Carl Van Vechten Papers Related to African American Arts and Letters, James Weldon Johnson Collection in the Yale Collection of American Literature, Beinecke Rare Book and Manuscript Library.

———. Letter to Gertrude Stein. February 1, 1928. Gertrude Stein and Alice B. Toklas Papers, Yale Collection of American Literature, Beinecke Rare Book and Manuscript Library.

———. "Monday." Letter to Carl Van Vechten. 1925. Carl Van Vechten Papers Related to African American Arts and Letters, James Weldon Johnson Collection in the Yale Collection of American Literature, Beinecke Rare Book and Manuscript Library.

———. "Tuesday 19th." Letter to Dorothy Peterson. July 19, 1927. Dorothy Peterson Collection, Yale Collection of American Literature, Beinecke Rare Book and Manuscript Library.

Larson, Charles R. *Invisible Darkness: Jean Toomer and Nella Larsen*. Iowa City: University of Iowa Press, 1993.

Latham, Sean. *The Art of Scandal: Modernism, Libel Law, and the Roman à Clef*. New York: Oxford University Press, 2009.

Levine, Paul. "J. D. Salinger: The Development of the Misfit Hero." *Twentieth-Century Literature* 4, no. 3 (October 1958): 92–99.

Lewis, David Levering. *When Harlem Was in Vogue*. New York: Knopf, 1981.

Lewis, Theophilus. Letter to Dorothy Peterson. January 29, 1929. Dorothy Peterson Collection. Yale Collection of American Literature, Beinecke Rare Book and Manuscript Library, Yale University.

———. "Wallace Thurman Is Model Harlemite." *Amsterdam News*, 1930.

Liggins, Emma. "The Misfit Lesbian Heroine of Inter-War Fiction." In *Odd Women? Spinsters, Lesbians, and Widows in British Women's Fiction, 1850s–1930s*, 163–206. Manchester: Manchester University Press, 2014.

Lilly, Mark. *Gay Men's Literature in the Twentieth Century*. New York: New York University Press, 1993.

Locke, Alain. "Enter the New Negro." Special issue of *Survey Graphic*, "Harlem: Mecca of the New Negro" (March 1925).

———, ed. *The New Negro: An Interpretation*. 1925. Reprinted as *The New Negro: Voices of the Harlem Renaissance*. New York: Touchstone Books, 1992.

Lorde, Audre. "The Uses of the Erotic: The Erotic as Power." 1984. In *Sister Outsider: Essays and Speeches*, 53–59. Berkeley: Crossing Press, 2007.

Love, Heather K. *Feeling Backward: Loss and the Politics of Queer History*. Cambridge: Harvard University Press, 2007.

———. "Introduction: Modernism at Night." *PMLA* 124, no. 3 (May 2009): 744–48.

———. Introduction to "Rethinking Sex." Special issue of *GLQ: A Journal of Lesbian and Gay Studies* 17, no. 1 (2011): 1–14.

Marcuse, Herbert. *Eros and Civilization: A Philosophical Inquiry into Freud*. 1966. Boston: Beacon, 1975.

———. *One-Dimensional Man: Studies in the Ideology of Advanced Industrial Society*. 1964. Boston: Beacon Press, 1991.

Mardorossian, Carine. "Franz Fanon: An Indispensable Theoretical Misfit Today." *College Literature* 45, no. 1 (Winter 2018): 18–23.

Martínez-Bonati, Félix. *Fictive Discourse and the Structures of Literature: A Phenomenological Approach*. Translated by Philip W. Silver. Ithaca: Cornell University Press, 1981.

McDowell, Deborah E. Introduction to *"Quicksand" and "Passing,"* by Nella Larsen, edited by Deborah E. McDowell, ix–xxxv. New Brunswick: Rutgers University Press, 1986.

McHale, Brian. "Free Indirect Discourse: A Survey of Recent Accounts." *PTL: A Journal for Descriptive Poetics and Theory of Literature* 3 (1978): 249–87.

McIntire, Gabrielle. "Toward a Narratology of Passing: Epistemology, Race, and Misrecognition in Nella Larsen's *Passing*." *Callaloo* 35, no. 3 (Summer 2012): 778–94.

McKay, Claude. *Home to Harlem*. 1928. Boston: Northeastern University Press, 1987.

Miller, Arthur. *The Misfits*. New York: Viking, 1960.

"Misfit." *Oxford English Dictionary Online*. 3rd ed. 2002.

Mitchell, Jennifer. "The Trouble with 'Victim': Triangulated Masochism in Jean Rhys' *Quartet*." In *Rhys Matters: New Critical Perspectives*, edited by Mary

Wilson and Kerry L. Johnson, 189–211. New York: Palgrave, 2013.

Mohanty, Satya P. "The Epistemic Status of Cultural Identity: On *Beloved* and the Postcolonial Condition." *Cultural Critique* 24 (1993): 41–80.

Moore, Gene. "Focalization and Narrative Voice in *What Maisie Knew*." *Language and Style* 22, no. 1 (1989): 3–24.

Moran, Patricia. "'A Doormat in a World of Boots': Jean Rhys and the Masochistic Aesthetic." In *Virginia Woolf, Jean Rhys, and the Aesthetics of Trauma*, 115–47. New York: Palgrave, 2007.

Muñoz, Jose Esteban. *Disidentifications: Queers of Color and the Performance of Politics*. Minneapolis: University of Minnesota Press, 1999.

Murray, Chris. "Coleridge, Isherwood, and Hindu Light." *Romanticism* 22, no. 3 (2016): 269–78.

Musser, Amber Jamilla. "Re-membering Audre." In *No Tea, No Shade: New Writings in Black Queer Studies*, edited by E. Patrick Johnson, 346–61. Durham: Duke University Press, 2016.

Nagarajan, S. "Christopher Isherwood and the Vedantic Novel: A Study of *A Single Man*." *Ariel* 3, no. 4 (1972): 63–71.

Naipaul, V. S. "Without a Dog's Chance." Review of *After Leaving Mr. Mackenzie*, by Jean Rhys. *New York Review of Books*, May 18, 1972. The Jean Rhys Papers, McFarlin Library, University of Tulsa, Oklahoma.

Nair, Sashi. *Secrecy and Sapphic Modernism: Writing Romans à Clef Between the Wars*. London: Palgrave Macmillan, 2012.

Nancy, Jean-Luc. *The Inoperative Community*. Translated by Peter Connor, Lisa Garbus, Michael Holland, and Simona Sawhney. Minneapolis: University of Minnesota Press, 1991.

Nandrea, Lorri G. *Misfit Forms: Paths Not Taken by the British Novel*. New York: Fordham University Press, 2015.

Nash, Jennifer C. *Black Feminism Reimagined: After Intersectionality*. Durham: Duke University Press, 2019.

Nealon, Christopher. *Foundlings: Gay and Lesbian Historical Emotion Before Stonewall*. Durham: Duke University Press, 2001.

Nève, Édouard de (Jean Lenglet). *Barred*. Translated by Jean Rhys. London: Desmond Harmsworth, 1932.

———. *In de Strik*. Amsterdam: Andries Blitz, 1932.

———. *Sous les verrous*. Paris: Librairie Stock, 1933.

The New York Amsterdam News. "Nella Larsen, Author of 'Quicksand,' Honor Guest at N.A.A.C.P. Tea." May 23, 1928.

Ngai, Sianne. *Ugly Feelings*. Cambridge: Harvard University Press, 2005.

Nguyen, Hoang Tan. *A View from the Bottom: Asian American Masculinity and Sexual Representation*. Durham: Duke University Press, 2014.

North, Joseph. "What's 'New Critical' About 'Close Reading'?: I. A. Richards and His New Critical Reception." *New Literary History* 44, no. 1 (Winter 2013): 141–57.

Nugent, Richard Bruce. Letter to Dorothy Peterson, n.d. (possibly November 7, 1928). Wallace Thurman Collection. Yale Collection of American Literature, Beinecke Rare Book and Manuscript Library.

———. "Smoke, Lilies, and Jade," *Fire!! A Quarterly Devoted to Younger Negro Artists* 1, no. 1 (November 1926): 33–39.

Patterson, Orlando. *Slavery and Social Death: A Comparative Study*. Cambridge: Harvard University Press, 1982.

Payne, E. George. "A Program of Educational Sociology." *Journal of Educational Sociology* 2, no. 8 (April 1929): 457–63.

Peterson, Dorothy. Letter to Carl Van Vechten. June 21 (postmarked June

22), 1943. Carl Van Vechten Papers Related to African American Arts and Letters, James Weldon Johnson Collection in the Yale Collection of American Literature, Beinecke Rare Book and Manuscript Library.

Plum, Steve. *Neue Sachlichkeit 1918–33: Unity and Diversity of an Art Movement*. Amsterdam: Rodopi, 2006.

Poe, Edgar Allan. "The Fall of the House of Usher." 1839. In *The Fall of the House of Usher and Other Tales*, 117–37. New York: Signet, 2006.

Price, Matthew Burroughs. "A Genealogy of Queer Detachment." *PMLA* 130 no. 3 (2015): 648–65.

Proust, Marcel. *À la recherche du temps perdu*. 1913–27. Edited by Jean-Yves Tadié. Paris: La Pléiade–Gallimard, 1999.

———. *In Search of Lost Time*. Translated by C. K. Scott Montcrieff, Terence Kilmartin, D. J. Enright, and Andreas Mayor. 6 vols. New York: Modern Library, 2003.

Puar, Jasbir K. *Terrorist Assemblages: Homonationalism in Queer Times*. Durham: Duke University Press, 2007.

Ramsay, Stephen. *Reading Machines: Toward an Algorithmic Criticism*. Urbana: University of Illinois Press, 2011.

Rhys, Jean. *After Leaving Mr. Mackenzie*. 1931. New York: Norton, 1997.

———. *Good Morning, Midnight*. 1939. New York: Norton, 1999.

———. The Jean Rhys Archive. McFarlin Library, University of Tulsa, Oklahoma.

———. *The Left Bank and Other Stories*. London: Jonathan Cape, 1927.

———. *Postures*. London: Chatto and Windus, 1928.

———. *Quartet*. 1929. New York: Norton, 1997.

———. *Tigers Are Better Looking*. New York: Harper & Row, 1974.

———. "Vienne." 1927. In *The Collected Stories*, 94–124. New York: Norton, 1987.

———. *Voyage in the Dark*. 1934. New York: Norton, 1982.

———. *Wide Sargasso Sea*. 1966. New York: Norton, 1998.

Richards, I. A. *Practical Criticism: A Study of Literary Judgment*. Edinburgh: Edinburgh Press, 1930.

Roche, Hannah. "An 'Ordinary Novel': Genre Trouble in Radclyffe Hall's *The Well of Loneliness*." *Textual Practice* 32, no. 1 (2018): 101–17.

Rubin, Gayle. "Sexual Traffic." Interview with Judith Butler. *differences* 6, nos. 2–3 (1994): 62–99.

———. "Thinking Sex: Notes for a Radical Theory of the Politics of Sexuality." In *The Lesbian and Gay Studies Reader*, edited by Henry Abelove, Michèle A. Barale, and David M. Halperin, 3–44. New York: Routledge, 1993.

Saloman, Randi. "Making Modernism Fit." Review of *Ford Madox Ford and the Misfit Moderns: Edwardian Fiction and the First World War*, by Rob Hawkes. *Journal of Modern Literature* 38, no. 4 (Summer 2015): 192–96.

Sanders, José, and Gisela Redeker. "Speech and Thought in Narrative Discourse." In *Spaces, Worlds, and Grammar*, edited by Gilles Fauconnier and Eve Sweetser, 290–317. Chicago: University of Chicago Press, 1996.

Savory, Elaine. *Jean Rhys*. Cambridge: Cambridge University Press, 1998.

———. "Jean Rhys, Race and Caribbean / English Criticism." *Wasafiri* 14, no. 28 (1998): 33–34.

Schavrien, Judy. "The Joyce Hero: Everywomanman [*sic*] and Misfit." *Abiko Quarterly with James Joyce Studies* 9, no. 17 (Fall/Winter 1997–98): 86–117.

Scott, Daniel M., III. "Harlem Shadows: Re-evaluating Wallace Thurman's *The*

Blacker the Berry." *MELUS* 29, nos. 3–4 (Fall/Winter 2004): 323–39.

Scott, Darieck. *Extravagant Abjection: Blackness, Power, and Sexuality in the African American Literary Imagination*. New York: New York University Press, 2010.

Sedgwick, Eve Kosofsky. *Epistemology of the Closet*. Berkeley: University of California Press, 1990.

———. Introduction to *Touching Feeling: Affect, Pedagogy, Performativity*, 1–25. Durham: Duke University Press, 2003.

———. "Paranoid Reading and Reparative Reading; Or, You're So Paranoid, You Probably Think This Essay Is about You." In *Touching Feeling: Affect, Pedagogy, Performativity*, 123–52. Durham: Duke University Press, 2003.

Shen, Dan. "Unreliability." In *The Living Handbook of Narratology*, edited by Peter Hühn et al. Hamburg: Hamburg University Press, June 27, 2011. Revised December 31, 2013. www.lhn. uni-hamburg.de/article/unreliability.

Shepherd, Reginald. "An Interview with Chad Parmenter." *American Poetry Review* 37, no. 5 (2008): 11–13.

Sherrard-Johnson, Cherene. "'A Plea for Color': Nella Larsen's Iconography of the Mulatta." *American Literature* 76, no. 4 (December 2004): 833–69.

Simmel, Georg. "The Stranger." 1908. In *On Individuality and Social Forms*, 143–49. Translated by Donald N. Levine. Chicago: University of Chicago Press, 1971.

Singh, Amritjit. "Introduction: Wallace Thurman and the Harlem Renaissance." In *The Collected Writings of Wallace Thurman: A Harlem Renaissance Reader*, edited by Amritjit Singh and Daniel M. Scott III, 1–28. New Brunswick: Rutgers University Press, 2003.

Singh, Amritjit, and Daniel M. Scott III, eds. *The Collected Writings of Wallace*

Thurman: A Harlem Renaissance Reader*. New Brunswick: Rutgers University Press, 2003.

Snediker, Michael D. *Queer Optimism: Lyric Personhood and Other Felicitous Persuasions*. Minneapolis: University of Minnesota Press, 2009.

Sneller, Judy E. "Bad Boys / Black Misfits: Ruth McEnery Stuart's Humor and 'The Negro Question.'" In *Images of the Child*, edited by Harry Eiss, 215–28. Bowling Green: Bowling Green State University Press, 1994.

Sorum, Eve. "Masochistic Modernisms: A Reading of Eliot and Woolf." *Journal of Modern Literature* 28, no. 3 (2005): 25–43.

Soskind, William. Review of *After Leaving Mr Mackenzie*, by Jean Rhys. *The New York Evening Post* (June 26, 1931). The Jean Rhys Archive, McFarlin Library, University of Tulsa, Oklahoma.

Spitzer, Robert L. "Homosexuality and Civil Rights: Position Statement." American Psychiatric Association. December 1973.

Stein, Gertrude. "Melanctha." In *Three Lives*. New York: Grafton Press, 1909.

Sullivan, John Jeremiah. "The Curses." *Sewanee Review* 125, no. 1 (Winter 2017): 1–23.

Summers, Claude. Foreword to *Isherwood on Writing*, by Christopher Isherwood, edited by James J. Berg, vii–xv. Minneapolis: University of Minnesota Press, 2007.

Thomas, Sue. "Adulterous Liaisons: Jean Rhys, Stella Bowen, and Feminist Reading." *Australian Humanities Review* 22 (2001). http://www .australianhumanitiesreview.org /adulterous-liaisons-jean-rhys-stella -bowen-and-feminist-reading.

Thompson, Ewa M. "The Russian Formalists and the New Critics: Two Types of the Close Reading of the Text." *Southern Humanities Review* 4 (1970): 145–54.

Thurman, Wallace. *The Blacker the Berry . . . A Novel of Negro Life*. 1929. New York: Arno Press & the New York Times, 1969.

——. "Cordelia the Crude." *Fire!! A Quarterly Devoted to Younger Negro Artists* 1, no. 1 (November 1926): 5–6.

——, ed. *Harlem: A Forum of Negro Life* 1 (November 1928; H. K. Parker Publishing Company).

——. "High, Low, Past, and Present." In *The Collected Writings of Wallace Thurman: A Harlem Renaissance Reader*, edited by Amritjit Singh and Daniel M. Scott III, 218–20. New Brunswick: Rutgers University Press, 2003.

——. *Infants of the Spring*. 1932. Boston: Northeastern University Press, 1992.

——. "Negro Artists and the Negro." In *The Collected Writings of Wallace Thurman: A Harlem Renaissance Reader*, edited by Amritjit Singh and Daniel M. Scott III, 195–99. New Brunswick: Rutgers University Press, 2003.

——. "Negro Artists and the Negro." *New Republic* 52 (August 31, 1927): 37–39.

——. "Nephews of Uncle Remus." *Independent* 119 (September 1927): 297–98.

——. "Notes on a Stepchild." In *The Collected Writings of Wallace Thurman: A Harlem Renaissance Reader*, edited by Amritjit Singh and Daniel M. Scott III, 235–40. New Brunswick: Rutgers University Press, 2003.

——. "Notes on a Stepchild." Wallace Thurman Collection. Yale Collection of American Literature, Beinecke Rare Book and Manuscript Library.

——. Notes—Short Review of *Flight*, by Rudolph Fisher. In *The Collected Writings of Wallace Thurman: A Harlem Renaissance Reader*, edited by Amritjit Singh and Daniel M. Scott III, 190. New Brunswick: Rutgers University Press, 2003.

——. Review of *Infants of the Spring*, by Wallace Thurman. In *The Collected Writings of Wallace Thurman: A Harlem Renaissance Reader*, edited by Amritjit Singh and Daniel M. Scott III, 226–28. New Brunswick: Rutgers University Press, 2003.

——. "This Negro Literary Renaissance." In *The Collected Writings of Wallace Thurman: A Harlem Renaissance Reader*, edited by Amritjit Singh and Daniel M. Scott III, 241–51. New Brunswick: Rutgers University Press, 2003.

Thurman, Wallace, and William Jourdan Rapp. *Harlem: A Melodrama of Negro Life*. 1928. In *The Collected Writings of Wallace Thurman: A Harlem Renaissance Reader*, edited by Amritjit Singh and Daniel M. Scott III, 306–69. New Brunswick: Rutgers University Press, 2003.

Tredgold, Roger F. "Changes in Social Responsibilities—and the Misfit." *Journal of the Royal Society of Arts* 104, no. 4987 (September 28, 1956): 870–82.

Vadde, Aarthi. *Chimeras of Form: Modernist Internationalism Beyond Europe, 1914–2016*. New York: Columbia University Press, 2016.

Van Notten, Eleonor. *Wallace Thurman's Harlem Renaissance*. Amsterdam: Rodopi, 1994.

Van Vechten, Carl. *Nigger Heaven*. 1926. New York: Farrar, Straus & Giroux, 1980.

Vilain, Philippe. "Autofiction." In *The Novelist's Lexicon: Writers on the Words That Define Their Work*, edited by Villa Gillet and Le Monde, 5–7. New York: Columbia University Press, 2011.

Walker, Alice. "Looking for Zora." *Ms.*, 1975, 74–79, 85–89.

——. *In Search of Our Mothers' Gardens: Womanist Prose*. New York: Harcourt, 1983.

Walker, Daniel. "Exploding the Canon: A Re-Examination of Wallace Thurman's Assault on the Harlem Renaissance." *Western Journal of Black Studies* 22, no. 3 (1998): 153–58.

Walker, Rafael. "Nella Larsen Reconsidered: The Trouble with Desire in *Quicksand* and *Passing*." *MELUS* 41 no. 1 (Spring 2016): 165–92.

Warner, Michael. Introduction to *Fear of a Queer Planet*, edited by Michael Warner, vii–xxxi. Minneapolis: University of Minnesota Press, 1993.

———. *The Trouble with Normal: Sex, Politics, and the Ethics of Queer Life*. New York: Free Press, 1999.

Washington, Mary Helen. "Nella Larsen: Mystery Woman of the Harlem Renaissance." *Ms.* 9 (December 1980): 44–50.

Watt, Ian. "The First Paragraph of *The Ambassadors*: An Explication." *Essays in Criticism* 10, no. 3 (July 1960): 250–74.

Wertheim, Bonnie. "Nella Larsen, 1891–1964." *New York Times*, March 8, 2018. https://www.nytimes.com/interactive/2018/obituaries/overlooked-nella-larsen-html.

West, Dorothy. "Elephant's Dance: A Memoir of Wallace Thurman." *Black World* 20, no. 1 (November 1970): 77–85.

West, Rebecca. "The Pursuit of Misery in Some of the New Novels." Review of *After Leaving Mr. Mackenzie*, by Jean Rhys. *Daily Telegraph*, January 30, 1931. Jean Rhys Papers, Series I. Box 5, McFarlin Library, University of Tulsa, Oklahoma.

White, Edmund. "A Tale of Two Kitties." Review of *Isherwood: A Life Revealed*, by Peter Parker. *Times Literary Supplement* (June 4, 2004): 3–4.

White, Walter F. *Fire in the Flint*. 1924. Athens: University of Georgia Press, 1996.

Williams, Andreá N. *Dividing Lines: Class Anxiety and Postbellum Black Fiction*. Michigan: University of Michigan Press, 2013.

Williams, Raymond. *Marxism and Literature*. Oxford: Oxford University Press, 1977.

———. *Reading and Criticism*. London: Frederick Muller, 1950.

———. "Structures of Feeling." In *Marxism and Literature*, 128–35. Oxford: Oxford University Press, 1977.

Wood, Dan. "Misfits, Anarchy, and the Absolute: Interpreting O'Connor Through Levinasian Themes." *Literature and Theology* 29, no. 1 (March 2015): 33–46.

Woolf, Virginia. *Mrs. Dalloway*. 1925. New York: Mariner, 1990.

———. *A Room of One's Own*. 1929. New York: Harcourt, 2005.

———. *To the Lighthouse*. 1927. New York: Harcourt, 2005.

Wyndham, Francis. Introduction to *Wide Sargasso Sea*, by Jean Rhys, 5–13. New York: Norton, 1992.

———. "Page proofs for *Art and Literature*, December 27, 1963, with handwritten revisions and additions to text by Jean Rhys." The Jean Rhys Archive, McFarlin Library, University of Tulsa, Oklahoma.

Žižek, Slavoj. "Philosophy, the 'Unknown Knowns,' and the Public Use of Reason." *Topoi* 25 (2006): 137–42.

INDEX

tragic mulatto trope, 60, 64, 70, 75

Tredgold, Roger, 21–22

Turn of the Screw, The (James), 141

Ulysses (Joyce), 17, 26–27

Uncle Tom's Cabin (Stow), 103

understanding *vs.* classification, 130, 133–36, 137–40, 152

universalism, 12–13, 22–24, 28, 30

Upward, Edward, 163

utopianism rhetoric, 5–6, 38–39

Vadde, Aarthi, 196n3

Van Vechten, Carl
    Larsen's relationship and correspondence with, 55, 56, 57, 58, 189, 190
    New Negro movement, place in, 56, 197n11
    and Thurman, 3, 97
    Nigger Heaven, 89, 102

Vedanta Hinduism, 155–56, 180

Voyage in the Dark (Rhys), 129

Walker, Alice, 53, 54

Walker, Daniel, 91, 199n12

Walker, Rafael, 54, 86

Walls of Jericho, The (Fisher), 88–89

Warner, Michael, 8, 9, 122–23, 161

Washington, Booker T., 63

Washington, Mary Helen, 53

Watt, Ian, 51, 197n12

Well of Loneliness, The (Hall), 18, 25–26, 38, 39, 188

West, Dorothy, 61, 91–92, 110, 198n5

West, Rebecca, 36

Wheatley, Phillis, 54

White, Edmund, 162

White, Walter F., 57
    Fire in the Flint, 103
    Flight, 95

white queer theory, and antisocial thesis, 5–7, 8–9

whitewashed queerness, 188–91

Wide Sargasso Sea (Rhys), 126, 129

Wilde, Oscar, 95, 190

Williams, Raymond, 41, 42–47, 48, 50, 51, 197n12

Women, The (Als), 184–85

Wood, Dan, 19

Woolf, Virginia, 25
    Mrs. Dalloway, 16, 27, 140, 185–87
    Room of One's Own, A, 187

Wright, Richard, 96, 106

Wyndham, Olivia, 198n31

Zola, Émile, 108

ЯМ REFIGURING MODERNISM   *(A Series Edited By)*
Jonathan Eburne

ARTS

LITERATURES

SCIENCES

Refiguring Modernism features cutting-edge interdisciplinary approaches
to the study of art, literature, science, and cultural history. With an eye
to the different modernisms emerging throughout the world during
the twentieth century and beyond, we seek to publish scholarship that
engages creatively with canonical and eccentric works alike, bringing fresh
concepts and original research to bear on modernist cultural production,
whether aesthetic, social, or epistemological. What does it mean to study
modernism in a global context characterized at once by decolonization and
nation building; international cooperation and conflict; changing ideas
about subjectivity and identity; new understandings of language, religion,
poetics, and myth; and new paradigms for science, politics, and religion?
What did modernism offer artists, writers, and intellectuals? How do we
theorize and historicize modernism? How do we rethink its forms, its past,
and its futures?